MW00887686

Civic Illiteracy and Education

Studies in the
Postmodern Theory of Education

Joe L. Kincheloe and Shirley R. Steinberg
General Editors

Vol. 23

PETER LANG
New York • Washington, D.C./Baltimore
Bern • Frankfurt am Main • Berlin • Vienna • Paris

John Marciano

Civic Illiteracy and Education

The Battle for the Hearts and Minds of American Youth

PETER LANG
New York • Washington, D.C./Baltimore
Bern • Frankfurt am Main • Berlin • Vienna • Paris

Library of Congress Cataloging-in-Publication Data

Marciano, J.D.
Civic illiteracy and education: battle for the hearts and minds of American
youth/ John Marciano.
p. cm. — (Counterpoints; v. 23)
Includes bibliographical references and index.
1. United States—History—Textbooks. 2. Vietnamese Conflict, 1961–1975—
Study and teaching—United States. 3. Persian Gulf War, 1991—Study and
teaching—United States. 4. Civics. I.. Title. II. Series: Counterpoints (New
York, N.Y.); vol. 23.
E175.85.M37   956.7044'2'07—dc20   95-31635
ISBN 0-8204-2879-5
ISSN 1058-1634

Die Deutsche Bibliothek-CIP-Einheitsaufnahme

Marciano, J.D.:
Civic illiteracy and education: battle for the hearts and minds of American
youth/ John Marciano. –New York; Washington, D.C./Baltimore; Bern;
Frankfurt am Main; Berlin; Vienna; Paris: Lang.
(Counterpoints; Vol. 23)
ISBN 0-8204-2879-5
NE: GT

The paper in this book meets the guidelines for permanence and durability
of the Committee on Production Guidelines for Book Longevity
of the Council of Library Resources.

© 1997 Peter Lang Publishing, Inc., New York

All rights reserved.
Reprint or reproduction, even partially, in all forms such as microfilm,
xerography, microfiche, microcard, and offset strictly prohibited.

Printed in the United States of America.

Dedication

To the teachers who have struggled against civic illiteracy by challenging the hearts and minds of our youth.

Contents

Acknowledgements

I wish to thank Charles Banner-Haley, Bill Griffen, and John Ryder for their helpful comments on the manuscript. Richard Brosio gave critical assistance throughout, sharing his fine and progressive insights on schools and society. Noam Chomsky took time from his incredible schedule to give detailed and invaluable suggestions. His steadfast fidelity to truth in the face of power and violence is always inspiring. Karla Alwes helped me "get the words right" in the original proposal and introduction; Bill Bigelow, Bruce Franklin, Gene Grabiner, Chris Sperry, and Maria Sweeney did likewise in individual chapters. Nona Reuter of Lang Publishing, and Joe Kincheloe and Shirley Steinberg, series' editors, provided important support; and Bruce Murphy's editing strengthened the manuscript. Finally, I wish to thank Gerald Coles, for his wise counsel on this and other important matters; Ann Wexler, for her reading and loving support; and my father, Dan Marciano, who designed the cover.

Introduction

Land of Promise; One Flag, One Land; Our Land, Our Time; America: The Glorious Republic; Spirit of Liberty: An American History; The Americans: A History of a People and a Nation; A Proud Nation; Heritage of Freedom; The Challenge of Freedom. These history textbook titles reverberate with visions of democracy, freedom, and patriotism—what America is all about. They inspire one to think about the glorious traditions and lessons that should move youth.

There is a different view of our history, patriotism and war, however, that rarely makes it into schools, textbooks and mass media. This "other side" must be presented if youth are to think about and challenge the distortions, omissions and lies that shape history lessons about the country and its wars. This book is about the contest for the hearts and minds of youth, about what is termed "civic literacy"—the ability to think critically and objectively about the nation's fundamental premises and practices.

Influential educators faithfully support a dominant-elite view that has fostered an uncritical patriotism and militarism, undermining thoughtful and active citizenship in a democracy. In contrast, I argue that education, often through history textbooks which are the primary source of civic literacy instruction, offers youth a distorted view of America, promoting civic illiteracy and turning civic responsibility into patriotic conformity. Allan Bloom's "Closing of the American Mind" has actually been fostered by those who influence educational policy. Dissenters, therefore, must challenge the empty patriotism, yellow ribbons, and militarism that shape the nation and our schools.

Today, there is a crisis of civic literacy and democracy; the representation of our history in schools will help to shape its outcome. This crisis has arisen because we do not educate students to criticize and challenge the nation's policies, especially those involving war. Despite the many claims that civic literacy is crucial to education and democracy, patriotic and militaristic propaganda has dominated history lessons in our schools. Such miseducation leaves students unable to make reasoned judgments, preparing them to give unthinking support to American wars.

The crisis of civic literacy that I wish to address, however, is not the one discussed by educational reports, and by corporate, educational and political leaders. It exists because the dominant elite that runs this country requires youth and citizens who can be manipulated. This elite is comprised of corporate officials, influential educators, and political figures who govern the nation and shape its civic debate. These leaders see the foundations of our country and educational system as sound and our institutions and leaders as decent and humane, but they believe that mistakes are made because purposes are not questioned. The source of this crisis is not merely youthful ignorance of the basic facts of important historical events, though this deficiency certainly exists. Its roots lie in the elite's fear that civically-literate youth will become informed and involved citizens; civic instruction, therefore, is organized to prevent such a danger. Civic illiteracy, which helps to keep youth and other citizens stupefied, is perfectly reasonable once we understand the purpose and nature of "citizenship training" in the schools: to undermine the critical and liberating potential of education.

The images and beliefs inspired by the titles listed at the beginning of this introduction are those that influential political figures and educators want youth to embrace. The dominant elite fears what Harvard professor and former Pentagon official Samuel Huntington called "the democratic distemper" in the people, especially youth. If youth question and challenge issues and policies, this elite will face an "excess of democracy" of the kind that emerged in the 1960s when social movements challenged respected authorities and established policies.[1] Such movements threaten the power and stability of established institutions. The history lessons about patriotism, war, and these movements, therefore, are simply one educational tool in the struggle to vaccinate the hearts and minds of youth against this "distemper."

Those who shape our perception of world events, including history textbook authors, present similar views on matters of state and war despite apparent differences on particular issues or policies. Their general position is expressed in high school and media history discussions and lessons. Rarely heard by youth, however, are radical views that challenge the fundamental beliefs about America and war that students and citizens learn and take for granted.

The radical or "other side" was expressed by the late Andrew Kopkind, writer and journalist for *The Nation*. Writing after the conclusion of the Persian Gulf War, Kopkind argued that "America has been in a state of war—cold, hot and lukewarm—for as long as most citizens now living can remember"; that this state of war has "been used effectively to manufacture support for the nation's rulers and to eliminate or contain dissent among the ruled." This "warrior state is so ingrained in American institutions . . . in short so *totalitarian*—that government is practically unthinkable without it."[2] But this war mentality is a good cure for "democratic distemper," because it "implies command rather than participation, obedience over agreement, hierarchy instead of equality, repression not liberty, uniformity not diversity, secrecy not candor, propaganda not information."[3] This war system permeates every institution in our society, including our schools. Opposed to the "kinder gentler" rhetoric that we hear in commencement and political addresses, it glorifies patriotism and war and profoundly shapes the crisis in civic literacy.

• • •

The Format of the Book: Chapter Outlines and Argument

Chapter 1: The Crisis in Civic Literacy and Foundational Principles
Chapter 1 will examine the "crisis in civic literacy" and fundamental principles, as presented by influential educational reports and theorists who have defined the debate. These will include the Carnegie Foundation for the Advancement of Teaching Report (*High School: A Report of Secondary Education*, 1983), the Education for Democracy Project Report (*Democracy's Untold Story*, 1987), the National Endowment for the Humanities' *American Memory: A Report on the Humanities*

in the Nation's Public Schools (1987), the *Report on the First National Assessment of History and Literature* (1987), and the perspectives of Allan Bloom, William Bennett, and R. Freeman Butts. This review will serve as the basis for the challenge in later chapters to the nature of American society and civic literacy.

Chapter 2: America: The Dominant-Elite View

In order to critique the principles of civic literacy and education, we must examine the dominant-elite view about the United States, including its history and stated ideals, as expressed through its professed commitment to human rights and its role in the world. This view shapes the debate on civic literacy, country, and war, and those presenting it define the issues to which citizens and youth then respond. They include Robert Bellah, Bennett, Bloom, and Paul Gagnon.

Chapter 3: America: A Dissenting View

The dominant-elite view of national reports and leading educators will be contrasted with dissenters such as Noam Chomsky, W.E.B. DuBois, bell hooks, June Jordan, Michael Parenti, and Howard Zinn, voices rarely heard in contemporary political discussions in the media, and virtually excluded from our secondary history classrooms. Their dissenting critique gives us a much more truthful understanding of American history and contemporary events. The chapter explores DuBois's and Manning Marable's insights on how racism ultimately shapes youth's knowledge about peoples and nations in the Third World, and what this has to do with American wars. Since 1945, for example, the United States has committed aggression against people of color in Cambodia, Cuba, Chile, El Salvador, Guatemala, Grenada, Iraq, Korea, Laos, Lebanon, Nicaragua, Panama, Southern Africa, and Vietnam. Racist justifications found in history lessons and textbook accounts of American domestic and foreign policies and wars have legitimized this aggression.

The dissenting view continues with Ward Churchill's and Annette Jaimes's insights on U.S. aggression against Native Americans; reflections on patriotism from Henry David Thoreau, Leo Tolstoy, and *The Nation*; and feminist reflections on nationalism, women, and war from Jean Elshtain, Linda Gordon, and Betty Reardon. A discussion of civic literacy and society must include an examination of the relationship of gender to patriotism and war. The indoctrination that results in the emulation of militarism is not just fostered by school history lessons, but is nurtured by cultural gender stereotypes that glorify U.S. military exploits.

Chapter 4: The Radical Tradition in Educational Criticism

To continue dissenting perspectives on the dominant-elite view of America found in chapter 3, it is necessary to review the critical/radical scholarship that has arisen in educational studies over the past three decades. This section will include a discussion of the insights of Michael Apple, Ann Bastian, Samuel Bowles and Herbert Gintis, Martin Carnoy, Maxine Greene, and Kathleen Weiler.

Chapter 5: Civic Illiteracy and American History Textbooks: The U.S.-Vietnam War

The dissenting views in chapters 4 and 5 establish the context and foundation for the argument that educational texts, as part of the schools' larger political purposes, have fostered civic illiteracy by promoting an uncritical patriotism. To illustrate the general thesis that civic illiteracy is fostered in schools, I will challenge the dominant-elite view with a concrete analysis of how the U.S.-Vietnam War is presented in American history textbooks. These texts remain a key source of civic learning for high school students, especially about past wars; they equate U.S. policy with honorable intentions and justice while acknowledging errors of judgment and horrible casualties.

History textbooks support the dominant-elite version of the basic premises and practices of the nation, including: the U.S. is a democracy run in the interests of the people; government and educational leaders desire civically-literate and informed youth; the U.S. pursues peace and justice and is always trying to do good; and that although aggression and violence have been a part of our history, they are accidental by-products of essentially humane policies. I will challenge this benign view by weaving a narrative view of 20 history texts published in the 1980s, describing the U.S.-Vietnam war in the language of the textbook authors. Distortions and inaccuracies will be examined by using dissenting sources that are rarely part of schools' curricula.

Chapter 6: The Persian Gulf War

To continue the discussion of education and war, chapter 6 discusses civic illiteracy in the context of a detailed history of the Gulf War. Part I reviews the war from the "yellow-ribbon"[4] or dominant-elite perspective; Part II offers a dissenting critique of the war based on evidence rarely encountered in the mass media or schools.

Chapter 7: Civic Literacy during the Gulf War: Critical Pedagogy and an Alternative Vision

This chapter will examine civic literacy efforts undertaken in schools during the Persian Gulf War, drawing upon available research and information provided by teachers. I will report on the views of some teachers who fostered the critical dialogue envisioned by the leading educational reports and theorists as essential to civic knowledge. This critical dialogue happened because they practiced the essential virtue of civic literacy in a democracy: engaging students and citizens in an informed and critical dialogue on an important historical event. These educators embrace the highest ideals of the nation and their vocation; they are the heroes and heroines in the struggle for civic literacy.

We must have a radically different vision of civic literacy in order to challenge the powerful influence of the dominant elite, and the school history lesson version of U.S. wars. This new vision and approach are needed to counter the patriotic and militaristic indoctrination that our youth receive. Our social and educational institutions continue to pledge allegiance to civic literacy, compassion, and peace, while the nation's leaders remain militaristic and violent. We need to understand how these destructive policies have been supported by educational institutions, and how a genuine civic literacy can help to transform them.

• • •

My interest in writing this book is not merely academic. Powerful personal and political experiences have moved me to address the subject and controversy that are the heart of this work: my involvement in the anti-Vietnam War movement of the 1960s and 1970s; my work with Vietnam veterans on the war and related issues; my brother's combat service in Vietnam, and the death of his best friend with whom he went through basic and advanced infantry training; my personal contacts with Noam Chomsky, Dr. Martin Luther King, Jr., Benjamin Spock, and Howard Zinn, all of whom have spoken and written eloquently about issues of war and peace; co-authoring *Teaching the Vietnam War* (1979); teaching students at the State University of New York, College at Cortland for the past 27 years; and my efforts as an activist on issues of education, peace, and social justice for the past 31 years.

Regardless of the judgment on the questions under discussion in this book, becoming civically literate about patriotism and war is not merely a minor debating point in another educational report or publication. What youth learn about the U.S.-Vietnam War and the Persian Gulf War can literally mean devastation or peace, especially for the peoples of the Third World and, ultimately, for America and the globe. As the historian Howard Zinn argues, "we can reasonably conclude that how we *think* is not just mildly interesting, not just a subject for intellectual debate, but a matter of life and death."[5]

Notes

1   Samuel Huntington, "The United States," in Michael Crozier, Samuel Huntington, and Joji Watanuki, *The Crisis of Democracy: Report On The Governability of Democracies To The Trilateral Commission* (New York: New York University Press, 1975), 102. Huntington's essay is a must for those who wish to understand the dominant-elite's response to the progressive movements of the 1960s and 1970s.

2   Andrew Kopkind, "The Warrior State: Imposing the New Order at Home," *The Nation*, April 8, 1991, 433.

3   Ibid., 447.

4   Millions of Americans wore the yellow ribbon as a symbol of support for the troops, and ultimately the war itself. The symbol represented the overwhelming view in the country, especially after U.S. combat action began. The yellow ribbon perspective totally overwhelmed any civically-literate dialogue on the premises, purposes, and strategies of the war. See chapter 7.

5   Howard Zinn, *Declarations of Independence: Cross-Examining American Ideology* (New York: HarperCollins, 1990), 1-2.

Chapter 1

The Crisis in Civic Literacy
and Foundational Principles

National Reports

More than 30 national reports on U.S. schools were published
in the 1980s; a few addressed the "crisis of civic literacy." To
challenge the dominant-elite view of the crisis, education, and
the country, reference to some reports, influential figures, and
guiding principles is necessary as the foundation for the discussion and challenge in later chapters to our society and civic
literacy in the schools. The primary concern of this book is
what educational and political leaders assert about the crisis
in civic literacy and the nation—not pedagogy or the manner
of presentation.

Concern over civic literacy is not a recent development of
the 1980s and 1990s: historian of education Donald Warren
reminds us that a "crisis in civic literacy" is a recurring theme
in our history. The lack of civic knowledge about societal issues and principles has been a constant concern in education
throughout this century. Warren states that those who are presently concerned about the state of civic literacy seem to have
"a short memory." Whether the goal is to get beyond the dissent and disruption of the 1960s, or to deal with the demographic changes in the nation and educational system (e.g.,
increasing racial diversity), there is a desire on the part of
political officials and educators to create a "unifying socialization" for our youth. Thus, civic literacy is vital because it will
presumably bring us together as one people with common beliefs in a time when stress and multicultural traditions are break-

ing us apart. Warren believes that those who advocate civic
education "tend to agree that somehow we have lost our way,
that originally citizenship preparation mattered more and was
accomplished more *effectively*. Historical evidence suggests,
however, that rather than a bygone 'golden' era, we find a tradition of recurring conflicts and messy consensus over the
purposes of public education."[1]

   Distress is a common theme in the reports that address civic
literacy. The late Ernest Boyer, former U.S. Commissioner of
Education and author of a major Carnegie Foundation report
on the American high school (1983), lamented the fact that
"the Jeffersonian vision of grass roots democracy fueled by
education increasingly is viewed as utopian, and what's especially disturbing is that the school reform movement of the
1980s has paid insufficient attention to educating students
about the nation's history and institutions."[2] Why don't we educate youth about the important issues affecting the survival of
the Republic—about civic literacy in a democracy? Does the
answer lie in what has been termed "mindlessness" (see page
15), because leaders and educators don't think carefully or
deeply enough about the purposes of society and schools? Perhaps the deeper and true reason is that genuine civic literacy
would undermine the elite's ability to maintain effective control. Boyer contends that we have not shown much concern for
citizenship education, and that "for those who care about government 'by the people,' this lack of concern cannot go unchallenged. . . . What we urgently need today are groups of
well-informed, caring individuals who band together in the
spirit of community to learn from one another and participate
as citizens in the democratic process."[3] His concern essentially
misses the target: educating youth in this spirit would threaten
existing power arrangements in the country. Boyer claims that
civic illiteracy is growing, and that

> unless we find better ways to educate ourselves as citizens, we run the
> risk of drifting unwittingly into a new kind of Dark Age—a time, when,
> increasingly, specialists will control knowledge and the decision-mak-
> ing process. In this confusion, citizens would make critical decisions
> on the basis of blind belief in another set of professed experts.[4]

This is an ironic claim, especially when one considers that the
Boyer Report and other major educational studies in the 1980s

were made by elite experts, with only rare participation by citizens, parents, and teachers. Although *High School* is perhaps the best of the major reports in terms of its concern about equality for poorer youth and civic literacy, it still reproduces the same elitism of experts that Boyer decries. He contends that "civics is an important part of the core of common learning. In a world where human survival is at stake, ignorance about government and how it functions is not an acceptable alternative."[5] Boyer is right, but only at the most abstract or general level where no one could disagree: a sound and vibrant democracy cannot afford such ignorance about history and institutions. In the concrete and real world in which we live, however, he is wrong and naive. Given the choice between ignorant and uninvolved youth or those who actively challenge our country's history and policies, the elite and influential allies will choose the former and avoid the conflicts that emerged when too many youth became infected with "democratic distemper" in the 1960s.

Asserting that "civic education, by its very nature, means helping students confront social and ethical concerns and applying what they have learned," Boyer joins conservatives like William Bennett and radicals such as Michael Parenti who argue that adults "must help them [students] to understand that not all choices are equally valid."[6] The problem arises, however, when the choices made run counter to those reflecting the needs and views of the elite and its influential allies. No reasonable thinker on civic literacy and education claims that all views are equally truthful—the fundamental issue remains to decide from among competing claims which one is the most truthful. Despite rhetorical support for the "free marketplace of ideas," however, it is clear that the marketplace has been limited to the ideas that benefit those in power, especially when it comes to designing high school history lessons and textbooks.

According to Boyer, civic literacy is absolutely crucial in this era when fast-paced technological change profoundly shapes our daily existence. "The study of history" is especially needed because it reveals an awareness of a "larger reality beyond the present." He pleads for "a sense of continuity with the past [that] can provide a kind of lifeline across the scary chasm of our contemporary situation." Through civic education, "all high school students deepen their understanding of our national heritage through a study of United States history, with special emphasis on the people, ideas, and issues that have shaped the nation."[7] This outcome depends, of course, upon whose version of history our youth learn, and its substantive truth claims, an idea that is not discussed by Boyer, the major educational reports, or influential theorists.

In *Democracy's Untold Story* (1987), a joint effort of the American Federation of Teachers, Education for Excellence Network and the Freedom House, historian Paul Gagnon asserts that young people are not learning the commitments essential for a democracy. These commitments, which are the foundation for civic literacy—are actually undermined because "among some educators . . . there appears a certain lack of confidence in our own liberal, democratic values, an unwillingness to draw normative distinctions between them and the ideas of non-democratic regimes."[8] This is because some educators and citizens insist "upon maintaining neutrality among competing values [a] tendency to present political systems as not better or worse but only different."[9] Gagnon argues that this neutrality is a mistake: there is a right and wrong historical position on international conflicts that civically-literate youth should understand and embrace, and educators and citizens in a democracy should not fall into the historical or value relativism that Allan Bloom bitterly criticizes. Gagnon and Bloom are both correct, though not for the reasons they state, as I shall discuss in chapter 3. According to Gagnon, a critical examination of American democracy "must rest on a solid base of factual knowledge" which rejects the notion that "no particular body of knowledge is worth knowing than any other."[10] Both of these assertions are true as abstract principles; however, a basic issue not addressed by Gagnon, the national reports, and influential theorists, is whether U.S. practices are actually, as they claim, "democratic and liberal." This claim is not examined with critical historical evidence.

In a report for the National Endowment for Humanities (NEH): *American Memory: A Report on the Humanities in the Nation's Schools* (1987), the chair of the Endowment, Lynne V. Cheney, supports the concerns expressed above. She believes, with Nobel Prize-winning poet Czeslaw Milosz, that "'a refusal to remember' is a primary characteristic of our age. Certainly there is abundant evidence that this is a primary characteristic of our nation. . . . Nationwide polls show startling gaps in knowledge." Cheney claims that "cultural memory flourishes or declines for many reasons, but among the most important is what happens in our schools. Long relied upon to transmit knowledge of the past to upcoming generations, our schools today appear to be about a different task. Instead of preserving the past, they more often disregard it." She also claims that our nation is "at risk" because young people do not know

> how the society in which they live came to be. Knowledge of the ideas
> that have molded us and the ideals that have mattered to us functions
> as a kind of civic glue. Our history and literature give us symbols to
> share; they help us all, no matter how diverse our backgrounds, feel
> part of the common undertaking.[11]

Cheney insists that when we allow youth to suffer an "erosion of historical consciousness, we do to ourselves what an unfriendly nation bent on our destruction might."[12]

Again, in the abstract or general sense, she is correct: we should teach youth to "remember" the past with all its tragedies and triumphs. But in the concrete reality of what *is* learned about patriotism and war in the nation, for example, young people have a long educational apprenticeship in historical amnesia that has been fostered by those like Cheney who are intellectual apologists for the dominant elite. She is right about the need for historical consciousness, a theme echoed by many other influential theorists who support the dominant-elite view; but a truthful historical consciousness for youth that might help them to undermine the national security state and culture that she supports is not what she has in mind. The irony is that Cheney never reflects on the role that Reagan-Bush conservatives played in the destruction of real historical memory by their violence and contempt for the truth.

In *A Report on the First Assessment of History and Literature* (1987), educators and former Department of Education officials (under Bush and Reagan) Diane Ravitch and Chester E. Finn, Jr. share their deep distress over students' lack of civic knowledge, especially history. A representative sample of high school juniors scored barely above 54 percent on the history portion of the assessment, leading Ravitch and Finn to conclude: "If there were such a thing as a national report card for those studying American history . . . [these] eleventh grade students earned failing marks."[13] They are justifiably upset by these results and claim that it is foolish to believe "that students can think critically or conceptually when they are ignorant of the most basic facts of American history," an important point that should not be ignored. They conclude that if "educators, parents, and citizens allow [civic] literacy" to diminish, the "quality of public . . . debate in our society will suffer," and this decline will surely undermine civic literacy.[14] Their judgment is blunt: "We merely conclude that it [the 'younger generation'] is ignorant of important things it should know, and that it and generations to follow are at risk of being gravely handicapped by that ignorance upon entry into . . . citizenship."[15] They remind us that not all youths are at risk, because some have a "decent reservoir of knowledge of history . . . and these . . . tend to be the children of the well-educated, the well-employed, the well-motivated, and the well-off." This elite will "do its best to equip its own children with this knowledge and to send them to schools that furnish substantial quantities of it. But neither our culture, our politics, our civic life, nor our principles of equal opportunity can be satisfactorily maintained if larger numbers of youngsters enter adulthood with little knowledge of this kind."[16]

Although I differ profoundly with Ravitch and Finn about civic literacy and this country, and will argue that they and the elite they cite fear an informed and activist youth, their basic conclusion on the factual knowledge of history is true. Students can't challenge anything if they don't know anything; they can't criticize national and international policies if they don't have the basic information upon which such judgments are made. In a co-authored article on civic literacy, Finn and Ravitch expand on the thesis of the elite nature of historical understanding and tracking in our schools. They assert that:

> elites have always understood that to be master of one's own affairs and the affairs of others requires a rigorous education in the humanities. While knowledge of literature, history, and poetry and the command of languages may not substitute for brute force or tribal loyalty . . . determined members of the 'ruling class' have consistently seized every opportunity for their children to acquire such knowledge.[17]

Thus the authors point out the class nature of education in the United States. Some demand and obtain the best education so they can govern the society and manage its social, economic, and cultural institutions. They will do their best to buy such education for their children, most of whom will study in elite private schools and prestigious institutions of higher education. While the course of study for those who are trained to govern and those who are trained to be governed is different, it is essentially similar when it comes to the basic civic lessons about war, patriotism, and the country. "My country right or wrong" is still the operative principle.

Although not intended as a study of civic literacy, Charles Silberman's report on U.S. schools for the Carnegie Corporation, *Crisis in the Classroom* (1970), examined issues that are crucial to the current discussion. Silberman, then an editor of *Fortune Magazine,* contended that our schools do not help students because they "keep youngsters in a state of chronic, almost infantile, dependency."[18] Schools do this because most are "organized and run to facilitate order."[19] This depressing state of affairs is not the result of a deliberate effort on the part of educators and other public officials—it does not happen because of "venality or indifference or stupidity" but is caused, rather, by "mindlessness." Mindlessness, "the failure or refusal to think seriously about educational purpose, the failure to question established practice," is found throughout the society.[20] Simply put, we are so bogged down in the details of governing the country and schools that we don't have the time to think clearly about such crucial matters as basic purposes and practices. Silberman's thesis captures the dominant-elite perspective, the worldview of influential leaders who shape the civic debate in the nation. I will challenge Silberman's thesis on every point, arguing instead that the crisis in civic literacy is not caused by mistakes that flow from humane and worthwhile premises and policies, but the logical result of organizing society and schools so that most youth will display the docility and civic illiteracy that Silberman, Ravitch and Finn, and other leading educators lament.

Leading Dominant-Elite Theorists

The crisis in civic literacy and the underlying foundational principles have gained the attention of a number of influential intellectuals. These include William Bennett, former Secretary of Education and a leading conservative spokesman; the late Allan Bloom, philosopher and author of the controversial *The Closing of the American Mind*; R. Freeman Butts, an historian of education who has written extensively on the subject; and E.D. Hirsch, Jr., author of *Cultural Literacy*. Their views have received wide distribution in the mass media and academe, and have influenced the debate on civic literacy in the country.

Bennett is deeply distressed by the civic illiteracy that is common among our youth. He quotes Paul Gagnon, who states that many come to college "after twelve years of school (presumably in the 'college track'), knowing nothing of the pre-Plymouth past, including the Bible! . . . They often know . . . next to nothing of the history of science, technology, industry, of capitalism and socialism, of fascism and Stalinism, of how we found ourselves in two world wars, or even in Vietnam."[21] These students are simply unprepared to engage in an intelligent dialogue about issues crucial to the country, and Bennett's dissatisfaction is blunt and uncompromising: "The point is clear. Our young people are woefully ill-educated about history and the basic principles of our nation and our civilization. For those who believe, with Thomas Jefferson, that a knowledge of history belongs at the very center of every American's general education, this lack of knowledge is cause for alarm."[22] What is not discussed by Bennett and those who agree with him, however, is whether the government wants students to be educated along these lines.

Bennett illustrates the fundamental principles of civic literacy by showing how an historical controversy should be handled.

> We'll consider an example from a turbulent era in our own history. . . . What manner of men were the abolitionists? A number of perfectly respectable historians have branded them as "extremists," "impractical," "trouble-makers" and "not free of racial prejudice themselves." Other historians, equally respectable, have defended the abolitionists as "men of conscience," "courageous," and "Christian." As it is not likely that this controversy will ever be definitely resolved, the only way that a student can arrive at a useful judgment . . . is by reading different histories . . . reading the actual words of the abolitionists and their critics, by being exposed to different points of view, and

then by thinking out the problem for himself. . . . And in the process
. . ., he acquires what is surely one of the most important skills of
democratic citizenship: the ability to think critically about society and
its affairs.[23]

First of all, students and citizens would not know from this
statement that many of the abolitionists, including some of
the most famous, were women. Also, Bennett's historical and
moral relativism in his claim implies that there are no criteria
and evidence that might allow one to move beyond the view
that critical and laudatory perspectives on abolitionists are
"equally respectable." This is not the same Bennett who argues that there are evil nations and acts in the world and we
should teach our youth about them—strong and truthful perspectives which oppose these things, and they should not be
equated with untrue and immoral political views (see chapter
2). Would this serious approach to evidence and critical thinking hold if it challenged the fundamental policies of the U.S.
and thus blocked its ability to wage war against the Third
World? When truth challenges the power of the state, Bennett
and other conservatives who decry the excesses of big government fall into line to support it, as witnessed by their defense
of U.S. aggression in the Third World.

Bennett stresses the crucial importance of historical understanding for democratic citizenship, quoting Jefferson, who
believed that history was essential to the civic education of
citizens because, "by apprizing [Americans] of the past, [it]
will enable them to judge of the future; it will avail them of the
experience of other times and other nations; it will qualify
them as judges of the actions and designs of men; it will enable them to know ambition under every disguise it may assume; and knowing it, to defeat its views."[24] For Bennett, such
a judgment indicates that "running through our nation's history like a golden thread" has been a deep commitment historically to "certain ideals and aspirations. We believe in liberty and justice and equality. We believe in . . . the betterment
of the human condition."[25] While these ideas are professed in
a general sense, and Jefferson's thoughts on civic knowledge
and responsibilities should be studied carefully, Bennett's assertion of the golden thread totally distorts the actual history
of the country (see chapter 3).

Bennett's views are echoed by a conservative academic who enjoyed widespread public exposure: the late Allan Bloom. In *The Closing of the American Mind,* Bloom bitterly criticizes the changes in schools and colleges brought on by the reforms of the 1960s, and claims that they caused a steep decline in civic illiteracy among youth because "civic education turned away from concentrating on the Founding."[26] Educators spent too much time on contemporary political concerns and making students feel good about themselves, and not on the basics and origins of our system of democracy and the ethical questions that are absolutely essential to a civically literate population. Rather than helping students understand and appreciate the great figures and principles of the nation, especially the inspiring political ideas of those great men who created it, civic literacy for youth today often consists of "hearing [that] the Founders [are] racists, murderers of Indians, representatives of class interests."[27] The key issue, however, is not whether students *hear* that these Founders were "racists [and] murderers of Indians": It is whether that assertion is *true,* and why it is rarely debated in classrooms, texts and the media so that youth can develop the skills and values of civic literacy many argue are crucial to an informed and democratic citizenry. If dissenting views are rarely examined, how and where will youth gain the intellectual skills they need to become such citizens?

Bloom states that contemporary civic literacy actually reflects "the new language . . . of *value* relativism," which allows educators to avoid helping youth to deal with the "perpetual tyranny of good and evil, with their cargo of shame and guilt."[28] He bitterly opposes the notion that all opinions about the country, the Founders, and ethical issues are equally valid; and he criticizes those who refuse to take a truthful and courageous position on the issues of right and wrong, guilt and evil. Even though he vastly exaggerates the extent to which "relativism" occurs in our schools and history textbooks, Bloom raises an important principle about good and evil in the country and the world, one that he does not apply to his own government. For example, there is no suggestion that the U.S. might be evil because of its genocidal treatment of African slaves and American Indians. Each day, educators make political judgments and take sides on issues; however, they invariably end up supporting the government on matters of state—actively or through their silent acquiescence. They may criticize the means used or excessive means, or suggest that mistakes were made because things did not work as planned, as in Vietnam and the Gulf War, but they seldom oppose U.S. violence on the principle that it is fundamentally wrong or criminal. The assertion that youth grow up without hearing clear right and wrong statements on moral and political issues is simply untrue. Virtually everything that they heard in schools and the media about the Gulf War, for example, lauded it as a patriotic and wonderful moment in our nation's history; they rarely heard any educator, political official, or media commentator condemn it. Civic literacy fundamentally consisted of yellow-ribbon support for the decisions that had already been made.

Another Bloom claim is that "almost every thoughtful observer knows that it is in the U.S. that the idea of rights has penetrated most deeply into the bloodstream of its citizens."[29] But the noble idea of civil rights was extended to American Indians, slaves, persons of color, women and workers only after long and arduous struggles that forced the substance of the ideal upon the dominant elite. The dominant elite and influential spokespeople espouse lofty principles and claims about civic literacy and the society; but these ideal notions of civic reflection are not applied in schooling and textbook history lessons, nor are they used to uncover the truth about the actions of the U.S. government in past wars.

A concluding thought from Bloom on civic education: "Prejudices, strong prejudices, are visions about the way things are. They are divinations of the order of the whole of things, and hence the road to a knowledge of that whole is by way of erroneous opinions about it. Error is indeed our enemy, but it alone points to the truth and therefore deserves our respectful treatment."[30] He is correct about the road to knowledge; thinkers on the right like Bloom and Bennett, however, have their claims of truth and error passed on in the schools while those on the left, like Chomsky, are not—even though an objective assessment of Bloom's and Bennett's views would reveal support for the most horrible policies, justifiable in the name of the national security state.

The historian of education R. Freeman Butts has devoted years of study to the issue of civic literacy, and writes with concern and passion about the social and educational crisis that he finds in our country. In "Public Education in a Pluralistic Society," he argues that many among the public "are losing confidence not only in the particular officials in the government, but in the basic regime itself. [There is] widespread disillusionment, disenchantment, discontent, distrust of public men in public institutions, with corresponding paucity of public knowledge of political affairs, apathy, cynicism, and lack of participation."[31] Education has a special obligation to turn these discouraging developments around, recapturing the legitimacy and moral authority that has been lost, and promoting vigorously "the basic values of the American civic community: liberty *and* equality *and* justice. It might just be, too, that not only was the future of public education at stake, but also the existence of the democratic political community itself."[32]

Butts raises important issues; the problem, however, is that his belief in the essential soundness of our political institutions and values undermines the very nature of what he defends. He asks, for example, "How are citizens to be prepared to judge the merits of public policies in domestic and foreign affairs conducted by officials in office or proposed by candidates. . . ." But think about the secrecy and the imperial presidency that we have witnessed, especially since the Vietnam War, that did not allow citizens to make informed and reasoned judgments, by blocking the quest for that information under the excuse of national security. Butts argues that meritorious policies "can best be achieved only by careful judgments informed by a reasoned historical perspective and a meaningful concept of the best values underlying our constitutional order."[33] Although it is true that we do need to bring a reasoned perspective to deliberations on the civic order and the fundamental issues that guide us as a people, we cannot make such reasoned judgments when the President and the Executive Branch continually and routinely break the constitutional safeguards on war, maintain secrecy, and oppose substantive democratic involvement by citizens.

Although E.D. Hirsch, Jr.'s *Cultural Literacy* is broader in scope than civic literacy because it also includes literature, I mention his concerns because he shares the dominant-elite view of the national reports and influential theorists. Some have challenged Hirsch's version of cultural literacy, with its Eurocentric, male, and white perspective, and I will not add anything here to criticisms of his work.[34] Hirsch asserts that "to be culturally literate is to possess the basic information needed to thrive in the modern world. . . . Many young people strikingly lack the information that writers of American books and newspapers have traditionally taken for granted among their readers of all generations. . . . Our children's lack of intergenerational information is a serious problem for the nation."[35] As others who support the dominant-elite perspective, he too identifies some basic knowledge that youth must have to take their place as citizens in a democracy. But once again, there is no suggestion that such knowledge and a critical challenge to it might not be in the interest of those who govern our nation and educational system, and that a truly democratic and civically-literate education would actually subvert the status quo.

Hirsch rests his assertions about civic literacy on the fundamental, traditional, and time-honored precepts laid out by the Founding Fathers, who preached the "idea of a literate and informed citizenry." Hirsch states that essential to this concept is the principle that, when desirable, [national issues] can be explained to literate and educated citizens. Economic issues can be discussed in public." Arguing that it is not "undemocratic or intolerant to make nationwide decisions" about what is studied in schools, he states that "to repudiate the idea of a shared . . . curriculum is necessarily to accept the idea of an *unshared* . . . curriculum."[36] His reflections on the decentralized nature of educational curricula must be examined, however; the United States has a de-facto national curriculum when it comes to the premises and principles of patriotism and war, and particular events such as the Gulf and Vietnam wars. There is little genuine pluralism and fragmentation when it comes to the national security state: an uncritical "pro-American" perspective flows throughout school history lessons, essentially a dominant-elite version.

Addressing the principles of civic literacy in *The Genius of American Education*, the late Lawrence A. Cremin, one of the most influential historians of education in the twentieth century, writes that "what the school is uniquely equipped to do . . . is to make youngsters aware of the constant bombardment of facts, opinions, and values to which they are subjected; to help them question what they see and hear; and ultimately, to give them the intellectual resources they need to make judgments and assess significance."[37] The school may be ideally equipped to do these things, but if we examine actual practice—the only true test we have of whether it is doing what Cremin claims it can do—we find another story. The teachers who used the Gulf War as a means of furthering the kinds of thinking that Cremin, Bennett, and others laud in the abstract, for example, were a small minority (chapter 7). Most teachers were silent on the war or cheered the troops on to victory, as sympathy for the troops replaced any real analysis of why they were there in the first place.

Cremin also lauds Jefferson's views on civic literacy and education. In the Rockfish Gap Report on the program at the University of Virginia, Jefferson argued that the "objects of primary education . . . were: To understand his duties to his neighbors and country, and to discharge with competence the functions confided to him by either; To know his rights; to exercise with order and justice those he retains; to choose with discretion the fiduciary of those he delegates; and to notice their conduct with diligence, with candor, and judgment."[38] Cremin makes an eloquent appeal based on Jefferson's conception of citizenship education: "On the basis of prudence alone, no modern industrial nation can fail to afford every one of its citizens the maximum opportunity for intellectual and moral development. . . . And beyond prudence, there is justice. No society that calls itself democratic can settle for an education that does not encourage universal acquaintance with the best that has been thought and said."[39]

Cremin's political perspective, however, does not allow him to confront what it is about America that has undermined the ideal of civic literacy for citizens and youth. He concludes with "Jefferson's faith—and the faith on which any democracy must rest . . . that the average man, properly educated, could indeed render such a judgment."[40] But the "average" citizen's insights on national power and war have been distorted because the skills and sentiments that are necessary for democracy have been undermined by the media and school history lessons. As my Foundations of Education colleague at Ball State University, Richard A. Brosio, has eloquently and persuasively argued, the conflicting imperatives of capitalism and democracy act upon the school, state and other arenas of civic life in ways that undermine the ethical and political vision and democratic ideals and principles that we pass on to youth.[41] Educators continue to do the very opposite of Cremin's ideal; to do otherwise is to confront power and hierarchical rule—something that no one in authority wants.

The social-political theorist Morris Janowitz opposes a "civic education [that is] limited to inculcation of traditional patriotism or conventional nationalist ideology [because it is] obviously inadequate for an advanced industrial society and a highly interdependent world." However, he still upholds the essence of the elite indoctrination view: after citizens shed their distorted chauvinism, they still end up supporting the national security state. What would Janowitz think if national chauvinism were not "inadequate for [our] advanced industrial society"? He finds "the words nationalism and patriotism limiting and [prefers] the term *civic consciousness*. It refers to positive and meaningful attachments a person develops to the nation-state. Civic consciousness is compatible with and required for both national and international responsibility and obligations."[42] Nothing in Janowitz's work suggests that the violent national security state does not deserve "meaningful attachments" but determined and principled opposition. Those who challenge an aggressive America are simply dismissed, and the "debate" over patriotism or hyper-patriotism can go on in a civically-literate manner.

In the research for this book, I did not find a single influential educator or national report that even considered the critique of the national security state violence made by Noam Chomsky (see chapter 3) or George Bradford (see chapter 6). Perhaps the image of American GIs as liberators during World War II remains the prevailing one for many in the U.S., thus blocking their ability to ask fundamental questions about the purposes of educational and other state institutions in furthering and explaining away the international aggression and violence of the present American garrison state.

Some Summary Reflections on the Dominant-Elite View

The influential reports and intellectuals cited in this chapter express deep concern about what they see happening to the country, educational system, and youth; they are quite accurate in many of their descriptions of the problems of knowledge facing youth and older citizens who need to think critically about the issues of patriotism and war. While they are long on description and lamentation, however, they are short on critical and theoretical insights into why things are as they are.

Before I discuss and then challenge the dominant-elite perspective on our country, human rights, and war in chapter 2, I wish to leave the reader with some beginning thoughts and questions on the crisis in civic literacy from a dissenting point of view which forms the basis for my profound disagreement with the dominant-elite. In *Democracy and Education*, John Dewey asks some questions that must be raised if the civic literacy that is critical to the well-being of the country and schools is to be nurtured. Can we have education that is "conducted by a national state and yet the full social ends of the educational process not be restricted, constrained, and corrupted? How [do we] reconcile national loyalty with 'superior devotion to things which unite men in common ends, irrespective of national political boundaries?'"[43]

The crisis in civic literacy and the underlying conflict of ideals and problems that are at the heart of this debate, are reflected in Dewey's questions. They have also been examined by Barbara Finkelstein, Professor of Education at the University of Maryland, who raises some disturbing ethical issues that must be confronted by those who are concerned with what is happening in the country and schools. Finkelstein believes that we need to think of civic literacy in terms of deeper "commitments to justice, freedom, and dignity" that strengthen "civic bonds built on mutuality and interdependence, cooperation and harmony, sociality and love."[44] I applaud her sentiments and vision, but we must ask why these fine ideals are not the guiding principles that move educational and social practice for all people in our country, especially youth. Is it not true that a genuine civic literacy built upon ethical ideals has been and remains a threat to the dominant elite's power? Finkelstein calls for a holistic vision of democratic citizenship and draws from the work of Robert H. Brown, who claims that for a true civic literacy to flourish we must involve ourselves as moral agents in the public arena.[45] Finkelstein contends that "if the conditions of modern life prevent the political exercise of moral agency—if the political economy precludes it, government ceases to require it, and education fails to model it—freedom and justice are threatened." People must show their personal commitment to a just society in a public manner. If they do not, "they cease to be citizens. . . . As a moral matter, their commitments to freedom, justice, and dignity become empty pieties, or worse, demagogic invocations of socially un-grounded rhetoric."[46]

Edward H. Berman of the University of Louisville has ana-lyzed the major national educational reports of the 1980s in light of what is at risk for the nation-state and the dominant elite that runs it. Berman asserts that although

> there are indeed differences among the most influential of the sev-eral reports, the commonalities are more striking: the decisive role of the United States in the world capitalist economy must be arrested and the nation's schools have a central role to play in order to accom-plish this.[47]

The dominant elite has influenced the current educational debate in a number of ways. First, most of the reports were "initiated, sponsored, or guided" by those who represent im-portant government agencies, multinational corporations, or influential foundations, which pass on the beliefs that shape the country, schools, and civic literacy. The seemingly demo-cratic dialogue on crucial issues ends up supporting the rules established by the dominant elite. Intense discussion and dis-agreement often take place, but within premises that are taken for granted and not open to critical challenge. The important concerns that face us—such as "social justice, the realization of individual potential, democratic empowerment [and] critical [or civic] literacy"—are essentially ignored by the major educa-tional reports, aside from the usual expression of concern about the importance of these qualities helping to foster economic growth.[48] Berman concludes on a note that should be kept in mind by the reader of this book: If the school were to educate "the majority of its students to analyze society's current organization it would perhaps encourage a possible reappraisal of— and perhaps revolt against—the existing arrangement that favor the few and disadvantage the majority."[49]

I close this chapter with some words from the influential American historian, Arthur Schlesinger, Jr., the Kennedy advisor whose views on multiculturalism complement Diane Ravitch's. He articulates the dominant-elite view on civic literacy, and is absolutely right on one count: "A struggle to redefine the nation's identity is taking place in many arenas . . . and in no arena more crucial than our system of education. The schools and colleges . . . train the citizens of the future. They have always been battlegrounds for debates over beliefs, philosophies, values. The debate about the curriculum is a debate about what it means to be an American. What is ultimately at stake in the shape of the American future."[50] He puts it well, for the school history lessons of the past represent what those in power and their educational allies wish to have passed on to youth—all in the name of historical objectivity, critical thinking and civic literacy. As I will show in chapter 3 and beyond, none of the above goals are fostered by the kinds of lessons that have been taught.

Notes

1   Donald Warren, "Original Intentions: Public Schools as Civic Education," *Theory into Practice*, Vol. 27, No. 4, Autumn 1988, 243-44.

2   Ernest Boyer, "Civic Education for Responsible Citizenship," *Educational Leadership*, Vol. 48, No. 3, November 1990, 5.

3   Ibid.

4   Ernest Boyer, *High School: A Report on Secondary Education in America*. The Carnegie Foundation for the Advancement of Teaching (New York: Harper and Row, 1983), 105-6.

5   Ibid.

6   "Civic Education," 7.

7   *High School*, 101.

8   Paul Gagnon, *Democracy's Untold Story: What World History Books Neglect* (Washington: American Federation of Teachers, Democracy Project, 1987), 15.

9   Ibid., 16.

10   Ibid., 19. The two democracy reports (the other was *Democracy's Half-Told Story: What American History Books Should Add*, 1989) were cosponsored with the Education Excellence Network and Freedom House, both of which support the agenda and policies of the dominant elite. The working relationship of the AFT with such organizations is yet another admission of the educational and political bankruptcy of its leadership, personified by its president of nearly 30 years, Albert Shanker. It is also a sad commentary on the civic literacy of many of its rank-and-file members. Gagnon was also the chief investigator for the *Bradley Commission Report on Historical Literacy in the Schools*—supported by the same Bradley Foundation that has funded the rightist work of the Heritage Foundation, American Enterprise Institute, and Charles Murray's classist and racist *The Bell Curve*. The AFT and Bradley Commission reports agree on basic societal and educational premises and principles that are shared by influential conservatives and liberals, who support the policies of the national security state. As used throughout the book, the term refers to, in the words of Noam Chomsky, the United States as "global enforcer." It has unleashed unrivaled violence throughout the Third World, especially since the creation of the Central Intelligence Agency in 1947. This military power, however, is the means used to maintain American corporate hegemony in the world. The ultimate goal of the na-

tional security state is to maintain corporate class control over the world's resources, keeping them in the hands of the U.S. and major capitalist nations by undermining and destroying any viable alternative to efforts by poorer nations to leave the global capitalist order. The reader should study the history of U.S. economic and military aggression against Chile, Cuba, El Salvador, Haiti, Nicaragua, and Vietnam to test this thesis.

11   Lynne Cheney, *American Memory: A Report on the Humanities in the Nation's Public Schools* (Washington: National Endowment for the Humanities, 1987), 5.

12   Ibid., 7.

13   Diane Ravitch and Chester E. Finn, Jr., *What Do Our 17-Year-Olds Know?: A Report on the First National Assessment of History and Literature* (New York: Harper and Row, 1987), 1.

14   Ibid., 17,20.

15   Ibid., 201.

16   Ibid., 251-2.

17   Finn and Ravitch, "Conclusions and Recommendations: High Expectations and Disciplined Effort," in *Against Mediocrity: The Humanities in America's High School*, eds. Finn, Ravitch and Robert T. Fancher (New York: Holmes and Meier, 1984), 240.

18   Charles Silberman, *Crisis in the Classroom: The Remaking of American Education* (New York: Random House, 1970), 134.

19   Ibid., 126.

20   Ibid., 11.

21   Paul Gagnon, quoted in William Bennett, *Our Children and Our Country: Improving America's Schools and Affirming the Common Culture* (New York: Simon and Schuster, 1988), 160.

22   Ibid., 161.

23   Ibid., 163-4.

24   Thomas Jefferson, quoted in Ibid., 160.

25   Ibid., 165.

26   Allan Bloom, *The Closing of the American Mind: How Higher Education Has Failed Democracy and Impoverished the Souls of Today's Students* (New York: Simon and Schuster, 1987), 29.

27   Ibid.

28   Ibid., 141-2.

29   Ibid., 166.

30   Ibid., 43.

31   R. Freeman Butts, "Public Education in a Pluralistic Society," *Educational Theory*, Vol. 27, No. 1, Winter 1977, 9.

32   Butts, *Public Education in the United States: From Revolution to Reform* (New York: Holt, Rinehart and Winston, 1978), 395.

33   Butts, *The Civic Mission in Educational Reform: Perspectives For The Public and The Profession* (Stanford, California: Hoover Institution Press, 1989), 280.

34   See Stanley Aronowitz and Henry A. Giroux, "Schooling, Culture and Literacy in the Age of Broken Dreams," *Harvard Educational Review*, Vol. 58, No. 2, May 1988.

35   E.D. Hirsch, Jr., *Cultural Literacy: What Every American Needs to Know* (Boston: Houghton Mifflin, 1987), 7.

36   Ibid., 144.

37   Lawrence Cremin, *The Genius of American Education* (New York: Random House, 1965), 23.

38   "Report of the Commissioners Appointed to Fix the Site of the University of Virginia," in Roy J. Honeywell, *The Educational Work of Thomas Jefferson* (Cambridge, Massachusetts: Harvard University Press, 1931), quoted in Ibid., 37.

39   Ibid., 46-7.

40   Ibid., 61.

41   Richard A. Brosio, *A Radical Democratic Critique of Capitalist Education* (New York: Peter Lang, 1994).

42   Morris Janowitz, *The Reconstruction of Patriotism* (Chicago: University of Chicago Press, 1983), x.

43   John Dewey, *Democracy and Education* (New York: The Free Press, 1966), 113-14.

44   Barbara Finkelstein, "Rescuing Civic Learning: Some Prescriptions for the 1990s," *Theory into Practice*, Vol. XXVII, No. 4, Autumn 1988, 251.

45   R.H. Brown, *Society as Text: Essays on Rhetoric, Reason and Reality* (Chicago: University of Chicago Press, 1987), cited in Ibid.

46   Finkelstein, 251.

47   Edward Berman, "The State's Stake in Educational Reform," in Christine Shea, Ernest Kahane, and Peter Sola, eds., *The New Servants of Power: A Critique of the 1980s School Reform Movement* (New York: Praeger, 1989), 58. See also his "Civic Education in the Corporatized Classroom," *Theory into Practice*, Volume XXVII, No. 4, Autumn 1988.

48   Ibid., 59.

49   Ibid., 61.

50   Arthur Schlesinger, Jr., "The Disuniting of America," *American Educator*, Winter 1991, 14.

Chapter 2

America: The Dominant-Elite View

The educational reports and influential theorists discussed in this chapter reflect premises and principles about American history and society that shape their views on such matters as the Founding and the Constitution, human rights, and the U.S. role in the world. Their dominant-elite perspective will then be contrasted in chapter 3 with those of radical dissenters whose insights are rarely found in schools and the mass media.

America: Leading Theorists and Fundamental Principles

The influential reports and individuals cited in this chapter begin with one fundamental premise about our country: despite recurring problems and inequalities, the United States is and has been a democratic and humane society, in many ways the last and best hope for freedom and justice in the world. This fundamental premise holds, for example, in *The Paideia Proposal* and other writings of the philosopher and educator Mortimer Adler. The *Paideia* report discusses the kind of educational system the country needs to raise children for a democratic and civil society. Arguing that the United States is a classless society because citizens are actually "the principal and permanent rulers,"[1] Adler asserts that the fundamental ideas shaping the nation are found in such documents such as the Declaration of Independence, the Constitution, and Lincoln's Gettysburg Address. These ideas include the basic concerns for "equality, inalienable rights (or human rights), pursuit of happiness, civil rights . . . the consent of the governed, the dissent of the governed." However, he reminds us that the principle of equality is "an ideal that we have not yet fully achieved."[2] This is also true for the "idea of democracy, for the Greek roots of that word mean precisely that: government by the *demos*, or people. . . . we can see that it is an ideal that is still far from being fully attained."[3] When they discuss the country, civic literacy and the schools, supporters of the dominant-elite view such as Adler admit that problems have blocked the realization of the lofty vision of the Founders, but these are contradictions within a democratic and humane history.

Adler states that in the Preamble to the Constitution there are other ideas, such as "justice, domestic tranquility . . . or civil peace, common defense . . . national security, general welfare, blessings of liberty," which are also ideals; some of these have been realized through "successive amendments to the Constitution."[4] He cites the Declaration of Independence, however, in a way that departs from any other report or individual discussed in this book: "a free people has another right: the right to alter or abolish any form of government that fails to protect or that violates their natural rights."[5] When the political rights of the American people are discussed in the mass media and education, this right identified by Adler is not mentioned; thus, students have no basis upon which to examine this Jeffersonian principle in light of the past and contemporary events. Adler honestly admits the contradictions within the founding democratic and egalitarian ideals of the country, discussing those who were not allowed to share in these ideals: women, blacks who were enslaved, and many poor white males who didn't have enough property to pay poll taxes. Although these groups were not part of "the people," they "were in fact an overwhelming majority."[6] This conservative and influential spokesperson for the dominant-elite perspective recognizes those left out of the egalitarian democratic community. He should have included Native Americans as well, although they have always claimed, rightly, that they are separate and sovereign nations that are not part of the United States.

Adler is concerned about the increasing power of the Presidency and the Executive Branch. He comments on the "enormous increase in the power of the President [over] Congress in the sphere of foreign policy, in leading the nation by gradual steps into undeclared war, and in deploying our military might in order to serve our national interests without consulting Congress about them." The country's military has changed from a small standing army to the present one which is "huge in size and arsenal, globally stationed . . . raising issues of security and using agencies of secret intelligence, and having immense impact not only on free people but also on domestic politics."[7] These are important insights that are not addressed by the dominant-elite reports or theorists cited in this book. Despite his perceptive comments about the realization of our founding ideals, and the impact on free people of the national security state—a development that has brought little outcry from conservatives who might be expected to oppose the massive and permanent militarization of the country—these negative developments are mentioned only as exceptions to what he sees as a sound and marvelous system. They are not considered as fundamental and undemocratic developments that have been unfolding since 1776.

In *Democracy's Untold Story*, Paul Gagnon discusses the bonds in our political heritage that have brought Americans together, "the vision of a common life in liberty, justice and equality as expressed in the Declaration of Independence and Constitution."[8] Given Gagnon's reputation as an historian, one wonders how he can ignore the actual conditions facing the majority of the people during the period of our Declaration and Constitution (as Adler touched on, above). Gagnon asserts that "informed, reasoned allegiance to the ideals of a free society rests on three convictions: First, that democracy is the worthiest form of human governance ever conceived. Second, we cannot take its survival or its spread—or its perfection in practice—for granted [because] we know that very much still needs to be done to achieve justice and civility in our own society." While applauding the honorable traditions that have made the country great, therefore, according to Gagnon we must recognize that there is much to do to insure that such blessings belong to all. This is a recurring theme among the dominant-elite reports and intellectuals, expressed again and again without any reasonable explanation of why these blessings are not already enjoyed by all more than two centuries after the Founding.

Gagnon's third point is that "democracy's survival depends upon our transmitting to each new generation the political vision of liberty and equality that unites us as Americans—and a deep loyalty to the political institutions our founders put together to fulfill that vision."[9] This view is found in the mass media and school history lessons. Despite fundamental contradictions (e.g., most people were not included in the democratic and revolutionary founding of the country; a genocidal destruction of the indigenous peoples who were here; a system of slavery lasted nearly another century, and racism blocked the achievement of formal political rights for African Americans until the Voting Rights Act of 1965; political voting rights were denied to women in national elections until 1920; and working people and the poor have been exploited throughout American history), *Democracy's Untold Story* can still claim that we are a society guided by "liberal and humane values." The work to attain these values continues, but democracy advocates are open to attack by the "extremists of Left and Right, well-armed with force and simple answers. The ongoing, worldwide struggle for a free center . . . is the best hope of the earth and we would make it the heart of a reordered curriculum for history and social studies."[10] Voiced here is another fundamental premise of the dominant-elite position: truth resides in the democratic center and not at the extremes, especially on the Left.

Democracy's Untold Story admits the problems and contradictions that undermine the noble ideals that marked the Founding and history of our country. It acknowledges that conflict and violence have influenced the development and history of democratic societies, since "all of the major self-governing states conquered and colonized weaker societies by brute military force in the several decades prior to 1914." Gagnon can "easily point to the contradiction between ideals expressed, and often adhered to, at home and injustice and the aggression and exploits practiced abroad; to the corruption of public life and political debate at home by the forces of imperialism; and finally, to the seeds of decline, even of self-destruction, sown by the imperialist urge." This "imperialist urge" appears to emanate from a biologically based human nature, as Gagnon puts forth some need on the part of countries or individuals that makes them unable

to withstand the temptations that come with power and success. Democracies have been no exception. Again and again, democratic ideals and their advocates at home have failed to contain the forces of
pride or greed or the ordinary desire for comfort and convenience at
the expense of others.[11]

This explanation for imperialist aggression and exploitation
sounds very familiar, similar to other human nature ideologies that have been put forth to defend class rule, male dominance, and white supremacy. In essence, they hold that there
is some natural or inborn tendency to domination and imperial rule, which even infects "democratic" societies.

William Bennett passionately defends the lofty principles
and traditions that have shaped the country. These include
"justice, liberty, government with the consent of the governed,
and equality under the law." These ideas are the "glue" that
hold this society together, the basic truths that should be taught
to our youth, who must be made to understand that they live
in a "free, self-governing society [that defends] those ideas
which together make for freedom and self-government."[12] I raise
here a central question that will be examined by dissenters in
chapter 3: Was this nation founded on such honorable principles, given the language and practice of the Constitution,
laws, and social life which excluded the majority from substantive involvement, enslaved millions, and sanctioned aggression
against the original inhabitants?

Alongside the fundamental principles and truths that youth
should know, however, Bennett sees a "dark side"—other societies and ideas that contrast with our devotion to freedom and
justice. For example, do youth know about the Berlin Wall?
About "terror as an instrument of state policy" and what happened in Cambodia? He claims that "our" principles and traditions have not guided all governments in this world, and
applying "universal" standards will show us that some nations
"are simply awful."[13] This statement is true, but U.S. enemies
are the "awful" ones, never its friends; and the United States
itself is never included among the "awful." The U.S. does not
have a principled objection to terror or oppression but rather
a political and expedient one that suits its national interests,
i.e., the interests of the dominant elite. Thus, the terrible ones
include Iraq but not Indonesia, Cuba but not Guatemala. The
"universal standards" are never applied to U.S. actions and

support of murderous regimes in the world; certainly that would not be the kind of civic literacy the dominant elites want. Bennett argues that we need to teach honestly about how such terrible realities contrast with our own democratic system; we need to teach youth "the whole truth" about other nations. But this "whole truth" cannot be taught, because it would drive the "democratic distemper" of youth to new and dangerous heights.

Bennett's celebration of Western and U.S. principles and history is complemented by Allan Bloom, who argues that despite the efforts of "radicals in the civil rights movement" to portray the Founding and American principles as "racist," the "United States is one of the highest and most extreme achievements of the rational quest for the good life according to nature." Despite the genocidal and horrible facts of American history (see p. 34), Bloom can accuse "radicals" of terrible attacks on the country and the men of principle who brought it to life. According to him, these Founders and the Revolution created a system of government that was based on "freedom and equality, hence on the consent of the governed," and Americans "were in general were satisfied with the result and had a pretty clear view of what they had done."[14] Bloom wrote in the late 1980s, when the U.S. was crushing the democratic Sandinista reforms in Nicaragua, continuing economic and military attacks on Cuba, supporting the South African government and the forces it sponsored in the terrorist wars in Angola and Mozambique, and blocking the efforts of many at home to obtain their full human rights. Still, this era is termed as the defining "American moment in world history, the one for which we shall forever be judged," because "the fate of freedom in the world" was the responsibility of our "regime."[15]

R. Freeman Butts argues that civic literacy's historic and contemporary importance is absolutely essential for the maintenance of a democratic and sound society. His views on the Founding, history, and guiding principles of the country are in line with the major national reports and leading intellectuals such as Bennett and Bloom; unlike the latter, however, he is not an uncritical cheerleader for the country's principles and policies. He agrees with the American Federation of Teachers that "democracy is the worthiest form of human government ever conceived" and the United States is part of the "great central drama of modern history . . . to establish, preserve, and extend democracy—at home and abroad."[16] As a people we have a noble heritage that citizens should support, despite the serious ills that have plagued us since the birth of the country.

> We have seen how the Republic's founders rejected military power, religious sanction, and the inherited prerogatives of kinship or hier-archical social class as the basis for the authority of the new Ameri-can community. They proclaimed instead that the democratic politi-cal community was to be the building element of social cohesion and that this political community was to be based upon such basic values as liberty, equality, and justice.[17]

As with Bennett and Bloom, however, it is difficult to recon-cile Butts's view with what actually happened in that period, when there was no justice for slaves, American Indians, women and the poor. He states that important and vital questions re-main, however, and must be considered if citizens are "to judge the merits of public policies in domestic and foreign affairs." They will do this "only by careful judgments informed by a reasoned historical perspective and a meaningful concept of the best values underlying our constitutional order."[18] Yet within this constitutional order, presidents have engaged in war without the congressional mandate required by the Con-stitution, and without any restraint by the courts, which have totally abdicated their responsibility with regard to state-sanc-tioned violence. Although lauding the founding ideals and our democracy like other dominant-elite reports and intellectuals, Butts does not ignore the serious problems facing the country. He asserts that while we rightfully look with pride at "building a genuine cohesive, as well as pluralistic democratic society," we cannot avoid the historical legacy of "persistent racism, nativism, segregation, discrimination, and inequality."[19] In addition, Butts is genuinely troubled and disturbed by the "lack of truth telling by governments of democratic and free societ-ies." This includes "deceptions" and "attempted cover-ups" that involved Vietnam, Watergate, and the Iran-Contra affair. All this caused citizens' trust in their leaders to decline, with a resultant risk to the foundations of our free society.[20]

Citizens who cannot separate truth from lies cannot critique historical events, and so "cannot retain their freedom." Butts continues: "Nor can a government that lies to its citizens continue to serve justice and equality, maintain its legitimate authority, or even expect loyalty from its citizens."[21] If we take Butts's criteria to heart, and apply them to an investigation of U.S. foreign policy, it becomes clear that the U.S. government has broken new ground when it comes to systematic lying to the people on the vital matters of state. A study of the historical record would bear out his concerns; therefore, why should youth or citizens give allegiance to such a government? The erosion of trust that Butts sees undermines the principles that he claims the Founders emphasized, such as "the individual's obligation for the public good in terms of civic virtue . . . patriotism and loyalty to the new emerging nation as well as duty, discipline, and obedience to moral and religious commands." These virtues are needed more than ever, because they are the "social and political glue" that will allow our democratic political system to survive as well as prosper.[22] But if the government is unjust and corrupt, why have this glue? Given its "deception," does it deserve to persist and thrive?

Diane Ravitch emphasizes "the unique feature of the United States," a "common culture" created out of the "interaction of its subsidiary cultures." She goes on to state that "it is a culture that has been influenced over time by immigrants, American Indians, African slaves, and their descendants." This is a mind-boggling statement, especially when one considers that everything that American Indians and African slaves brought to this "common culture" was assaulted. She contends that we are "a single nation knitted together by a common set of political and moral values . . . how do we reconcile our *pluribus* and our *unum*?" Students and citizens need to understand and appreciate that "we are one people. . . . We are all Americans." Her passionate allegiance to the dominant-elite perspective comes through loud and clear in her view of patriotism: "*True patriotism celebrates the moral force of the American idea as a nation that unites as one people the descendants of many cultures, races, relations, and ethnic groups.*"[24] This perspective to which Ravitch refers is a hegemonic celebration of patriotism and moral force which is passed on uncritically to youth in schools. The "truth" and "moral force" represented undermine the civic literacy so often touted as essential to learning.

In her editorial comments for *The American Reader: Words That Moved A Nation*, Ravitch returns to the fundamental themes and stirring thoughts that form the basis for the dominant-elite view of the Founding and its basic principles. "The settling of America began with an idea . . . . citizens of a society could join freely and agree to govern themselves by making laws for the common good."[25] This idea was reinforced in 1776 by the Declaration of Independence, which Jefferson felt was "an appeal to the tribunal of the world." The founding principles in such documents as the Mayflower Compact and the Declaration of Independence "have resounded throughout the world," and those seeking to reform America, "whatever their cause . . . have reminded the public that 'all men are created equal.'" These sentiments from our country's history have moved people throughout the world as they struggled "against undemocratic regimes"; they have used "Jefferson's words, that governments derive 'their just powers from the consent of the governed.'"[26] She is right on one point: these are genuine and powerful symbols that have inspired historic struggles by other peoples—such as the Vietnamese, who declared their independence from France in 1945 by using the opening lines of our Declaration of Independence. That struggle for independence, however, was opposed by the United States.

The dominant-elite view of country, democracy, and national unity is also found in the writings of Arthur Schlesinger, Jr. Discussing the issues of civic literacy and multiculturalism that are at the heart of current debate and controversy, Schlesinger asks the same question as that "famously asked two centuries ago by French immigrant J. Hector St. John de Crèvecoeur in his book *Letters from an American Farmer*: "what then, is this American, This new man?" 'The American is a new man, who acts upon new principles. . . . *Here individuals of all nations are melted into a new race of men.*'"[27] This "new race of men," of course, meant white men and excluded the vast majority of those living in the nation at that time. Schlesinger does not see a fundamental problem with this exception to the humanist rule of justice and equality and the other noble principles that inspired the Founding and historical evolution of our nation.

America and the National Security State

I close this chapter with the reflections of Robert N. Bellah et al., authors of the insightful *Habits of the Heart: Individualism and Commitment in American Life*, and the follow-up discussion of themes raised in that book, *The Good Society*. Combined with fine insights on the nature of our country, civic concerns and democracy, and the pressing need for community, are premises about the principles of the nation, human rights, and U.S. foreign relations that fall within the dominant-elite perspective. This view is evident in their analysis of National Security Council Document 68 (1950), perhaps the most important single statement of the national security state to emerge in the post-World War II era. NSC 68, which laid the foundation for U.S. aggression throughout the world, is a blunt and detailed statement of the dominant-elite view on foreign policy that has remained with us up to the present under both Democratic and Republican administrations. My decision to place Bellah et al. on the side of the dominant elite will become evident when I compare their treatment of NSC 68 with the interpretation of the same document by the country's leading dissident intellectual, Noam Chomsky (see chapter 3).

In their reading of NSC 68, *The Good Society* authors assert that the goal of the U.S. after World War II "was to create a new, morally superior world order."[28] For the NSC, America's fundamental goal was to "assure the integrity and vitality of our free society, which is founded upon the dignity and worth of the individual." There is a deep concern on the part of the NSC authors that they are living in a momentous time in history, facing "the fulfillment or destruction not only of this Republic but of civilization itself."[29] With such issues at stake, therefore, Bellah et al. assert that the nation "had to make itself powerful in order to defend the cause of freedom in the world. Today such talk seems excessively idealistic. Realists in and outside of government are more wont to talk about regaining our competitive edge, keeping on top, staying on as Number One."[30]

The Good Society asserts that those who wrote NSC 68 and guided the nation's foreign policy after 1945 "rooted that policy deeply in ideals of freedom and responsibility. However, their formulations were not profound enough to prevent the eventual and continual resort to means that would undermine them."[31] American ideals and ends of freedom and responsibility are therefore honorable but often undermined in practice. Bellah and colleagues miss an evident point: the premises of NSC 68 and policies that flow from it are consistent with maintaining dominant-elite interests in the world, and aggression is a legitimate means to this end. Basic to the document's vision "was the familiar American idea 'freedom under a government of laws.'" It reflected principles that

> flowed from a quintessential American combination of virtues and vices. It was bold and generous in its conception of ultimate goals. Not afraid to reach for high ideals, it dared to commit itself uncompromisingly to the defense of the dignity of each individual human person in the world.[32]

We must recall that in the period when this document was written, the CIA was undermining democratic movements in Europe led by those who had resisted fascism in WW II, racist segregation existed in the country, and the United States supported South African apartheid and the French attack on the Vietnamese.

Despite the laudable goals and vision of NSC 68, however, the authors remind us that it was "recklessly simplistic in its characterization of 'free society' as anything outside the Soviet system. . . . there were many other threats to freedom and dignity in the world, arising . . . from hatreds produced by class inequalities, racism, radical nationalism."[33] What was wrong with "the utopianism of NSC 68 was that there could be no coherent relation between the idealistic goals and the realistic means chosen to pursue them."[34] Drawing from the work of such writers as Noam Chomsky and Michael Parenti, however, I will argue that there has indeed been a close and "coherent relation." The professed "ideals" in the NSC document were those of a dominant elite aiming to preserve its economic and political interests in the world after the war, and assertions of justice, equality, freedom and democracy were really smokescreens to cover more important ends. The professed ideals have never been put into practice by those running the national security state, as the historical record of support for vicious and violent tyrants clearly demonstrates (see chapter 3).

Bellah and his co-authors develop a connection between the vision of NSC 68 and our founding principles as put forth by John Winthrop, Puritan leader and oft-times Governor of the Massachusetts Bay Colony, whose thoughts "remained archetypal for one understanding of what life in America was to be: 'We must delight in each other, make others' conditions our own, rejoice together, mourn together, labor and suffer together, always having before our eyes our community as members of the same body.'"[35] Winthrop's vision of our purpose as a people is part of the Puritans' religious tradition, whose "fundamental criterion of success was not material wealth but the creation of a community in which a genuine ethical and spiritual life could be lived."[36] This community of genuine ethical and spiritual values did not extend to the women of that community, nor to Native Americans, of whom Winthrop said: "But for the natives in these parts, God hath so pursued them, as for 300 miles space the greatest part of them are swept away by the smallpox which still continues among them. . . . God hath thereby cleared our title to this place."[37]

The authors share the guiding principles of a key Founder, James Madison, who writes in *The Federalist Papers* that "the public good, the real welfare of the great body of people, is the supreme object to be pursued; and that no form of government whatever has any other values than as it may be fitted for the attainment of this object." He begins with the "great republican principle, that the people will have virtue and intelligence to select men of virtue and wisdom."[38] This principle flowed from the basic premise that "the virtue of the people would lead them to choose for their officials and representatives men who would be great-spirited enough to place the public good above their own."[39] I shall return to the issue of the public good in chapter 3 with a radical and dissenting view, one that challenges Madison and the other wealthy and white Founders' perspective on the public interest and private class interest. The common or civic good as we now understand this term was not their primary concern: they had a much narrower definition of what constitutes this good. For all Madison's insights on the class nature of this system and the dominance of power related to the ownership of private property, the dissenting view is correct: the public good—and the civic literacy that is supposed to help youth to see and understand it—has never been a supreme object to be pursued in this nation.

The essential principles that form the elite perspective profoundly influence our national policies, school history lessons, and mass media commentary on important issues. But the professed principles are abstract and vague, and bear little relationship to actual dominant elite and government policies. These professed sentiments are captured by George Bush, former President and head of the CIA, and the prime architect of the Gulf War and Panama invasions. Accepting the Republican Party's nomination for reelection 1988, he said: "I see America as the leader, a unique nation with a special role in the world. This has been called the American century, because in it we were the dominant force for good in the world. . . . now we are on the verge of a new century, and what country's name will it bear? I say it will be another American century."[40] This is the ideology of empire and imperialism that has been fostered by the dominant elite and its educational allies.

The dominant elite and its allies are "the chosen people" who have tried to make good on this "Manifest Destiny"—even if it meant genocide, slavery, and terror. Bush's dominant-elite perspective shapes our destiny as a people—and no discussion of noble visions or national documents, commencement addresses or history lessons, will hide its arrogant and imperial assumptions. It has formed the basis for indoctrinating generations of youth.

Notes

1   Mortimer Adler On Behalf of the Members of the Paideia Group, *The Paideia Proposal: An Educational Manifesto* (New York: Macmillan, 1982), 17.

2   Adler, *We Hold These Truths: Understanding the Ideas and Ideals of the Constitution* (New York: Macmillan, 1987), 30.

3   Ibid., 29-30.

4   Ibid., 30.

5   Ibid., 76.

6   Ibid., 85.

7   Ibid., 112.

8   Paul Gagnon, *Democracy's Untold Story: What World History Books Neglect* (Washington: American Federation of Teachers, Education for Democracy Project, 1987), 13.

9   Ibid., 14.

10   Ibid., 21.

11   Ibid., 101.

12   William Bennett, *Our Children and Our Country: Improving America's Schools and Affirming The Common Culture* (New York: Simon and Schuster, 1988), 203.

13   Ibid., 203-4.

14   Allan Bloom, *The Closing of the American Mind: How Higher Education Has Failed Democracy and Impoverished the Souls of Today's Students* (New York: Simon and Schuster, 1987), 39.

15   Ibid., 158.

16   *Education for Democracy: A Statement of Principles; Guidelines for Strengthening the Teaching of Democratic Values* (Washington: American Federation of Teachers, 1987), quoted in R. Freeman Butts, *The Civic Mission in Educational Reform: Perspectives for The Public and The Profession* (Stanford, California: Hoover Institution Press, 1989), 10.

17   Ibid., 133.

18   Ibid., 280.

19 Butts, "International Human Rights and Civic Education," in Marga-
    ret Stimmann Branson and Judith Torney-Purta, eds., *International
    Human Rights, Society, and the Schools* (Washington: National Council
    For The Social Studies, Bulletin No. 68, 1982), 25. On this book, SUNY
    Cortland philosopher and colleague John Ryder commented on my
    critique of Butts and the Founders: "There's an interesting question
    that addresses this general point. Certainly you're right to point out
    that these commentators speak in grandiose terms about the Founders
    and their principles without taking seriously the majority . . . to whom
    these principles presumably didn't apply. But can one be guilty of the
    converse mistake, i.e., emphasizing . . . that the majority were excluded,
    while not realizing or acknowledging the fact or possibility that the
    Founders were serious about their principles and that their principles
    . . . were and to some extent still are, progressive?" See chapter 3 for
    more discussion on these questions.

20 Butts, *Civic Mission*, 298.

21 Ibid.

22 Ibid., 298-99.

23 Diane Ravitch, "Diversity and Democracy: Multicultural Education in
    America," *American Educator*, Spring 1990, 18.

24 Ibid., 19.

25 Ravitch, ed., *The American Reader: Words That Moved A Nation* (New
    York: HarperCollins, 1990), 3.

26 Ibid., 149.

27 Arthur Schlesinger, Jr., *The Disuniting of America: Reflections on a
    Multicultural Society* (New York: W.W. Norton, 1992), 12.

28 Robert Bellah, Richard A. Madsen, William M. Sullivan, Ann Swidler,
    and Stephen Tipton, *The Good Society* (New York: Random House,
    1992), 223.

29 National Security Document 68, in Thomas H. Etzhold and John Lewis
    Gaddis,"United States Objectives and Programs for National Secu-
    rity, NSC 68, April 14, 1950," in *Containment: Documents on American
    Politics and Strategy, 1945-1950* (New York: Columbia University Press,
    1978), quoted in Robert Bellah, et al., Ibid.

30 Bellah, et al., 224.

31 Ibid.

32 Ibid., 227.

33 Ibid.

34   Ibid., 228.

35   Robert Bellah, Richard A. Madsen, William M. Sullivan, Ann Swidler, and Stephen Tipton, *Habits of the Heart: Individualism and Commitment in American Life* (Berkeley: University of California Press, 1985), 28.

36   Ibid., 29.

37   Quoted in Howard Simpson, *Invisible Armies: The Impact of Disease on American History* (Indianapolis: Bobbs-Merrill, 1980), 7.

38   James Madison, *Federalist No. 45*, quoted in Bellah, et al., *Habits of the Heart*, 253. John Ryder commented here as well on my discussion of Madison and the Founders. "I don't think that Madison and the others did not have the public good in mind. The real question is 'what counts as the public?' For them, the public simply did not include women, the poor, etc. The analogy may be with the fact that when we speak about the importance of public participation in political life, we simply do not include children. We take it for granted that they are not capable of such participation. That's what the Founders thought about most of the people, so that most of 'the people' were not part of 'the public.' This may mean that we should no longer accept their concept of 'the public good,' but it does not mean that they didn't take it seriously."

39   Madison, quoted in Ibid., 255.

40   George Bush, quoted in *The Good Society*, 245.

Chapter 3

America: A Dissenting View

I begin with a simple and powerful statement from the historian Howard Zinn: We should "never lose the perception between the world as it is, and the way it should, or ought, to be." This is an important distinction, because the educational reports and theorists discussed in chapters 1 and 2 have used the professed ideals of America to undermine a civically literate understanding of its actual history.

Civic Literacy and the National Security State

Chapter 2 ended with Robert Bellah and colleagues' analysis of National Security Council Document (NSC) 68 (1950). I wish to critique that document and fundamental assumptions about our government and history from the perspective of the country's leading dissident intellectual, Noam Chomsky.[1] In contrast to these authors' analysis of NSC 68, Chomsky reveals how U.S. aggression throughout the world logically flows from the premises of the national security state and this document. As the reader recalls from Chapter 2, the essence of NSC 68 was that, unlike the Soviet Union, the "fundamental purpose [of the United States] is to assure the integrity and vitality of our free society, which is founded upon the dignity and worth of the individual."[2] This statement was written while the United States was, according to historian Melvyn Leffler, pursuing Cold War policies despite the fact that the dominant elite admitted in private that the USSR was unable to mount aggressive policies because of its huge losses in World War II and its "defensive posture" after the war in the 1940s.[3]

In a review of a section of NSC 68 that was not examined in *The Good Society* discussion, Chomsky points to the blunt language used by the dominant elite to "manufacture consent" among the public to achieve the wondrous ends dictated by its Cold War policies:

> To achieve these essential goals [against the USSR], we must overcome weaknesses in our society, such as "the excesses of a permanently open mind," "the excess of toleration," and "dissent among us"; we will have to learn to "distinguish between the necessity for tolerance and the necessity for just suppression," a crucial feature of "the democratic way." It is particularly important to insulate our "labor unions, civic enterprises, schools, churches, and all media for influencing opinion" from the evil work of the Kremlin, which seeks to subvert them and "make them sources of confusion in our economy, our civil culture and our body politic."[4]

NSC 68's assumptions prevail today when it comes to the good intentions of the United States. These are taken for granted by the reports and theorists cited in Chapters 1 and 2. These "good intentions" include "[invading] South Vietnam, [overthrowing] the democratic capitalist government of Guatemala in 1954 and [maintaining] the rule of murderous gangsters ever since, [running] by far the most extensive international terrorist operations in history against Cuba from the early 1960s and Nicaragua through the 1980s . . . [backing] Trujillo, Somoza, Marcos, Duvalier . . . the racist rulers of Southern Africa, and a whole host of other major criminals."[5] These facts from the historical record force us to ask basic questions that are at the heart of the debate over civic literacy: How do we sort out truth from untruth on these important issues that affect the country and world? How are the professed assertions of concern for human rights and democracy to be evaluated in light of the U.S. actions listed above, which resulted in the deaths of millions?

Chomsky's documentation is provided by the dominant elite itself. More realistic than its ideals is the view put forth in 1948 by George Kennan, an influential spokesmen for that dominant elite:

> . . .we have about 50 percent of the world's wealth, but only 6.3% of its population. . . . In this situation, we cannot fail to be the object of

envy and resentment. Our real task in the coming period is to devise
a pattern of relations which will permit us to maintain this position of
disparity without positive detriment to our national security. . . . We
need not deceive ourselves that we can afford . . . the luxury of altru-
ism and world-benefaction. . . . We should cease to talk about . . .
unreal objectives such as human rights, the raising of living standards,
and democratization.[6]

Idealistic youth, teachers, and citizens believe the professed
principles put forth about human rights and helping oppressed
peoples, but the dominant elite knows what it really takes to
maintain U.S. control over the resources to which Kennan referred. Few students have ever read his words or heard of him.
How can they become civically literate if such insights and
critiques of them are not examined?

What is simply not considered by the dominant-elite reports
and theorists is that during the decades of the Cold War, the
United States engaged in "worldwide subversion, aggression
and state terrorism" which strengthened the "military-industrial
complex," of which former President Eisenhower spoke in his
January, 1961 farewell address.[7] This process has brought increased power and influence to the dominant elite, and has
used up more than ten trillion public tax dollars since World
War II to support that powerful corporate-Pentagon alliance.
The national security state has been strengthened at the expense of the civic literacy, human rights, and popular involvement that are essential aspects of a democracy.

In contrast to dominant-elite assertions about the democratic
and egalitarian nature of our society, Chomsky's view of the
premises of our "capitalist democracy" is far more accurate:
"the primary concern of everyone must be to ensure that the
wealthy are satisfied; all else is secondary. . . . Only to the extent that the demands of the wealthy . . . are satisfied can the
population at large hope for a decent existence in their role as
servants of private power."[8] As applied to international life and
death matters of war and peace, this principle is articulated as
follows: "The central—and not surprising—conclusion that
emerges from the documentary and historical record in that
the U.S. international and security policy . . . has as its primary goal the preservation of what we might call 'the Fifth
Freedom,' understood crudely but with a fair degree of accu-

racy as the freedom to rob, to exploit and to dominate, to undertake any course of action to ensure that existing privilege is protected and advanced."[9] A civically-literate education for youth would expose them to such truths, thus allowing the most reasonable assessment of our nation's history based upon the evidence, not unsubstantiated beliefs paraded forth in history lessons and the mass media. Readers may judge for themselves whether this or any other of Chomsky's truthful assertions has ever surfaced in their school history lessons.

The concern that the dominant elite and its allies express regarding civic literacy, war and peace, has been exposed as wanting by dissident African Americans; perhaps the foremost of these is W.E.B. DuBois, the internationally-renowned and respected intellectual and activist. At the end of World War II, DuBois discussed the nation's commitment to human rights and democracy for people of color; he contended it would be *the* issue of the twentieth century in the United States. As contemporary events and tensions make clear, DuBois's prophecy has come to pass throughout the world. In 1945, he argued that World War II

> made it clear that we can no longer regard Western Europe and North America as the world for which civilization exists; nor can we look upon European culture as the norm for all peoples. Henceforth the majority of the inhabitants of the earth, who happen for the most part to be colored, must be regarded as having the right and the capacity to share in human progress and to become copartners in that democracy which alone can ensure peace among men.[10]

At that time, there was little mention of the "imperial ownership of the disenfranchised colonies" which are exploited because those living there are "regarded mainly as sources of profit for Europe and North America." This truth meant that the imperialist white dominant elite was "planning not peace but war, not democracy but the continued oligarchical control of civilization by the white race." This process continues today through economic, political, and military means, because that elite knows that there is a "rivalry for power and prestige, race dominance and income arising from the ownership of men, land, and materials." As long as this imperialist struggle continues, "there can be neither peace on earth nor goodwill toward men."[11]

DuBois understood that steps to remedy the racism and exploitation that enriched a few in the West at the expense of people of color throughout the world would not come without arduous struggle, because "most modern countries are in the hands of those who control organized wealth, and the just and wise distribution of income is hindered by this monopoly. . . . The retention of this power is influenced tremendously by the propaganda of newspapers, by radio, and by social organization." The "hand of organized wealth guides the education of youth,"[12] including American history lessons. He concluded by asserting that "democracy has failed because so many fear it. They believe that wealth and happiness are so limited that a world full of intelligent, healthy and free people is impossible."[13] While many dramatic changes in the world have been brought about since 1945 by struggles to alter colonial relationships, the fundamental injustice that DuBois addressed has not changed, and racist exploitation remains in place.

Early in the twentieth century, DuBois wrote that "the first and fundamental and inescapable problem of American democracy was Justice" for Black Americans.[14] Manning Marable, political activist and scholar, argues that it was not simply that the nation had failed to deal with race relations in the country; DuBois saw racism "at the core of the system, including power, economic production, culture and society." By the end of World War II, Marable asserts that DuBois clearly understood that the "twin pillars of white capitalist oligarchy were domestic racism and colonialism. Until international and domestic racism were smashed, no serious discussion of democracy could even occur in the US."[15] According to Marable, DuBois also "concluded early in his career that *no real democracy has ever really existed in the U.S.* (emphasis added)." The "great problem of American democracy was that 'it had not yet been tried.' Neither Blacks nor whites had been freed to exercise democratic principles of governance because of the powerful controls of white capitalist America's upper class."[16] In *The Education of Black People*, DuBois argued that democracy should mean that "all men are created equal and should have an equal voice in their own government." It should mean "the opening of opportunity to the disinherited to contribute to civilization and the happiness of men." He believed that "given a chance for the majority of mankind to be educated, healthy and free to act, it may well turn out that human equality is not so wild a dream as many seem to hope."[17] This eloquent hope has not been shared by the Founders, dominant elites, and influential theorists who comment on such matters.

Marable has built upon the critical foundation that DuBois established. He states that "the most striking fact about American economic history and politics is the brutal and systematic underdevelopment of Black people. . . . Blacks have never been equal partners in the American Social Contract, because the system exists not to develop, but *to underdevelop Black people*."[18] Judging by their admission of racial ills but their overall laudatory comments on the just nature of American democracy, this harsh but all-too-true indictment of racism would be unacceptable to educators such as Bennett, Bloom, Gagnon and Ravitch. This indictment is not part of the civic literacy they want nourished in our youth. The wealthy delegates to the Constitutional Convention in 1787 "were unconcerned about the 'inalienable rights' of Afro-Americans. Their chief concern was the creation of a strong national government that would guarantee property rights—slavery being counted among them."[19]

Marable brings DuBois's critique on peace and race to the present international setting. Third World peoples "think of 'peace' [in the] broader political context of social justice and Third World self determination. . . . Peace is an active, self-aware relation between human beings, not the absence of struggle. Our task is to root out patriarchy, national oppression, and racist exploitation, in order to create the social environment for peaceful and egalitarian relations."[20] His testimony on behalf of those in the Third World is rarely heard by youth in their history and civics lessons or encounters with mass media, because it challenges the premises and practices that have dominated our society since 1776. This lesson should serve as a reminder that civic literacy for youth on issues of war and peace, oppression and justice, is impossible as long as the perspectives of those like DuBois and Marable are left out of the dialogue.

Marable's insights contradict the dominant-elite perspective, which places an extraordinary emphasis on the noble and democratic ideals of the country, especially its professed commitment to human rights and dignity for all people. He asserts that the plight of African and African-American people in the United States has been one of unrelenting exploitation based upon racist and capitalist oppression. This brutal reality was in place prior to the Founding, yet the phenomenon is seen by the dominant elite and its educational allies as an aberration within the humane and democratic unfolding of U.S. history.

DuBois's and Marable's insights about racism and capitalism are also present in the work of African-American educator and writer bell hooks, who has analyzed the nature of institutionalized oppression against people of color and women and challenged the premises and practices of this system. While arguing that feminism is "a struggle to end sexist oppression," she also critiques the nature of feminism that has ended up supporting U.S. and Western imperialism and militarism. Her own family experiences among Black anti-war males taught her that "all men do not glory in war, that all men who fight in wars do not necessarily believe that wars are just, that men are not inherently capable of killing or that militarism is the only possible means of safety." In her critique of sexism, racism, and imperialism-militarism, she challenges those feminists who equate militarism and patriarchy in a way that suggests "that to be male is synonymous with strength, aggression, and the will to dominate and do violence to others; and that to be female is synonymous with weakness, passivity, and the will to nourish and affirm the lives of others."[21]

In her critique of a reformist feminism that supports the premises and practices of the national security state, hooks reminds us that "rather than clarifying for women the power we exert in the maintenance of systems of domination and setting forth strategies for resistance and change, most current discussions of feminism and militarism further mystify women's role." Feminist advocates "who are concerned about militarism must insist that women (even those who have children) are not inherently more life-affirming or non-violent." They must also recognize that "masses of women in the United States are not anti-imperialist, are not against militarism, and until their value systems change, they must be seen as clinging, like their male counterparts, to a perspective on human relationships that embraces social domination in all its forms." She concludes by arguing that "imperialism and not patriarchy is the core foundation of militarism."[22] Since there is no monolithic women's perspective on the national security state, many women support the assault on human rights in poor countries and help to block civic literacy education for youth that might uncover such racist and imperialist policies.

hooks's view of feminism directs our attention to systems of domination and the links between sex, race, and class oppression. She openly challenges the prevailing view on the country, government and war. Unlike some feminists who work hard for reforms within the basic premises and structures that have shaped the history of the nation, but are silent about or supportive of U.S. wars in the Third World against people of color, hooks links the country's social, economic and political policies to women, placing the demands made by women and other oppressed groups within the context of the broader international policies of the United States. Her internationalist and anti-imperialist view places her with Chomsky, DuBois, Marable, and others who are outside the tolerated discourse on U.S. foreign policy, human rights, freedom, patriotism, democracy, and war. When such dissenting critiques are kept from the mass media and the schools, youth cannot develop the civic literacy that so many claim is essential in a democracy.

The essayist, poet, and political activist June Jordan is also part of the rich African-American dissident heritage. Despite the dominant-elite mythology about the Founding and the history of the country, Jordan asserts that African Americans and other citizens have not had and deserve "the intact legacy of the Declaration of Independence. Every single freedom guaranteed by the Constitution. A coherent foreign policy consistent with the principles of nonintervention and human rights."[23] To secure these rights and freedoms, she believes that as a nation "we cannot permit any one of us to slip outside the covenant of the Fourteenth Amendment to the Constitution," and that all our people "must be bound by the law of our country that, in turn, shall entitle him or her to the awesomely powerful privileges of American citizenship."[24]

This substantive citizenship has been denied to African Americans and others of color in particular, but also to all Americans. Jordan states that the country has become

> a beacon for tyrants, greed-driven entrepreneurs, and militaristic fantasies. As a people we have become accustomed to the homeless, beggars, the terrorized minorities, and the terrified elderly, As an electorate, we have become the craven subjects of deceitful, lawless,and inhumane leadership.[25]

She points out that, contrary to the dominant-elite history that students learn in schools, "democracy was never the goal of the Founding Fathers. 'The richest man in America,' George Washington, and his autocratic, slaveholding comrades wanted political autonomy for themselves and a comfortable continuation of their elitist wealth and privilege. . . . Indeed, most of the Fathers of America occupied public positions of power under the British. These white men were not egalitarians or rebels for justice!"[26]

Jordan also challenges "our ignorance of power—*why* it happens that some have while other have not/*when* power can change hands or move from the few to the many/*how* we may easily lose what we have gained with so much difficulty—this ignorance among us grows more dangerous, day by day!" She claims that we

> can know and must see . . . the truth of our predicament: It is they, the powerful few, who have never been the People. It is they, the would-be ruler aristocrats of politics and commerce, who composed those Founding Documents that value property as much as or more than human life, and it is they who have dared to evaluate other human beings for hire or for sale. . . . It is they . . . who rush to wars that they, themselves, refuse to fight. . . . It is they, the cowardly, lying, mean, egomaniacal, and irrepressibly avaricious ruling elite who invent and promulgate the ideology and practice of racism, throughout the world.[27]

The political economy that needs the national security state does not escape Jordan's critical challenge. This present dominant-elite system cannot "provide for the well-being of most of its citizens: our economic system increasingly concentrates . . . wealth in the hands of fewer and fewer interest groups" be-

cause it "increasingly augments the wealth of the richest sector of the citizenry while it diminishes the real wages and the
available livelihood of the poor." This class-controlled political economy "remains insensitive to the political demands of a
democracy,"[28] a fact that simply is not confronted by the dominant-elite reports and theorists discussed earlier. There is a
clear "operating principle" and imperative behind the system
that Jordan brilliantly dissects: to give to those who have and
take from those who do not.[29] Such radical perspectives are
rarely found in the history and civics lessons presented to our
youth; therefore, they cannot judge them in light of the historical record as part of the process of becoming civically literate.

The Founders and Founding Principles

Given the laudatory references in Chapters 1 and 2 to the
Founders and their supposedly magnificent principles, and the
contradictions embedded in these principles exposed by the
dissenting writers reviewed above, it is appropriate here to
present some critical thoughts on the Constitution and on one
of those Founders, James Madison. When we are moved by the
lofty rhetoric of the founding principles and insights—and there
is much to be learned from the words of those leaders who
gave serious attention to important political matters—we must
never forget that those sentiments were written in an era of
slavery, denial of basic rights for women, and genocide against
Native Americans. What people actually did—as opposed to
what they said, or what influential educators laud them for
saying—is the historical reality in the context of which the talk
of "liberty and the pursuit of happiness" must be seen. This
context is simply not addressed by our influential intellectuals
and reports.

One dissident who has exposed the chasm between the high
ideals and the brutal reality of America is the political theorist Michael Parenti. In *Democracy for the Few*, Parenti discusses
the civic illiteracy and mis-education of millions of youths who
learn a "somewhat idealized textbook version of American
government . . . the United States was founded by persons dedicated to building a nation for the good of all its citizens [and]

the nation's political leaders . . . are for the most part responsive to the popular will."[30] He disputes the idealism of the dominant-elite reports and theorists by addressing the actual nature of power, which "belongs to those who possess the
resources that enable them to control the behavior of others,
such as jobs, organizations, technology, publicity, media, social legitimacy, expertise, essential goods and services . . . and
the ingredient that often determines the availability of these
things—money."[31] To understand political power in the United
States, one must confront the fact that "*almost all the social institutions existing in the society ... are under plutocratic control, ruled
by non-elected, self-selected, self-perpetuating groups of affluent corporate representatives who are answerable to no one but
themselves.*"[32]

Parenti challenges the prevailing view of the "national interest." The dominant-elite reports and theorists argue that
the government acts for the common good. But this ideological view blocks citizens' understanding that "*national* policy is
usually the policy of dominant groups strategically located"
within an institutional structure which invariably responds "to
the powers and needs of the corporate system" embraced by
the major educational reports and leading intellectuals.[33] The
national interest argument is especially crucial when it comes
to such issues as war and human rights. Within these international concerns, the dominant elite "justif[ies] military intervention" on the grounds that it is "defending democracy from
communism." Actually, it is "defending the capitalist world
from social change—even if the change be peaceful, orderly,
and *democratic*."[34] In Central and South America, for example,
the CIA "has used military force [and] terror . . . to bring down
democratically-elected governments and install reactionary
dictatorships friendly to American corporate interests."[35] This
documented historical record is simply ignored in the elite
discussions of civic literacy, the country, and human rights.
Since the objective record is a non-issue unworthy of review in
the school history textbook lessons, students cannot develop
the civic literacy that Bennett, Ravitch, and other authors claim
is important to a democratic citizenry.

Howard Zinn has written and lectured extensively on the
state of the country, the Founders, and the Constitution. His

insights provide the basis for a dissenting and radical look at our society, and present a vision of a civic literacy that youth and citizens need and deserve. In *Declarations of Independence*, Zinn asserts that "we grow up in a society where our choice of ideas is limited and where certain ideas are dominant: We hear them from our parents, in the schools, in the churches, in the newspapers, and on radio and television. . . . They constitute an American *ideology*—that is, a dominant pattern of ideas."[36] These are the thoughts that we as citizens are expected to hold . . . the ones we quickly learn are the most acceptable. . . . The result is an obedient, acquiescent, passive citizenry—a situation that is deadly to democracy."[37] The existence of so many passive citizens is clear evidence that we do not foster civic literacy in our schools, but a civic illiteracy that cannot embrace the true meaning of democracy. Real democracy, Zinn contends,

> rests on the idea that, except for technical details for which experts may be useful, the important decisions of society are within the capability of ordinary citizens. Not only *can* ordinary people make decisions about these issues, but they *ought* to, because citizens understand their interests more clearly than any experts.[38]

What youth are taught in their history lessons about the country and the Founders rarely includes those like Zinn who offer a democratic and principled opposition to the dominant-elite perspective.

Civic Literacy and Native Americans

The dominant-elite reports and the influential theorists who discuss democracy and the origin of the nation state do not address the connections between the founding documents and Native American principles. These influences are absent from the glowing comments about the Constitution and the Founding discussed above in chapter 2. Professors Donald A. Grinde, Jr. and Bruce E. Johansen point out that the origins of the United States rested on indigenous principles in place before Europeans arrived. That these contributions are ignored or buried is not surprising, for as the respected Native American scholar Vine Deloria, Jr., tells us, "history is too often the privilege of the winners. It is the luxury in which they indulge themselves in order to cover up their shortcomings and prevent further discussion of actual events and personalities." Such historians "cling tenaciously to their myths."[39] Grinde and Johansen state that among the suppressed facts is this: The League of the Iroquois, with its democratic governance structure, "not only predated the United States Constitution but also influenced the evolution and development of the ideas that shaped the document, as well as other fundamental expressions of the American character." Evidence of this influence "is clearly present in the colonial, revolutionary, and early national records of the United States and in the oral and written traditions of the Iroquois."[40]

The development of American democracy reflects "a synthesis of Native American and European political theories; there is an abundance of inferential and direct evidence to support the thesis that American government was influenced by Native American political concepts."[41] The Founders and other commentators discovered in existing Native American political development "the values that the seminal European documents of the time celebrated in theoretical abstraction—life, liberty, happiness, and a model of government by consensus, under natural rights, with relative equality of property." Native Americans governed themselves without a monarchy under "a practical model for a philosophy of government based on the rights of the individual, which they believed had worked, did work, and would work for them in America."[42] This history reveals the tragic irony of a genocidal assault upon the Native Americans who supplied the indigenous roots of democratic principles, subjects about which the major reports and theorists who discuss the Founding remain silent.

The contrast between the more democratic and egalitarian Native American nations and the "America" lauded by educational reports and theorists as the beacon of democracy and human rights is striking. The influence of Native American political principles and practices has been recognized by legal scholars; one of these, Felix Cohen, argued that

it is out of a rich Indian democratic tradition that the distinctive political ideals of American life emerged.Universal suffrage for women as men, the pattern of states we call federalism, the habit of treating chiefs as servants of the people instead of their masters, the insistence that the community must respect the diversity of men and the diversity of their dreams—all these things were part of the American way of life before Columbus landed.[43]

What we really find as we look backward to the Founders is that the foundations for civic literacy that the dominant-elite reports and educators proclaim as necessary for a decent and free society were in place when Europeans arrived. But despite their adulation about the founding of the nation, the dominant-elite theorists and reports do not recognize this fact.

The historical record of the interaction between Native Americans and Europeans supports the radical and dissenting thesis about violence and aggression presented in this chapter. Discussing the Sand Creek Massacre of 1864, M. Annette Jaimes of the Center for the Study of Ethnicity and Race at the University of Colorado shows that the U.S. military engaged in immoral and illegal warfare against indigenous peoples, including the kinds of systematic slaughter that we associate with the Nazis in World War II and death squads in Central America. For example, "the creation of the State of Colorado . . . [was] utterly predicated upon the physical destruction of most Cheyennes and Arapahos and the forced relocation of the remainder into Oklahoma."[44] What happened at Sand Creek was not an exception to U.S. policy, thus supporting the thesis that the attempted physical and cultural destruction of an entire race of people (defined as a war crime at Nuremberg), or "genocide," was integral to the nature and development of the United States. As a result of this historical fact and other aspects of the Euro-american invasion, Native Americans now suffer "the most extreme poverty of any sector in the present North American population [with] far and away the greatest rates of malnutrition, plague disease, death by exposure, infant mortality, and teen suicide of any group on the continent."[45]

Civic literacy about Native Americans and the U.S. must come to a reckoning of the actual, as opposed to mythical, history of what is now the American nation state. American Indian Movement (AIM) activist and scholar Glenn T. Morris points out that when the first European settlements were established here, "without exception, these colonists were greeted by native peoples with friendship and openness, as Columbus had been before them. In return, indigenous nations were confronted with racism, massacres, religious bigotry, and systematic fraud."[46] The historical evidence is indisputable and overwhelming; yet dominant-elite scholars and educational reports continue to picture the United States as a democratic nation built upon "liberty and justice for all." Those who admit to some "ills" still see these as flaws in an otherwise marvelous political experiment, and they most certainly do not view Native American nations as constituting independent entities. They ignore Morris's point "that the founding documents and laws of the United States remove any doubt that the [new country] recognized the national sovereignty of indigenous nations; the intention to recognize indigenous sovereignty is clear." He points an obvious fact that should be known by any civically-literate youth or citizen: the United States "negotiated treaties with the sovereign indigenous peoples of North America," and "these treaties were, and continue to be, recognized under Article VI of the U.S. Constitution as the supreme law of the United States, and continue to warrant the same respect and enforcement as any other international treaty."[47]

Ward Churchill, an AIM activist and scholar, points out that the historical evidence is absolutely clear regarding the destruction of these treaties and the wars between Native Americans and the U.S. government:

> There is no historical record of any war between [Indian nations] and the United States which was initiated by Indians. Each known outbreak of open warfare was predicated upon documentable invasion of defined (or definable) Indian lands by U.S. citizenry. The defensive nature of Indian participation in these wars is thus clear. Logically, they should thus be termed "settlers' wars" or, more accurately, "wars of conquest."[48]

The U.S. belief in "Manifest Destiny," which allowed this relentless march to the west, has much in common with Adolph Hitler's concept of *Lebensraumpolitik*—"the idea that the Germans were innately entitled by the virtue of their racial and cultural superiority to land belonging to others and that they were thus morally free to take it by aggressive military action." This connection included the "clearing of inferior racial stock" by the Third Reich and "such U.S. precedents as the 1830 Indian Removal Act and subsequent military campaigns against the indigenous nations of the Great Plains, Great Basin and Sonora Desert Regions. Even the Nazi tactic of concentrating 'undesireables' prior to their forced 'relocation or reduction' was drawn from actual U.S. examples."[49] This is the horrific reality beneath the rhetoric of concern and the admission in the dominant-elite reports and theorists' writings that some terrible things did indeed happen in the history of this nation.

The historian David Stannard claims that the aggression against native people who were living in North America is a genocidal assault that has no parallel in human history. The population of North America "prior to the European invasion remains a subject of much academic debate, with most informed estimates ranging from a low of about 7 million to a high of 18 million." By the end of the nineteenth century, there were about 250,000 Native Americans left in the United States and Canada. From the first European arrival to the Wounded Knee massacre in 1890, therefore, "between 97 and 99 percent of North America's native people were killed." In New England as elsewhere, "disease laid the groundwork for the massacres that followed. The epidemics were regarded by the English as the handiwork of God. . . . One after another after another, Indian towns and villages were attacked and burned, their inhabitants murdered or sold in foreign slavery." Most political figures supported the assault against Indians, but "few did so with such evident glee as Andrew Jackson. . . . On [one] occasion he ordered his troops to slay all the Indian children they could find, once they had killed the women and men." As President, Jackson must take responsibility for the infamous Trail of Tears, when U.S. Army troops "drove the dwindling remnants of the Cherokee nation out of their homes and across the country in a march. . . . the 50 percent death rate on the Trail of Tears, like that of numerous other presidentially ordered death marches of Indian peoples, was approximately the same as that suffered by the Jews in Germany, Hungary and Romania between 1939 and 1945."[50]

Those who support the dominant-elite view of U.S. history object to the use of the term genocide to describe what was done to Native Americans. Stannard points out, however, that "the UN Genocide Convention lists five techniques, ranging from mass murder to 'deliberately inflicting on [a] group conditions of life calculated to bring about its physical destruction in whole or in part.'"[51] The actions of the Founders and other U.S. government officials clearly fall within the officially recognized international standards on genocide. The violence against Native Americans should put to rest the notion that this was a democratic and compassionate nation led by men of vision and daring—that this reality still does not shame us speaks volumes about the country and its schools.

Stannard asserts that U.S. citizens are "so bombarded" with the "unexamined ideology of 'worthy' and 'unworthy' victims' . . . that only by imaginatively substituting the word 'Jew' or the collective name of some other group of worthy victims each time 'Indian' or 'native' appears in essays . . . is there any hope of recognizing the grotesque nature" of what actually happened in the Americas. And the slaughter continues: "Year in and year out confirmed reports are published of the torture, enslavement and murder of Indians of Central and South America—almost 10,000 dead and 'disappeared' annually in Guatemala alone during much of the 1980s . . . virtually all of it carried out with the complicity of the United States government."[52] Stannard's conclusions are rarely examined in our schools, and the crimes against indigenous peoples are ignored or downplayed; yet educators regularly discuss the Holocaust against European Jews and Stalinist crimes in the Soviet Union. Since they do not object to disturbing youth with the horrible events in other lands, one must conclude that it is not violence as such that moves the dominant elite and its educator allies to express concern about human rights, but who the victims are and their relationship to American policy.

Civic Literacy and Patriotism

One of the most taken-for-granted principles in civic life and education is patriotism. Although little discussion of the concept appears in the educational reports and theorists' comments, it is assumed that civically-literate youth and citizens will be patriotic: they will support the U.S. government and dominant traditions. This view of patriotism is in contrast to the dissenting thoughts on the subject that appeared in the special issue of *The Nation* in July 1991. Shortly after the glow of yellow-ribbon support for the Persian Gulf War, an alternative perspective challenged the patriotic ideology that defines and distorts U.S. history and civic education. Considerations were raised that are not examined in the dominant-elite commentaries or in the textbook history of the U.S.-Vietnam War.

Seymour Melman, Professor Emeritus at Columbia University, has written extensively on the Cold War political economy and the massive Pentagon budgets that have fueled it. He reflects on Webster's definition of a patriot ("One who loves his country and supports its authority/ies and interest") and states that part of this definition "implies a love for . . . people. . . . But what about support for a country's 'authorities and interest'?" He contends that "the interests of top managers of government and corporations are different from those of working people [but the] top decision makers of national establishments/ruling classes identity the interests of a country as a whole with *their* interests." Patriotism is essentially bound up with

> the beliefs and rituals of the state religion, in which the state is god and its top managers and senior military officers a priesthood. This state religion has patriotic rituals . . . that mask the system of authoritarian control by proclaiming affection for the country as a whole.[53]

In order to challenge ideological hegemony, therefore, it is vitally important that youth become civically literate, and that they gain the tools of critical knowledge and thinking to make this possible. This kind of civic literacy, however, is missing in the textbook treatment of the Vietnam War, and surfaced during the Gulf War only through the courageous and principled efforts of a minority of teachers.

Writer Michele Wallace is deeply disturbed by the idea of patriotism, stating that

> after all, it has only one purpose: to make war. I don't think that patriotism has anything to do with loving one's country or the people in it. It's the cover word for keeping the war machine tuned.[54]

The elite and influential educators, however, are able to speak to concerns about love of country and yet keep Wallace's assertion about the war machine under wraps. Part of the development of civic illiteracy and ignorance among our youth is found in the use of code words that hide the true meaning of our history and present-day struggles; these words, however, cannot be exposed without an objective and systematic study of history that makes youth examine the most fervently-held beliefs about the country and its policies. Such a study, however, has never happened in our schools or textbooks.

Raising an issue that is ignored in the textbook discussion of the Vietnam War and history lessons for students, psychologist Naomi Weisstein argues that "we can no longer ignore the connections between macho and murder, between a triumphal jingoism and the victimization of the weak, between adoration of power and the sanctification of world leaders who would rather kill hundreds of thousands than risk the unmanly ignominy of backing down." She concludes that the patriotism we find in the U.S. today is "the patriarchal justification for legally sanctioned murder."[55] Weisstein links nationalist and male violence in a way that has been placed out of bounds in education; thus, youths cannot think critically because they don't get to explore the tough questions in a civically-literate manner, which would allow them to examine the macho and nationalistic values they have absorbed without reflection.

The insights on patriotism in *The Nation* were uttered in the nineteenth century by the writers Henry David Thoreau and Leo Tolstoy. In the midst of slavery and U.S. aggression against Mexico, Thoreau declared:

> I walk toward one of our ponds; but what signifies the beauty of nature when men are base? . . . Who can be serene in a country where both the rulers and ruled are without principle? The remembrance of my country spoils my walk. My thoughts are murder to the State, and involuntarily go plotting against her.[56]

When he reflected on the nature of the government in his era, Thoreau felt he could not "without disgrace be associated with it."[57] The nation now honors Thoreau with a first-class postage stamp and many revere his thoughts on literature and nature; however, leaders in the U.S. certainly do not wish youth to follow his example and end up with such a "negative" attitude about the government. The dominant elite and its influential allies may be able to withstand concern and even deep protest over a particular war or policy, but they cannot endure millions of civically-literate youths who embrace Thoreau's deep distrust of the government's basic nature and actions.

In his *Writings on Civil Disobedience and Nonviolence*, Tolstoy complements Thoreau's harsh insights on the state, patriotism, and war, challenging his fellow Russians to examine their views on these matters. He asserts that in order "to destroy the root of war [one must destroy] the exclusive desire for the well-being of one's own people; it is patriotism. . . . But to destroy patriotism, it is first necessary to produce a consciousness that it is an evil."[58] Such contentions about the nature of our society and its nationalist tendencies do not make their way into the civic consciousness or history lessons. These strong but necessary words must be considered carefully and critically if civic literacy is to have some real meaning for youth, for they cannot fully examine their own history unless those who speak such controversial truths are given a fair hearing. Tolstoy also finds that patriotism is entirely incompatible "with the truly understood teaching of Christ," and reflects "the very lowest demands of morality in a Christian society"[59]—a penetrating point that should be raised given that many Christians throughout America give uncritical support to national security state violence. Tolstoy concludes with a profound and heartfelt question, one that is rarely if ever asked in the civic education of our youth: "*How can this patriotism, when come human suffering incalculable . . . be necessary, and be a virtue?*"[60]

Howard Zinn believes that U.S. citizens "are intimidated by the word *patriotism*, afraid to be called unpatriotic," and he draws from the words of the anarchist and feminist Emma Goldman to support his views. She argued that

> conceit, arrogance and egotism are the essence of patriotism. . . . patriotism assumes that our globe is divided into little spots, each one surrounded by an iron gate. Those who had the fortune of being born on some particular spot, consider themselves better, nobler, grander, more intelligent than the living beings inhabiting any other spot. It is, therefore, the duty of everyone living on that chosen spot to fight, kill, and die in the attempt to impose his superiority upon all others.[61]

Zinn claims that if we thought of patriotism

not as blind obedience to government, not as submissive worship to flags and anthems, but rather as love of one's country, one's fellow citizens (all over the world), as loyalty to the principles of justice and democracy, then patriotism would require us to disobey our government, when it violated those principles.[62]

Given what we learn in history lessons about the colonial war of independence against England, one might think civil disobedience would be affirmed as a civic virtue. How, after all, are students to embrace the call of the Declaration of Independence for revolution, without accepting the possibility that revolution against the present U.S. government would be civically literate, patriotic, and responsible? But such thoughts are not in the dominant-elite reports nor the writings of influential allies, and certainly not in the mass media. As Zinn points out: "It seems that the closer we get to matters of life and death—war and peace—the more undemocratic is our so-called democratic system."[63] This assertion must be examined if civic literacy is to be nourished among our youth, for these life-and-death matters remain the most crucial, which is why they are avoided in our educational institutions.

Civic Literacy: A Feminist Critique

The dominant-elite view on the crisis in civic literary, the country, founding principles, patriotism, and war steadfastly avoids feminist criticism. The absence of any discussion in the major reports and by influential theorists of women's struggles in society and education, and the relevance of feminist views for civic literacy, indicate the extent to which such concerns are trivialized by those who shape social and educational policy. The feminist critique of the male-dominated system of war and violence confronts the dominant-elite masculine perspective. Some feminist educators and social theorists have focussed particularly on the connections between gender and power as it relates to war and conflict; their insights must be examined if one is to understand and challenge the dominant-elite view. At the same time, however, they have also asked whether women's views are truly different when it comes to issues of war and peace. While polling data tell us that women are more likely than men to reject state-sanctioned violence, there is not a fundamental difference between the two; e.g., women as well as men cheered the troops in Vietnam and Iraq. Some of the feminist theorists discussed in this chapter recognize a difference of degree when it comes to support for war and patriotism, but also remind us that women are not immune to nationalist propaganda for war and violence.

One respected scholar on war and violence is Jean Bethke Elshtain of the University of Chicago. She contends that those of us who live "in the west are the heirs of a tradition that assumes an affinity between women and peace, between men and war . . . the persona of Just Warriors and Beautiful Souls."[64] However, she looks critically at that tradition and cautions us to avoid the simplistic equation of men with war and women with peace. Elshtain cites the nineteenth century suffragette Elizabeth Cady Stanton, who in 1868 proclaimed the often-believed position of male evil and female healing: "the male element is a destructive force, stern, self-aggrandizing, loving war, violence, conquest, acquisition, breeding in the material and moral world alike discord, disorder, disease and death. . . . The need of this hour is . . . a new evangel of womanhood, to exalt purity, virtue, morality, true religion, to lift man up into the higher realms of thought and action."[65] Much of what Stanton proclaimed is true—socialization and miseducation have made many men brutal and violent. But Elshtain argues that the split between men and women regarding war is not as simple as it might appear: "We are now four decades beyond . . . the last 'good' war. Much has been changed or challenged . . . but it would be unwise to assume that the combined effects of Vietnam, feminism, the involvement of over 50 percent of American women in the labor force . . . undercut received webs of social meaning as these revolve around men, women and war."[66]

Women have been "invited to turn away [because] war is men's: men are the historic authors of organized violence. Yet, we have been drawn in—and the young have been required to observe, suffer, cope, mourn, honor, adore, witness, work." Generally, women have "[accepted] some rough and ready division between male life takers and women life givers."[68] The issues of war and peace are not only the province of men, but are deeply connected to the political life of a people as "citizens, human beings in their civic capacities."[69] Women are not fundamentally different in nature when it comes to patriotism and war; Elshtain critiques the feminist viewpoint of Betty Friedan, showing that it is naive to believe that women would change war and violence as a result of their increasing involvement in the military. In *The Second Stage*, Friedan "assured readers . . . that women warriors would, as women, have more sensitive concern for life than do male warriors, hence would be a force for caution against brutality in any future war." This "sentimentalism," as Elshtain calls it, "strains credulity. Women soldiers do not speak that way. They are soldiers. Period."[70] She asserts that feminists and all civically-minded individuals should reconsider the argument that having women soldiers will lead to a "kinder gentler" military. She does not believe the "naive liberal [view] that women if drafted in large numbers will transform the military and war fighting. I *know* the military will transform women."[71]

Historian Linda Gordon supports Elshtain on the nature and civic views of women, pointing out that women "have also been active and influential in far-Right social movements," including the great "enthusiasm with which many Germans and Austrian women's groups supported the Nazis." Women in the U.S. embraced Gerald L.K. Smith's America First, "a racist, anti-Semitic, patriotic movement of the 1940s . . . [which] was not only dominated numerically by women, but made gender issues extraordinarily prominent."[72] In addition, the women's peace movement in the early twentieth century "was based on arguments that women were naturally gentler and more peace-loving" than men, and that women are somehow "special" when it comes to issues of war and violence.[73] Thus, Gordon joins Elshtain in arguing that war and patriotism are not always women's issues, despite the apparently common belief that the "gentler sex" is more concerned about destruction and more nurturing.

In her feminist critique of society and war, *Sexism and the War System*, educator Betty Reardon asserts that "halting the arms race and reversing the planetary trend toward militarization" are "not possible unless the problems are addressed within the context . . . raised by feminists," because sexism and war are part of the same "common problem: social violence."[74] The war system as a logical outcome of a social order that

is based on authoritarian principles, assumes unequal value among
and between human beings, and is held in place by coercive force.
The institutions through which this force is currently . . . applied are
dominated by a small minority [of men] who run the global economy
and conduct the affairs of state.[75]

They primarily represent the Western industrial countries, and
their "common objective [is] the maintenance of their own
control and domination." She views war as the "legally sanctioned, institutionally organized armed force" used by male
"authorities [to] maintain social control [and] protect vital institutions. . . . The 'security' of the state depends on its ability
to wage war."[76] Reardon thus challenges the view of the United
States as a democratic nation based on just and noble founding principles that should be passed on to youth as part of
their civic legacy. This critique is not touched on by Bennett,
Ravitch and others who articulate the dominant-elite perspective.

The feminist theorists discussed above raise profound and
disturbing questions that go to the heart of gender and patriotism. What are the obligations of women, for example, who
have been shut out of the civic life of the nation, with little
power to influence vital events and issues? Do they owe anything to the government that denies them substantive civic participation? Their challenge to the male dominant-elite view of
war and patriotism is not addressed by any of the national
educational reports or leading educators and intellectuals discussing civic literacy. The feminist critique, which is essential
to any civic literacy on war or dissenting challenge to the patriarchal dominant-elite view that saturates the mass media and
schools, is simply not examined.

Notes

1   One could write a book on the exclusion of Chomsky's views from mainstream educational and media sources. "Arguably the most important intellectual alive today," in the words of one *New York Times Book* reviewer, Chomsky personifies the grand tradition of the struggle of truth against power—as does W.E.B. DuBois—by courageous and admirable movements and individuals to extend the ideals and sentiments in the Constitution and Declaration (limited as they were) to all. But Chomsky's thoughts are ignored in and maligned by schools and the media. His works on society and foreign policy, alone and with Edward S. Herman, are outstanding and accurate. They include, *The Fateful Triangle: The United States, Israel, and the Palestinians* (Boston: South End Press, 1983); *The Culture of Terrorism* (Boston: South End, 1988); *Manufacturing Consent: The Political Economy of the Mass Media* (New York: Pantheon, 1988), with Herman; *The Political Economy of Human Rights, Vol. I: The Washington Connection And Third World Fascism* (Boston: South End, 1979) and *Volume II: After the Cataclysm: Postwar Indochina & The Reconstruction of Imperial Ideology* (South End, 1979), with Herman; *Necessary Illusions: Thought Control in Democratic Societies* (Boston: South End, 1989); *Deterring Democracy* (New York: Hill and Wang, 1992); *JFK, the Vietnam War, and U.S. Political Culture* (Boston: South End, 1993); *World Orders, Old and New* (New York: Columbia University Press, 1994); and *Powers and Prospects: Reflections on human nature and the social order* (Boston: South End Press, 1996). Civically-literate citizens would be able to understand and appreciate Chomsky's analysis of the country's economic and political policies. It is a testimony to the influence and strength of the dominant-elite view that Chomsky, who is known and respected worldwide, is relatively unknown in the U.S. I have taught more than 5,000 students in 27 years at the State University of New York at Cortland: few have heard of him or the other dissenters discussed in this book, and it is rare to find anyone who has read his writings.

2   "United States Objectives and Programs for National Security, NSC 68, April 14, 1950," in Thomas H. Etzold and John Lewis Gaddis, eds., *Containment: Documents On American Policy and Strategy, 1945-1950* (New York: Columbia University Press, 1978), 386.

3   See Melvyn Leffler, *A Preponderance of Power: National Security, the Truman Administration, and the Cold War* (Stanford, California: Stanford University Press, 1992).

4   Chomsky, *Deterring Democracy*, 11.

5   Ibid., 14.

6   George Kennan, "Policy Planning Study (PPS) 23," February 1948, quoted in Chomsky, *On Power and Ideology: The Managua Lectures* (Boston: South End Press, 1987), 15-16.

7   Chomsky, *Deterring Democracy*, 21.

8   Chomsky, On *Power and Ideology*, 116.

9   Chomsky, *The Culture of Terrorism* (Boston: South End Press, 1988), 1.

10   W.E.B. Dubois, *Color and Democracy: Colonies and Peace* (New York: Harcourt, Brace and Company, 1945), Preface.

11   Ibid., 103.

12   Ibid., 75.

13   Ibid., 99.

14   DuBois, "Opinion," *Crisis*, Vol. 21 (March 1921), quoted in Manning Marable, *How Capitalism Underdeveloped Black America* (Boston: South End Press, 1983), 11.

15   DuBois, "The Negro in America Today," *National Guardian* (January 16,23,30, February 13, March 5, 1953), cited in Ibid.

16   DuBois, "Is Man Free?," *Scientific Monthly*, Vol. 66 (May, 1948), 432-3, quoted in Ibid.

17   DuBois, *The Education of Black People* (New York: Monthly Review Press, 1971), 118-9.

18   Ibid., 1-2.

19   Ibid., 4.

20   Marable, "Peace and the Color Line: Third World Perspectives on Coalitions and the Curricula," *Radical Teacher*, June 1984, 82.

21   bell hooks, *Talking Back: thinking feminist, thinking black* (Boston: South End Press, 1989), 93-4.

22   Ibid., 94-5.

23   June Jordan, *Technical Difficulties: Selected Political Essays* (London: Virago Press, 1992), 39.

24   Ibid., 52-3.

25   Ibid., 56.

26   Ibid.

27   Ibid., 59-60.

28   Ibid., 70.

29   Ibid., 96.

30 Michael Parenti, *Democracy for the Few, 5th Edition* (New York: St. Martin's Press, 1988), 1.

31 Ibid., 6.

32 Ibid., 37.

33 Ibid., 69.

34 Ibid., 95.

35 Ibid., 148.

36 Howard Zinn, *Declarations of Independence: Cross-Examining American Ideology* (New York: HarperCollins, 1990), 3. See also his *People's History of the United States, Revised and Expanded Edition* (New York: Harper and Row, 1995).

37 Ibid., 5.

38 Ibid., 6.

39 Vine Deloria, Jr., "Foreward," in Donald F. Grinde and Bruce E. Johansen, *Exemplar of Liberty: Native America and the Evolution of Democracy* (Los Angeles: UCLA American Indian Center, 1991), ix.

40 Grinde and Johansen, xxii.

41 Ibid., xxiv.

42 Ibid., 3.

43 Felix Cohen, "Americanizing," quoted in Ibid., 234.

44 M. Annette Jaimes, "Sand Creek: The Morning After," in *The State of Native America: Genocide, Colonization, and Resistance* (Boston: South End Press, 1992), 4.

45 Ibid., 8.

46 Glenn T. Morris, "International Law and Politics: Toward a Right to Self-Determination for Indigenous People," Ibid., 63.

47 Ibid., 65.

48 Ward Churchill, "The 'Trial' of Leonard Peltier," in Jim Messerschmidt, *The Trial of Leonard Peltier* (Boston: South End Press, 1983), quoted in Rebecca Robbins, "Self-Determination and Subordination: The Past, Present, and Future of American Indian Governance," Ibid., 91.

49 Churchill, "The Earth is Our Mother: Struggles for American Indian Land and Liberation in the Contemporary United States," Ibid., 145.

50 David Stannard, "Genocide in the Americas: Columbus's Legacy," *The Nation*, October 19, 1992, 430.

51 Ibid., 431.

52   Ibid.

53   Seymour Melman, *The Nation*, July 15/22, 1991, 112.

54   Michele Wallace, Ibid., 130.

55   Naomi Weisstein, Ibid., 132.

56   Henry David Thoreau, *Anti-Slavery and Reform Papers* (Montreal: Harvest House, 1963), 40.

57   Ibid., 127.

58   Leo Tolstoy, *Writings on Civil Disobedience and Nonviolence* (Philadelphia: New Society Publishers, 1987), 140.

59   Ibid., 142.

60   Ibid., 144.

61   Emma Goldman, *Anarchism and Other Essays* (New York: Dover, 1969), quoted in Zinn, *Declarations of Independence: Cross-Examining American Ideology*, 118.

62   Ibid., 118.

63   Ibid., 120.

64   Jean Bethke Elshtain, *Women and War* (New York: Basic Books, 1987), 6.

65   Elizabeth Cady Stanton, in Stanton, Susan B. Anthony, and Matilda Joslyn Gage, eds. *History of Women's Suffrage*, Vol. 2, 351-52, quoted in Ibid., 7.

66   Elshtain, 7.

67   Ibid., 164.

68   Ibid., 165.

69   Ibid., 241.

70   Ibid., 243.

71   Ibid., 244.

72   Linda Gordon, "The Peaceful Sex? On Feminism and the Peace Movement," *National Women's Studies Association Journal*, Vol. 2, No. 4, Autumn 1990, 625.

73   Ibid., 627.

74   Betty Reardon, *Sexism and the War System* (New York: Teachers College Press, 1985), 4.

75   Ibid., 10.

76   Ibid., 15.

Chapter 4

The Radical Tradition in Educational Criticism

Introduction

Perhaps the most fundamental of the premises and practices of civic education is gaining students' support for the dominant-elite narrative of "America" and U.S. aggression against other nations. The theorists discussed below form an educational link to the societal critique in chapter 3, and provide the basis for the analysis that follows on the Vietnam and Persian Gulf Wars. Their works have exposed inequalities and ideological hegemony, and have offered a challenging alternative to the conception of civic literacy offered by most educators, who rarely examine the right of the United States to inflict violence upon the Third World, and instead promote the dominant-elite view of the national security state found in history textbooks.

A number of premises guided the selection of the educational works in this chapter, which emphasize an analysis of education and society that places class and national issues in the forefront of the critique; understand schools within the larger political economy; recognize the Rightist assault on the civic order and the very conception of a public education in a democracy; and in some cases, pursue a Marxist critique which is clearly out of fashion in an educational discourse that allows deep-seated ills to be examined without reference to how they are caused by the capitalist political economy. The scholars discussed here go beyond important single-issue concerns; some of them offered radical and Marxist critiques of education that appeared in the 1970s which have increasingly fallen out of favor because of their alleged one-dimensionality and reductionism. While open to critical debate as any theoretical model, the Marxist analysis put forth by theorists Samuel Bowles and Herbert Gintis in 1976, for example, seems more relevant today after two decades of relentless class assault on the public sector and the standard of living of most Americans and those in the Third World. Their critique has stood the test of time, as one may discover by examining the recent economic data provided by Holly Sklar and Edward N. Wolff.[1]

Their data reveal a great shift in wealth over the past two decades from the middle and lower classes to the upper 5 percent of Americans. I believe that the fundamental reason for this shift is to be found in the class dynamics of multinational capitalism and the necessity to defend this system through the national security state (as discussed in chapter 3). This emphasis on the class nature of capitalism and the national security state is not meant to divert attention from analyses and struggles around gender and race that have been undertaken in the nation—all of which are now under assault by the Right. It is simply a plea and reminder that coalitions need to be developed between class, gender and racial movements for change, so that single-issue politics can be transcended in order to get at the basic premises and policies of the national security state. While people understandably respond to oppression on the basis of race and gender, for example, they seldom develop a critique of the system that creates such oppression. Their responses are necessary but not sufficient if we are to sustain and defend life in our country and on the planet, and challenge the state managers who provoke wars and other forms of violence against peoples in the Third World. Unless the separate identity-issue movements now waging defensive struggles against the reactionary backlash of the 1980s and 1990s connect their efforts to reveal how internal U.S. societal ills are connected to international and national security state issues, there will not be any fundamental change in this nation.

The Radical/Critical Tradition

A dissenting national report of the 1980s was that of Ann Bastian and colleagues for the New World Foundation. They looked at education in light of the Rightist assault that emerged

in the 1980s with its attack on the public sector and democratic possibilities of schooling, and the real crisis in education, which is a crisis of inequality. The Right attempted, with
varying degrees of success, to redirect "the education debate
with the same objectives that guide [its] economic and social
welfare policies: to reduce government responsibility for social needs, to reinforce competitive structures of mobility, to
lower expectations for security, and to popularize Social Dar-
winist thinking."[2] This was part of the Reagan agenda, which
brought together a coalition of "ultra-conservatives, religious
fundamentalists, and entrepreneurs" who wished to replace
public education with the magic of the private marketplace.
This Rightist attack on public education included calls for the
"reinstatement of school prayer and mounting censorship campaigns against the teaching of evolution and other humanist
features of modern curriculum."[3] But Bastian and her authors
believe that there is "a far more fundamental crisis in our
schools," represented by "our failure to provide even minimal
levels of quality to the school population that is working class
and poor."[4] This failure has grown to "epidemic proportions,"
especially for lower-income and minority students, and its roots
lie in the "chronic inequality in the school resources allocated
to poor and declining communities, in ways that learning is
stratified and structured, [and] in ways that schools treat diverse needs and potentials."[5]

In their groundbreaking yet much-criticized Marxist critique
of education, *Schooling in Capitalist America*, Samuel Bowles
and Herbert Gintis argue that "the roots of inequality in the
United States are to be found in the class structure and the
system of sexual and racial power relationships. The school
system is then but one of several institutions which serve to
perpetuate this structure of privilege."[6] The roots of privilege
and inequality "lie not in human nature, not in technology,
not in the education system itself, but in the dynamics of economic life."[7] Education is thus bound up within a fundamental
contradiction: preparing youth for democratic life in an inherently hierarchical and undemocratic capitalist system. This
systemic reality is the root cause of civic illiteracy on historical and societal issues, because it demands a dominant-elite
organization and control of society that allow hierarchical
power relations to continue unchallenged.

Their insights about the fundamental importance of the political economy and work in determining personal development bring them to support John Dewey's thesis that education can foster personal development and economic equality only if democracy is extended to all parts of society. Dewey, they state, "offered a most incisive observation. Education can foster personal development and economic equality while, at the same time, integrating youth into adult society only under one condition: a thorough extension of democracy into all parts of the social order." This Deweyan ideal "can only occur, we now see, when economic life is itself democratized—when all relations of power and authority are based on participation and democratic consent. But the social relations of economic life in the U.S. are by no means democratic and egalitarian."[8] Therefore, Dewey's ideal cannot happen in the present hierarchical and corporate capitalist society. This assertion is even more disturbingly accurate today, given the growing economic inequality of the past twenty years. Their critique of capitalism and support for Dewey's thesis lead Bowles and Gintis to argue that liberal educational reform has failed because the school cannot change the political economy; instead, the essential task is to legitimize it and the class system.

This legitimation is partly accomplished through a facade of meritocracy that fosters a belief in equality of opportunity for all, especially those in the lower classes and racial minorities—resulting in a form of ideological hegemony that hides the reality of a hierarchical and unjust system and its schools. Education "fosters and reinforces the belief that economic success rests on the possession of technical and cognitive skills—skills which it is organized to provide in an efficient, equitable, and unbiased manner on the basis of the meritocratic principle." In the contemporary United States, meritocracy serves to legitimate power just as surely as the "divine right of kings" did in its time; the dominant-elite's need for a "stable social order" has forced it to create and sustain "these ideological facades and . . . [block] the emergence of alternatives."[9]

Another important educational work that emerged in the 1970s to critique the nature of American capitalism and education, was by Stanford University economist and educator Martin Carnoy. *Education as Cultural Imperialism* is a rare critical study that places U.S. history and educational development in an international political economy context. Carnoy argues that "even within the dominant [Western] countries . . . schooling did not offset social inequities. The educational system was no more just or equal than the economy and society itself—specifically . . . because schooling was organized to develop and maintain, in the imperialist countries, an inherently inequitable and unjust organization of production and political power."[10] Carnoy addresses the social class control over property and resources that allows the few to decide vital national and international issues. He reminds us of an essential truth about the role schooling in this process: it serves to provide higher status for

> a *small percent* of the urban poor and an even smaller number of rural poor, and it may also contribute to dissent and original thinking. Nevertheless, these are not the *primary purposes* or functional characteristics of school systems. They are by-products of schooling which occur as it attempts to achieve its main function of transmitting the social and economic structure from generation to generation.[11]

We must thank a small minority of courageous and principled teachers for this civic dissent in our schools, for it is not the conscious result of what dominant-elite planners have in mind when they use the term "critical thinking."

Despite assertions about the transformative potential of schools, one must keep in mind the historical and structural features of education which, according to Carnoy, mean "that the quantity and the nature of the schooling process can be and is used to maintain the hierarchical roles of different groups in the society. . . . the school system becomes less of an agent of change and more and more an agent of *maintaining* the social structure."[12] In the desire to reconstruct schooling and society while not falling prey to a simplistic impositionist theory that reduces educational and societal dynamics to the political economy alone, one cannot ignore the structural limits on political economy that Carnoy, and Bowles and Gintis identify. They point to the objective realities in America that are established by the dominant elite; the dominated classes must operate within these hierarchical and undemocratic parameters. As part of the struggle for transformative possibilities, one must understand the schools' basic purpose within the larger political economy. For Carnoy, internationally and domestically, they "are *colonialistic* in that they attempt to impose economic and political relationships . . . *especially* on those children who gain least (or lose most) from those relationships. . . . While this is logical in preserving the status quo, it is also a means of colonizing children to accept unsatisfying roles."[13] Citizens and educators must confront the issue of whether their analysis is more in line with the class realities of multinational capitalism than critiques that underplay the objective structural limits and oppression that are found in corporate America.

Carnoy asserts that colonialistic or imperialistic schooling occurs because "powerful economic and social groups *acting in their common self-interest* succeeded through legislation and influence to use schooling to further their own ends." This happens not because the powerful conspire against the weak, but because the wealthy support "institutions and ways of life which maintain their position of wealth and power. . . . They are obviously not going to *help* the poor of the world take *control* of the world's resources for their own use, by schooling or by any other means. Schooling as a colonialistic and imperial institution is eminently reasonable once we understand who influences it and who controls the public funds which support it."[14] Supporting the Italian Marxist-Communist Antonio Gramsci's analysis of hegemony, Carnoy asserts that the colonial and imperialist relationships are legitimated by dominant ideologies which must be understood within the context of the political economy that shapes the idea-producing institutions such as the media and schools. Unless this foundational context is understood, it is simply impossible to explain why one view about the country and war, for example, becomes dominant over another. In the struggle to understand ideological hegemony in education, it appears that Gramsci's Marxist analysis and activism—he taught workers in Turin, Italy as part of his involvement with that country's Communist Party—is muted by others. When it comes to some critical educational theorists' analysis of his work, historian T.J. Jackson-Lear's assertion is on the mark: Gramsci has been made into "the Marxist who's safe to bring home to mother."[15]

In 1985, Carnoy and Stanford colleague Henry Levin returned to the political economy thesis Carnoy laid out a decade earlier. In *Schooling and Work in the Democratic State*, a book that moved away from the alleged Marxist reductionism for which *Education as Cultural Imperialism* was criticized, they stated that "the challenge today is to explain how the public school can at one and the same time be an institution that reproduces the unequal class relations of capitalist society and an institution that is more democratic and equal than the workplace for which it produces students. We reject both a mechanistic correspondence between work and school and a clear separation of the two."[16] They went on to argue that

> the school is necessarily caught up in the larger conflicts inherent in the capitalist economy and the liberal capitalist state. . . . [It] is essential to the accumulation of capital and the reproduction of the dominant relations of production, and it is valued by parents and youth as a means to greater participation in economic and political life.[17]

One must assess, however, the relative weight given each part of the relationship, and recognize that the capitalist hegemonic role is overwhelming and dominant. Critical theorists who stress contestation undervalue capitalist power and inflate the resistance side of the education relationship. Carnoy and Levin conclude that "the educational system is not an instrument of the capitalist class. It is the product of conflict between the dominant and the dominated."[18] In this conflict one must ask who has consistently and overwhelmingly dominated whom regarding the fundamental decisions affecting society, economy and schools? Furthermore, in terms of the struggle over civic literacy within the schools, whose view of the national security state and wars has been dominant?

One of the most humane and perceptive commentators on American schools is Michael Apple. In numerous works covering nearly two decades, he has urged educators to see the links between schools and social and economic ills. Although he criticized the Marxist political economy analyses of the 1970s because they were reductionist, he wrote a comradely and supportive review of *Schooling and the Democratic State* in 1986, arguing that it is not to fall back into the trap of reductionism to recognize that in this society . . . there exist general priorities and interests that provide what might be called its "historical center of gravity". . . . I do not think that the class dynamics and the economic relations of capitalism explain everything of social importance to critically minded educators; but to ignore their utter import is to cut oneself off from some of the most insightful analytic tools we possess.[19]

He believes that most educators do not see the links between schools and larger social ills, however; instead, they respond to these conditions by ignoring them. "The world of capital flight, unemployment, the degradation of labor, disintegrating cities and communities—all of this is not about education, after all."[20] Educators do not see that these ills are connected to larger issues, as well as their own position in the crisis. Mistakenly, they often compartmentalize educational questions, thus blocking an understanding of how "the relations of class, gender and racial power . . . give education its social meaning."[21] Educational and social ills thereby continue in some schizophrenic manner as if they were not part of the same totality.

Apple has criticized the impositionist and reductionist strains in Marxist educational and social analyses, arguing instead for a more complex theory of conflict within the schools that would allow for resistance while recognizing the dominant-elite's power to set the agenda to which educators often respond. Although he believes that there has been much progress toward rejecting an impositionist theory, which argued that "dominant classes had self-identifiable and coherent interests" and "equally coherent strategies . . . to guarantee that dominant interests were in fact met," he does recognize that dominant class strategies are in place: "Witness the growing influence of capital on the bulk of the national reports on education and in many of the state legislatures."[22] While he is critical of some aspects of Marxist political economy, Apple is keenly aware that the dominant-elite's undemocratic power and decisions profoundly affect the lives of everyone in the country.

Apple also critiques the national reports of the 1980s in the context of what Piven and Cloward call the "recurring conflict between property and subsistence [or person] rights, which originated with the emergence of capitalism itself."[23] This conflict was deepened by the Reagan assault on the public sector and democratic possibilities in schools and society. The national reports blamed education for the country's ills, diverting attention from the real source of those ills—the multinational corporate system. They focused the blame for our economic problems on the educational system and the lack of high-tech industry: For the authors of the national reports, "only the economic problems as defined by industry are significant enough to cause a crisis. Thus, a large part of the solution lies in making our schools and their curricula more responsive to industrial and technological needs."[24] Apple, however, prefers to place responsibility with the corporate sector, which "bears a significant portion of the blame for our social and educational crisis. . . . The investment and employment decision that business has made have in large part generated 'dislocation, discrimination, declining real wages, high unemployment, pollution, poor transportation systems, and run down crime-ridden cities.'"[25]

Rare among educators for his sharp critique of the social and historical nature of technology and computers, Apple argues that the undemocratic technological nature of capitalism now found in the workplace compels us to resist it in education and ask basic questions about purpose, benefits, and control. In the U.S., "technology is seen as . . . if it had a life of its own, independent of social intentions, power, and privilege. . . . By thinking about technology [relationally] . . . we can begin to ask political questions about [causes and effects]. Whose idea of progress? Progress for what? And fundamentally, once again, who benefits?"[26] The very language used in education is determined by the dominant social order and speaks to a concern for "efficiency, production, standards, cost-effectiveness, job skills, work discipline, and so on" that is hegemonically defined, and this "[threatens] to become the dominant way we think about schooling."[27] We need to address the dominant-elite premises and policies that are displacing the "concerns for a democratic curriculum, teacher autonomy, and class, gender, and race equality."[28] These concerns must then be linked with "convincing answers to some very important questions about our future society and the economy before we turn our schools into 'production plants' for creating new workers."[29]

Within schools, similar questions also arise regarding technological benefits, power, and purposes. Apple asserts that a "considerable part of the curriculum would be organized around questions concerned with social literacy," and quotes Douglas Noble on this technological-educational issue: "Where are computers used? What are they used to do? What do people *actually* need to know in order to use them? Does the computer enhance anyone's life? Whose? Does it hurt anyone's life? Whose? Who decides when and where computers will be used?"[30] Apple states that unless these questions "are *fully* integrated in a school program at *all* levels, I would hesitate to advise the use of the new technology in the curriculum."[31]

His critique challenges those educators who do not look outside the schools to blame "an unequal economy and a situation in which meaningful and fulfilling work is not made available," or analyze how the so-called technological revolution "is 'creating a growing underclass of displaced and marginal workers.'" Therefore, they and their students personalize the issues and thus miss the social context. Thus, "it becomes the students' or workers' fault for not being computer literate."[32] Few educators recognize and understand that "the new technology is not just an assemblage of machines and their accompanying software. It embodies a *form of thinking* that orients a person to approach the world in a particular way. Computers involve ways of thinking that are primarily *technical*. The more the new technology transforms the classroom in its own image, the more a technical logic will replace critical political and ethical understanding."[33] Apple's insights are needed in the schools and country; however, will they be embraced by educators and students? Given the history of education in the United States, and the failure of educators to challenge the dominant-elite's view of technology and other matters, the prognosis is not good.

Apple's critique and his insistence upon the humane and liberating potential of schooling are also the concern of the highly-respected philosopher of education, Maxine Greene. She is distressed that "talk of the free world today is intertwined with talk of economic competitiveness, technology, and power. Talk of personal freedom refers to self-dependence and self-determination; it has little to do with connectedness or being together in community."[34] Rarely do we hear leading educators and civic leaders discuss "reconstituting a civic order, a community. There are no clearly posed proposals for creating what John Dewey called an 'articulate public.'"[35] Greene urges us to see the need for civic imagination and literacy in our time, amidst the overriding concern for technology, competition, and power. The need remains, in even more pressing ways than when she wrote in the late 1980s.

Greene pleads for a special kind of critical understanding to help us from being overwhelmed by technology, media, and everyday life—and especially for the young, who are not becoming thoughtful citizens but rather consumers and processed people, rendered wholly uncritical about the ills facing them and the country. This deficiency is most evident in their inability to think critically about civic issues such as war and patriotism. "A special sort of critical understanding is required, therefore, if persons are not to be overwhelmed by the necessities and determinants that work on every life."[36] Present discussions of freedom are mostly framed in individualistic terms and do not concern themselves with democracy and community; this undermines John Dewey's notion of critical intelligence, which is an absolute necessity if civic literacy is flourish. The task for educators, therefore, is to sustain it in these difficult times. "Finding it difficult to stand forth from what is officially (or by means of media) defined as real, unable to perceive themselves in interpretive relation to it, the young (like their elders) are all too likely to remain immersed in the taken-for-granted and the everyday." Many youth are trained for "an unreflective consumerism; for others, it means a preoccupation with *having* more rather than *being* more."[37] The nature of community and the safety nets that sustained the "disadvantaged and the sick have been chipped away. . . . Civil rights legislation and affirmative action arrangements are treated as infringements on people's liberties; social programs are considered not only 'wasteful' but injurious to 'character.'. . . And, quite, obviously, the wealthy, the advantaged, benefit from this new attention to freedom."[38]

Greene reiterates a point that John Dewey made nearly 60 years ago: "When obstructions are removed from in the economic domain, the 'robber barons,' the bankers, the finan-

ciers always have benefitted. . . . it left all the others at the
mercy of the new social conditions brought about by the freed
powers of those advantageously situated." The idea that we are
all "equally free to act if only the same legal arrangements
apply to all—irrespective of differences in education, in command of capital, and the contribution of the social environment which is furnished by the institution of property—is a
pure absurdity."[39] In addition to Dewey's insights, Greene asserts that the Jeffersonian "argument for education, like the
argument for freedom, did not touch upon the satisfaction of
personal desire or need. Rather, it had to do with the survival
of the republic, which presumably offered all its citizens a
chance to play a part, to be autonomous, to speak for themselves."[40] The historical evidence shows that this ideal has been
forced upon the dominant elite and its educational allies by
oppressed groups, but even it is now deemed anachronistic by
many today in this era of adulation for private and marketplace solutions to public issues.

Activist and writer Jonathan Kozol has articulated his radical critique of U.S. schools for nearly three decades, in eloquent and principled terms. Perhaps his harshest critique came
in *The Night is Dark and I Am Far From Home*. Education's greatest failure, according to Kozol, has nothing to do with basic
skills; rather, it is its "hesitation or refusal to ask remorseless,
penetrating questions concerning the intended or potential
uses of those skills."[41] Education is not inept, however, for

> it does the job . . . for which it was originally conceived. It is only if
> we try to lie and tell ourselves that the true purpose of a school is to
> inspire ethics, to provoke irreverence or to stimulate a sense of out-
> rage at injustice and despair, that we are able to evade the fact that
> public school is a spectacular device, flawed beyond question but ef-
> fective beyond dreams. The problem is not that public schools do *not*
> work well, but that they do.[42]

Because the schools foster civic illiteracy, Kozol believes that
educators and citizens who oppose it cannot avoid some adult
imposition because education is not neutral and the dominant
elite uses schools to domesticate and pacify children for its
purposes. "I am not in political or pedagogical opposition to
the risk of adult imposition on a child's mind. I am in stron-
gest opposition to the present social order of the U.S. and, for

this reason only, to the lies which are inevitably purveyed by schools which stand in service to its flag and anthem."[43] Education is here to serve those who run the nation, not the students; thus, the latter are trained to trust authority and not to think critically—especially on important civic matters.

Since the major purpose of U.S. education is the perpetuation of the value system articulated by the dominant elite, it explains the lies about good intentions and the real indoctrination: "Children do not go to school 'for their own good,' they go to school for something called 'their nation's good.' They go to school to learn how *not* to interrupt the evil patterns that they see before them, how *not* to question and how *not* to doubt . . . to kill on orders and to sleep eight hours without grief."[44] This elitist indoctrination is presented as the "national" value system that should be shared by all Americans; it "dominates both how we think and how we feel about those people who do *not* live in this land, or else who *do*, but live here in those Third World colonies which are the non-white ghettos."[45] Since education serves to inure youth to the hegemonic value system, it cannot be "compatible with private ethics or unmanageable dissent."[46]

Kozol links education's role to civic illiteracy in his discussion about what happened at My Lai:

> It is not the U.S. Army that permits a man to murder first the sense of ethics, human recognitions, in his own soul, then to be free to turn the power of his devastation outward to the eyes and forehead of another human being. Basic training does not begin in boot camp. It begins in kindergarten. It continues with a vengeance for the subsequent twelve years.[47]

Because of the need for national security state indoctrination, schools are "not in business to produce Thoreaus and, even less, young citizens who may aspire to lead their lives within the pattern of his courage and conviction."[48] Students are ethically quarantined from the truth about what the U.S. has done in their name. They are not helped to see the relationships between this country and the world, and the connections between historical events, victims, and victimizers. Most importantly, they are not helped to think critically so that they might condemn the government for its crimes against humanity—a taboo subject in nearly all classrooms.

Peter McLaren is an influential contemporary critical educational theorist. He writes passionately from a dissenting perspective that links schools and society in a unity; his critical theoretical stance is especially important because we now face a present crisis of education dominated by a "new public philosophy [which] has emerged along with the rise of the Christian Right," one that "celebrates the virtues of the nuclear family, defends at all costs America's God-fearing cultural tradition, and interprets world events according to a literal reading of the Bible." This frightening viewpoint is undermining progressive educational and social programs and efforts that have emerged since the 1960s, and it will not be transformed without a pedagogy that combines critical theoretical insights with practical and progressive political and educational practice. McLaren pleads for the students in the 1990s who have "inherited an age in which liberalism and democracy are in retreat."[49] At the heart of this retreat that is destroying the liberating potential of learning, is the attempt by powerful educators and national reports to define "academic success almost exclusively in terms of capital accumulation and the logic of the marketplace." The major reports have pushed their reforms under the guise of a "resurgence of chauvinistic patriotism . . . along elitist lines." This assault erodes the democratic and civic imperatives of education, making it merely an arm of the business sector. Combined with the New Right philosophy, we are witnessing a historical development that "undermines what it means to be a critical citizen."[50]

The social and educational system is producing an underclass among many communities of color in urban ghettos—merely the most recent expression of the historical emphasis on social class and race in U.S. schools. Schools, like other social institutions "reinforce [an] inegalitarian stratification" and "are reduced to credentialling mechanisms, protected enclaves that favor the more affluent."[51] The special mechanism supporting this inequality is tracking, the practice of separating students into ability groups ostensibly along meritocratic lines. Citing Jeannie Oakes's study of American schools and tracking, McLaren shows how tracking "alienates students and undermines their social aspirations and feelings of self-worth," especially for those poor whites and students of color who are at the bottom of the tracking hierarchy.[52] The practice of tracking and the dramatic difference in allocation of funds for rich and poor students in the nation show that the professed "American commitment to equality of opportunity is violated at its very roots."[53] The class and racial inequality that undermines the educational rhetoric about justice and meritocratic success hits the most oppressed groups the hardest, and is exacerbated by the lack of a critical pedagogy to provide them with "the ability to think critically, a skill that would enable them to better understand why their lives have been reduced to feelings of meaningless, randomness and alienation and why the dominant culture tries to accommodate them to the paucity of their lives."[54]

As they face the difficult 1990s, McLaren claims that citizens in the United States are "living collectively the American nightmare, *Death of a Salesman*, and like Willy Loman we are realizing that the exchange value of dead labor is empty hope."[55] Examining and confronting this assertion presupposes certain foundational principles of critical educational theory that underlie all dissenting insights and practice in schools. They reflect the true meaning of the Hebrew symbol *Tikkun*—"to heal, repair and transform the world, all the rest is commentary."[56] They include a political theory to help teachers "understand the role that schooling plays in joining knowledge and power, in order to use that role for the development of critical and active citizens"; a cultural theory that reveals how schools rationalized "the knowledge industry into class-divided tiers: that reproduce inequality, racism, and sexism; and that fragment democratic social roles through an emphasis on competitiveness and cultural ethnocentrism"; and an economic theory that asserts that schooling "for self and social empowerment . . . is *ethically prior*" to educational training that is "primarily tied to the logic of the marketplace."[57] Rather than serving as a means for a "democratic and egalitarian social order," schools "do *not* provide opportunities in the broad Western humanist tradition for self and social empowerment and in fact often work against these opportunities."[58] In sum, McLaren and other critical educators argue instead that schools "serve the interests of the wealthy and powerful, while simultaneously disconfirming the values and abilities of those students who are most disempowered in our society already: minorities, the poor, and the female."[59]

In the present anti-theoretical and pragmatic era, McLaren draws from the work of Gramsci to argue for the importance of theory and an understanding of *hegemony*, through which the dominant elite is able to "'fix' the meaning of signs, symbols, and representations to provide a 'common' worldview, disguising relations of privilege through the organs of mass media and state apparatus such as schools."[60] Hegemony could not continue without the support of ideology, those values and beliefs that people use to understand their world and the events that comprise it, which are accepted as "*natural and common sense.*"[61] It is crucial to see how hegemony needs and feeds civic illiteracy, and how the dominant-elite ideology influences the views of youth and citizens. Few students and citizens arrive at these through a reflective, democratic, and civic process; rather, they are conditioned by uncritical educators and the media. The development of hegemony must remain a major concern of critical educators, who attempt to understand "how schools are implicated in the process of *social reproduction . . .* to explore how schools *perpetuate or reproduce the social relationships and attitudes needed to sustain the existing dominant economic and class relationships of the larger society.*"[62]

Stephen Tozer, Paul C. Violas and Guy Senese, professors and scholars in history and philosophy of education, have also developed a critical analysis of American society and schooling within the context of hegemony and political economy, the latter being "an old-fashioned term which includes the social, cultural, economic, political and demographic arrangements in society. To study the political economy of a society is to examine how that society is organized."[63] One of the keys to understanding the nature of the educational system, therefore, is to explain how it passes on ideologies that promote and defend the multinational corporate political economy. Despite the common belief that the United States is an exception, the authors point out that "every society explains and justifies its [political economy] to the outside world in terms of what is members understand and value about the world. . . . In each case, those who are doing the explaining are revealing the underlying values that support their respective ideologies." Despite the rhetoric about a democratic and civic order in which there is a free and informed dialogue among equals who define and practice the important principles of the country's principles, "the ideology which becomes dominant in a society is almost always articulated by those who derive the most power, goods, and prestige from the community."[64] In terms of important national and international issues, therefore, youth must be taught to accept the existing dominant-elite definitions of truth, rather than to challenge them as civically literate individuals. Otherwise, they might disrupt business as usual in the social and educational order.

Supporting the class analysis of Bowles and Gintis and Carnoy, Tozer and his co-authors stress the deep impact of class in shaping the hegemonic societal and educational process in the country. They cite the research of political scientist Thomas Dye in support of their contention that class is "significant because different classes wield more political and economic powers than others." Such research reveals an unequal social and educational structure in the nation, which is justified through the dominant ideology of meritocracy put forth in our schools and media.[65] This ideology helps to undermine any critical and civic understanding of how society actually works—the starting point of civic literacy. Social class is a key to understanding the political economy and schools, for it "may be a more effective determinant of future opportunities than either race or gender. . . . In the case of poor and working-class children . . . the evidence strongly indicates that neither the processes nor outcomes of schooling are the same as they are for the children of the upper classes."[66] After decades of evidence-gathering on the impact of social class on tracking, for example, one would have expected that this issue was settled, and that measures to alleviate such inequality would have been taken.[67] It is testimony to class hegemony that mountains of objective evidence challenging the dominant meritocratic ideology has had little impact on changing our schools and society.

Their critique of the political economy, class domination, and hegemony leads these authors to dissent from the naive notions that those in control of the economy—the American business class—will provide the answers to the dilemmas currently facing the schools. They are not enamored of corporate America's commitment to democratic and egalitarian ideals in the society or schools. Therefore, they ask, why should parents and teachers give it free rein when it comes to civic literacy? To support their contention, the authors point to the obvious facts that emerged from the conservative corporate-driven policies of the past two decades, which "appear to have benefitted the rich at the expense of the poor and middle class . . . and there has been an ideological shift in favor of business at the expense, says educator Henry Giroux, of democracy itself."[68]

A vital part of the radical tradition in education has been a growing awareness that to bring about substantive change in the country and schools, we must confront the reality of an increasingly multiethnic society and student body. This awareness is the core and strength of Sonia Nieto's *Affirming Diversity*. Nieto, a professor at the University of Massachusetts, Amherst, emphasizes the necessity of a creative and sensitive approach to the differing premises and cultural values that youths bring from home to school. She addresses the intimate links between multiethnic realities within the context of a society that is classist, racist, and sexist. She emphasizes the ethnic and racial aspects of the totality, but never loses sight of the context in which these "isms" unfold.

Nieto writes about the cultural imperialism in the U.S. by which "the norm generally used to measure all others is European American, upper-middle class, English-speaking, and male. Discrimination based on perceptions of superiority is part of the structure of most schools."[69] This cultural imperialism, identified by Carnoy, Freire and others as essential to Western capitalism, establishes the framework within which the heritage and hopes of an increasingly diverse student body unfold—whose lived experiences and insights are not as valued as the dominant Euro-American norm. While she agrees with critical theorists who look to the structural features of this society for the "major causes of school failure," Nieto uses a multicultural social and educational theory that begins with such systematic insights but reminds us that "structural inequality and cultural incompatibility . . . work *differently* in different communities."[70]

Nieto believes that a multicultural analysis and educational program are necessary for all students, not just those from marginalized and oppressed groups—an effort that must be undertaken to help youth understand the undemocratic features of the country and schools and to act on those ills. The struggle for such a multicultural education is *"antiracist," "basic," "important for all students," "pervasive," "education for social justice," "a process"* and an important *"critical pedagogy"* that allow educators to reflect upon the context in which school failure and success occur, as well as to take the measures necessary to foster the kind of interracial and inter-ethnic solidarity and community that will help make youth intelligent citizens of a genuinely democratic and inclusive society.[71]

Kathleen Weiler is a critical feminist educator, whose *Women Teaching for Change: Gender, Class and Power* is based on a study of progressive educators in Boston secondary schools. These educators, "like all progressive teachers, are struggling against the increasingly technocratic control of public schools, a greater reliance on standardized testing, a public cry for the 'basics' in education." Despite these socially-driven technological and educational changes, they "have achieved a great deal and continue to fight for progressive and feminist goals."[72] As a critical-feminist educator, Weiler critiques the dominant classist and sexist ideologies, but shares with radical colleagues the belief that there is resistance to such domination, namely by feminist and progressive teachers who have fought for important changes.

Drawing from the critical tradition represented by Antonio Gramsci, Weiler appreciates the difficulty of doing critical and theoretical work in a society where the emphasis is on pragmatism, and in which people "have tended to be deeply suspicious of theoretical studies." While some of this resistance understandably arises from the inability of many people to comprehend the language that critical academics employ, she cautions against "a rejection of all theoretical analysis. That rejection can leave us limited in our ability to analyze the relationship between the actions of individuals and the social totality which has so profoundly shaped them."[73] Weiler thus joins other critical theorists who plead for an accurate and coherent explanation of everyday events that cuts through the fog that has been created to block such knowledge. She states this belief simply: A "clearly articulated theoretical perspective is necessary in order to understand the empirical data gathered through observation and to come to a deeper understanding of society, and individuals acting within it." Only when we understand the "complexity of social forces can we begin to transform them."[74]

Because critical theoretical work is necessary to understand and change unjust social and educational situations, Weiler is also drawn to Gramsci's insights on how the dominant elite maintains its hegemony in apparently democratic societies without having to continually resort to force. Central to these insights, in her words, is how this elite imposes its "concept of reality on all subordinate classes, and the possible ways in which the oppressed can create alternative cultural and political institutions to establish their own understanding of oppression in order to oppose and change it."[75] Understanding the dominant-elite's ability to shape the worldview of the subordinate groups is not a simple or reductionist process, however, and Weiler supports Gramsci's belief that people are not totally uncritical automatons. They are, in Gramsci's words, "strangely composite"; their thinking "contains Stone Age elements and principles of a more advanced science, prejudices for all past phases of history at a local level and intuitions of a future philosophy which will be that of a human race united the world over." He did not believe that the student was merely a "passive and mechanical receptacle." Instead, he held that "the relations between these education forms and the child's psychology are always active and creative, just as the relation of the worker to his tools is active and creative."[76] Thus, the hegemonic process is an active and "contested" one, not the mere depositing of dominant-elite ideologies into the heads of the students. The extent to which the dominant-elite views about the U.S.-Vietnam and Gulf Wars and the national security state have been internalized by citizens and youth, however, causes one to question any ambitious contestation model of explanation.

Weiler returns often to this issue of domination and resistance within schools, a fundamental concern of critical theorists. She comments that "teaching in public schools, although more professionally bounded by institutional constraints, also contains the possibility of transformative work. This does not imply that this work will be achieved without enormous and sometimes overpowering opposition." Agreeing with Freire, she states that "critical teaching in dominant institutions means that teachers are constantly living a contradiction. But possibilities for critical work exist within that very contradiction."[77] Thus, Weiler joins those critical theorists who seek to address the deep ills of education with a creative approach that admits powerful forces that are allayed against change and equality, without forgetting that each day teachers within these institutions carry on heroic efforts to promote the kind of critical civic literacy that is essential to a vibrant democracy. One must acknowledge and appreciate the marvelous and humane insights and struggles of these and other teachers.

At the same time, the degree to which teachers are able to act within oppressive institutions to challenge the dominant-elite view and its policies on civic issues is a matter of debate. I certainly agree with Weiler that "learning and teaching *can* take place in the interests of human liberation, even within institutions created for social control." But her study revealed "the complexity of that project and the need to recognize and to fight for critical thinking and learning as a means of empowerment."[78] Despite her support for progressive feminist teachers who address the deep-seated ills of schools and society (a view I wholeheartedly share), Weiler is not naive about the daunting task they face, because

> a society so shaped by racism, sexism, classism, and with great economic, political, and military power in the hands of a few cannot be transformed by the most dedicated and critical teaching alone. . . . It is vital that feminists and other progressive teachers remember the power that social forces exert on themselves and on their students and that they recognize the limits of what is possible to accomplish in the classroom.[79]

I remain more skeptical than she and other critical theorists, however, about the possibilities for radical educational and social change emerging from within the schools, particularly regarding the civic issues central to this book. For example, there is no evidence to suggest that more than a minority of

American teachers or students have ever challenged the foundational premises and policies of the national security state—even during the 1960s. The historical record seems clear, and the unfolding present situation does not offer much hope for the thesis that educators and youth will "contest" the system at its roots.

Schooling in Capitalist America: Another Look

In this context, we must consider Richard Brosio's analysis of critical educational theorists who have challenged what they perceive as Bowles's and Gintis's overly pessimistic and deterministic analysis of corporate capitalism and the schools. Brosio's fair-minded review of their work should be heard amid the scholarship that celebrates human agency and change by teachers and students. In his fine and powerful book, *A Radical Democratic Critique of Capitalist Education*, Brosio asserts that Bowles and Gintis were

> criticized for being overly deterministic, i.e., giving too little emphasis to the real and potential power of popular democratic resistance . . . to capitalist hegemony and its powerful imperative. Scholars . . . feared that Bowles and Gintis presented . . . a "black box" within which capitalism simply reproduced persons who were useful to the continuation of the system. The concern was that teachers, democrats, progressives, et al. could do little about the "black box."

Brosio goes on to state that their "seemingly pessimistic analysis . . . was criticized successfully by theorists who insisted upon the efficacy of the democratic imperative, although it has never been made clear whether [these] advocates believe that capitalist hegemony is altered seriously by the existence of occasional, and partial, popular victories."[80]

In an earlier article on the "economic sea changes" and educators' role in reproducing dominant-elite ideologies about the national security state and political economy, Brosio also addressed Bowles's and Gintis's thesis and criticisms of it. These "economic sea changes have been mainly caused by the actions of specific men who have exercised power" within the corporate and banking sectors, the military, and the government. Brosio argues that "these actions occurred within a certain context of historical and institutional reality . . . since 1970," and "have brought intense pressures to bear upon less powerful, and dependent, institutions such as schools, colleges and universities," with the goal of "convincing, cajoling, or forcing the educational communities to march correspondingly along the path that those who are mainly responsible for the sea changes have chosen."[81] The entire process tries to make educational institutions, for example, "subservient to the requirements of capital—as represented by the multinational corporation."[82] In the "contested terrain" of schools fought over by the dominant elite and democratic forces, "the advantage lies with those who make the macro-economic decisions. The contesting parties do not fight on equal ground, nor with equal power."[83]

Brosio believes that "some of the reaction and analysis to *Schooling in Capitalist America* may have been inaccurate and overwrought. A whole industry emerged—one that was made up of thinkers and scholars who warned us about Bowles and Gintis's overemphasis on economic tilt in Marx and Marxist tradition. . . . But when one has studied and re-studied [their work], one realizes that there are many ideas within it that are not as deterministic as critics have claimed." Despite the contention that it was a pessimistic book that did not leave progressive forces any room to challenge the economic system and change schools, they called for a "mass-based democratic party" and discussed the long march through the institutions that would be necessary to replace the capitalist political economy with a democratic and egalitarian socialism.[84]

Brosio reminds us that "historical actors do in fact act, contest terrain, become mediated by their gender, ethnic, racial, nationality membership; however, this occurs within an arena most importantly established by an economic system which is not fundamentally democratically answerable."[85] This truth must be acted upon if progressive educators are truly to counter the power of the national security state and its dominant elite, which is far more entrenched than in 1970. The principles and policies of the national security state that require civic illiteracy have not been altered by the contestation of the past 25 years within schools and other institutions. In the two wars discussed, those who resisted this state did not stop its dominant-elite rulers from killing and maiming millions of people.

Even the courageous and militant anti-Vietnam War resisters, at home and in the military, were not able to stop the orgy of bloodshed.

During the Persian Gulf War, the contest between the U.S. government and the anti-war movement was totally dominated by the former. It was about as much of a "contest" as that between the U.S. basketball "Dream Team" and Angola in the 1992 Summer Olympics. Despite the marvelous efforts of some dissident teachers to claim the true mantle of civic literacy in their schools (see chapter 7), the slaughter of Iraqis was not stopped. What "contest" ends up with a balance of 125,000 to 148 in the estimated military death toll, with perhaps another 576,000 children dead from the U.N. sanctions (see chapter 6)? On this and other contested terrains, the dominant elite has triumphed over the resistance, both inside and outside the schools. Those who suggest otherwise are profoundly naive and ignorant of twentieth century American history.

Writing on the theme of contestation in 1990, Brosio tells us that the contemporary era of "rightist reaction has not given way to human agency in the form of collective political action on the part of the democratic left."[86] For example, the contesting forces represented by democratic and progressive groups and organizations in the United States did not block terrorist aggression against El Salvador, Grenada, Guatemala, Nicaragua, and Panama. Those who resisted these policies in courageous and principled ways must be applauded, studied, and emulated, but their efforts must not blind us to the essentially defensive nature of these responses. Brosio addresses the realities that progressive educators face and questions the critical theorists' analysis of education—especially in areas of ideological hegemony and civic knowledge. Speaking "for many . . . who have worked with students since the end of the 1960s" and who have critically examined the "lived experiences within the institutional school and the larger society," Brosio states it is difficult to have much optimism about young persons' ability or desire to contest and challenge the dominant order" or about "the positions taken by many of our colleagues throughout the education/schooling community."[87]

In one of my courses, an undergraduate class discussion of the U.S.-Vietnam War based on James Loewen's fine book, *Lies*

My Teacher Told Me, brought Brosio's claim home—although one could pick any major educational or social issue of the past 20 years to illustrate his assertion. On every issue that has emerged since the mid-1970s, nearly all of my senior-level teachers in training and their graduate student colleagues have been unable to defend any political position with reasoned and logical arguments. They can't because their knowledge of American history and contemporary conflicts is woeful, the result of years of conditioning by schools and the mass media.

Based on Loewen's discussion of the treatment of the Vietnam War in history textbooks, I asked students some questions about that conflict and the more recent Persian Gulf War, including who fought (a give-away question) and an estimate of casualties for each side (more difficult). Nearly all of these senior-level students, who will later be teachers, have little or no knowledge of the basic facts of these wars—a fact that was also verified during class discussion. While most students knew that the U.S. and Vietnam fought, a few thought that the U.S. fought Korea in that war, and some thought that the Gulf War was, variously, between the U.S. and Kuwait, Saudi Arabia, Iran, the "Kuwaitians," or the Persians. I asked students to tell me how many American names are on the Vietnam Memorial in Washington, D.C.—the death toll. Their estimates were from 5,000 up to the millions; their estimates of the dead and wounded for the Vietnamese ranged from 6,000 to 6,000,000. The dead and wounded totals for the Gulf War ranged from 20,000 to 75,000 for Americans, and 100 to 1,000,000 for the Iraqis. Not one student response was accurate and many simply left the questions blank. The tragic truth about these and other life-and-death matters, is that students are often "clueless," having been made so by the media, political and educational authorities, textbook authors, and teachers at all levels. Those who wish to change this situation have to contend with their mass denial and begin from this basic starting point.

If students are ignorant of the basic information that forms the foundation for civic literacy about the history and premises of these two conflicts, how are they to critically "contest" the dominant-elite viewpoint? On what basis do radical educational theorists argue that students and their teachers are able and

willing to criticize and challenge the dominant hegemonic ideologies? When it comes to the issues of war, the national security state, and civic literacy, the inflated claims of critical contestation is fantastical, a distortion of the truth. This does not
mean that radicals stop doing important critical theory, or that
some teachers stop doing their marvelous work in classrooms
(see chapter 7 for a discussion of what some did during the
Gulf War). Rather, it means that we must stop having illusions
about what has happened in American history and what is happening now, and proceed on the basis of this hard-headed assessment.

Brosio's view does not lead him to a hopeless conclusion,
however, for he continues "to believe that more persons can
be educated to understand the issues and convinced that empowerment of all citizens is worthwhile; however, the tac-
tics and strategy to accomplish such improvement must be
based upon sound theoretical [and historical] insights." However, he also asserts that

> it is important for educational theorists to realize that while there
> may be room for oppositional maneuvering within an advanced capi-
> talist society, the great power of hegemonic capitalism must never be
> overlooked. We must resist making untenable motivational or inspi-
> rational claims for the power of teachers and students which ignore
> the massive greater power of capital and its allies.[88]

His conclusion captures the weakness of any position that argues for a substantive "contest" in society between the dominant elite and resistance forces, and such theory that may in
essence be the contemporary version of largely discredited plu-
ralist political theories. As Brosio concludes, "How could any
serious student of school and society in the United States maintain that the power of workers, common people, minorities,
and so forth, equals the power of capital?"[89]

Kathleen Weiler's and Brosio's critical insights get at the
core of the problem: How do we admit that structural limits
block progressive change without becoming paralyzed and
thinking that little can be done? How do we avoid the tendency to think that the social and educational realities shaped
by multinational capitalism and its dominant elite are really
being "contested" in such a way as to overcome them? A sober

assessment of present reality would show that critical dissent-ers in education, unlike those of 20-25 years ago, are losing the contest—badly. But this does not mean that a radically different vision of schools and society and the struggle to attain it are not worthwhile. This dilemma will be addressed in chapter 7.

With this review of the radical and critical tradition in edu-cational theory as the context and supplement to the dissent-ing view of America presented in chapter 3, I now turn to a critique of the treatment of the U.S.-Vietnam War in Ameri-can history textbooks.

Notes

1   Holly Sklar, *Chaos or Community: Seeking Solutions, Not Scapegoats for Bad Economics* (Boston: South End Press, 1995); Edward N. Wolff, *Top Heavy: A Study of the Increasing Inequality of Wealth in America* (New York: The Twentieth Century Fund Press, 1996).

2   Ann Bastian, Norm Fruchter, Marilyn Gitell, Colin Greer, and Kenneth Haskins, *Choosing Equality: The Case for Democratic Schooling* (Philadelphia: Temple University Press, 1986), 14.

3   Ibid., 14-15.

4   Ibid., 26.

5   Ibid., 27.

6   Samuel Bowles and Herbert Gintis, *Schooling in Capitalist America: Educational Reform and the Contradictions of Economic Life* (New York: Basic Books, 1976), 85.

7   Ibid., 88.

8   John Dewey, *Democracy and Education* (New York: The Free Press, 1966), cited in Ibid., 101.

9   Bowles and Gintis, 125.

10 Martin Carnoy, *Education as Cultural Imperialism* (New York: David McKay, 1974), 3.

11 Ibid., 13.

12 Ibid., 15.

13 Ibid., 19.

14 Ibid., 24.

15 Quoted in Christopher Phelps, "Lenin, Gramsci, and Marzani," Correspondence, *Monthly Review*, Vol. 47, No. 6, November 1995, 54.

16 Martin Carnoy and Henry Levin, *Schooling and Work in the Democratic State* (Stanford, California: Stanford University Press, 1986), 3-4.

17 Ibid., 4.

18 Ibid., 50.

19 Michael Apple, "Review Article—Bringing the Economy Back into *Educational Theory*," Educational Theory, Fall 1986, Vol. 36, No. 4, 403. The "historical center of gravity" comment comes from Robert Heilbroner, *The Nature and Logic of Capitalism* (New York: W.W. Norton, 1985), 85.

20 Apple, *Teachers and Texts: A Political Economy of Class and Gender Relations in Education* (New York: Routledge, 1988), 4.

21 Ibid., 5.

22 Ibid., 25.

23 Frances Fox Piven and Richard A. Cloward, *The New Class War: Reagan's Attack on the Welfare State and Its Consequences* (New York: Pantheon, 1982), 41, quoted in Ibid., 132.

24 Apple, 136.

25 Martin Carnoy, Derek Shearer, and Russell Rumberger, *A New Social Contract* (New York: Harper and Row, 1983), 61, quoted in Ibid., 138.

26 David Noble, *Forces of Production: A Social History of the Industrial Revolution* (New York: Alfred A. Knopf, 1984), xv., cited in Ibid., 151. See also his fine critique of capitalist automation and technology in *Progress Without People: In Defense of Luddism* (Chicago: Charles H. Kerr, 1993).

27 Apple, *Teachers and Texts*, 154. See Apple, *Ideology and Curriculum* (Boston and London: Routledge and Kegan Paul, 1979) and Ira Shor, *Culture Wars* (Boston and London: Routledge and Kegan Paul, 1986).

28 Ibid.

29 Ian Reinecke, *Electronic Illusions* (New York: Penguin Books, 1984), 234, cited in Ibid., 160.

30 Douglas Noble, "The Underside of Computer Literacy," *Raritan* 3 (Spring 1984), 40, quoted in Ibid., 172-3.

31 Ibid., 173.

32 Noble, quoted in Ibid., 168.

33 Ibid., 171.

34 Maxine Greene, *The Dialectic of Freedom* (New York: Teachers College Press, 1988), 1-2.

35 John Dewey, *The Public and Its Problems* (Athens, Ohio: Swallow Press, 1954), 184, quoted in Ibid., 2.

36 Greene, 4.

37 Ibid., 7.

38 Ibid., 17.

39 John Dewey, "Philosophies of Freedom," in *On Experience, Nature and Freedom*, ed. R. Bernstein (New York: The Liberal Arts Press, 1960), 271, quoted in Ibid., 28.

40 Ibid., 28.

41   Jonathan Kozol, *The Night is Dark and I Am far from Home: A Political Indictment of the U.S. Public Schools* (New York: Continuum Publishers, 1980), Preface.

42   Ibid., 1.

43   Ibid., 2.

44   Ibid., 7.

45   Ibid., 9.

46   Ibid., 10.

47   Ibid., 54.

48   Ibid., 66.

49   Peter McLaren, *Life in Schools: An Introduction to Critical Pedagogy in the Foundations of Education*, 2nd Edition (New York: Longman, 1994), 5.

50   Ibid., 6.

51   Ibid., 9.

52   Ibid., 10.

53   Ibid., 16.

54   Ibid., 18.

55   Ibid., 29.

56   Ibid., 168.

57   Ibid., 168-170.

58   Ibid., 170.

59   Ibid., 171.

60   Ibid., 183.

61   Ibid., 185.

62   Ibid., 194.

63   Steven E. Tozer, Paul C. Violas, and Guy Senese, *School and Society: Educational Practice as Social Expression* (New York: McGraw-Hill, 1993), 5.

64   Ibid., 6.

65   Ibid, 298-9. See Thomas Dye, *Who's Running America?: The Bush Era* (Englewood Cliffs, New Jersey: Prentice Hall, 1990).

66   Ibid., 303. For more on ideological hegemony, see Gramsci's *Prison Notebooks*.

67   See especially the work of Jeannie Oakes, *Keeping Track: How Schools Structure Inequality* (New Haven: Yale University Press, 1985). Oakes presents an extensive review of tracking, including the research from *A Study of Schooling*, a comprehensive examination of tracking through a national sample of schools. It was reported in John I. Goodlad, *A place called school* (New York: McGraw-Hill, 1984).

68   Tozer, et al., 399.

69   Sonia Nieto, *Affirming Diversity: The Sociopolitical Context of Multicultural Education* (New York: Longman, 1992), 21. Nieto's fine concrete and theoretical synthesis of diverse student experiences helps us understand the dynamic interplay of race and gender, and enlightens us on the realities of a multicultural society. However, multiculturalism as presently advocated by many does not challenge the fundamental premises of the capitalist national security state—the root of the demand for civic illiteracy. The progressive effort to diversify education and other institutions of power by race and gender, should not blind us to the fact that at the ultimate centers of power in the country (multinational corporate boardrooms, the Executive Branch, the Pentagon and CIA), the policy simply means changing the composition of those who continue the brutal and exploitative policies of this state. The fundamental issue is the groundrules and practices of this state, not the increasingly diverse multiethnic and gender makeup of those who lead and speak for it. Whether it was Jeanne Kirkpatrick promoting aggression in Central and South America or Colin Powell defending it in the Middle East, the issue remains, what is done and why—not who. Only a radical and civically-literate understanding of this fact will save what is left of civic and democratic traditions in the nation.

70   Ibid., 203.

71   Ibid., 208. In the "New World Order" of multinational capitalism, those who comprise the dominant elite are diverse in ethnicity and gender. But they are essentially alike when it comes to class perspective and dominant-elite allegiance. Their allegiance is not to community, country, or democracy, but to greed, power and the "market."

72   Kathleen Weiler, *Women Teaching for Change: Gender, Class and Power* (South Hadley, Massachusetts: Bergin and Garvey, 1988), 1.

73   Ibid., 2.

74   Ibid., 3.

75   Ibid., 13.

76   Antonio Gramsci, *Selections from the prison notebooks*, eds. Quintin Hoare
     and Geoffrey Nowell-Smith (New York: International Publishers, 1971),
     324, quoted in Ibid, 14,16.

77   Ibid., 52.

78   Ibid., 152.

79   Ibid., 152-3.

80   Richard A. Brosio, *A Radical Democratic Critique of Capitalist Educa-
     tion* (New York: Peter Lang, 1994), 21.

81   Brosio, "The Present Economic Sea Changes and the Corresponding
     Consequences for Education," *Educational Foundations*, No. 3, Fall
     1987, 5.

82   Ibid., 7.

83   Ibid., 20.

84   Ibid.

85   Ibid., 21.

86   Brosio, "Teaching and Learning for Democratic Empowerment," *Edu-
     cational Theory*, Vol. 40, No. 1, Winter 1990, 69.

87   Ibid., 72.

88   Ibid., 77.

89   Ibid.

Chapter 5

Civic Illiteracy and American History Textbooks: The U.S.-Vietnam War

In thirty years of "limited war" . . . the number of [Vietnamese] casualties perhaps totalled between 5,245,000 and 6,140,000 killed and wounded, plus 300,000 MIAs.

Jeffrey Kimball, 1989

At this moment of national disgrace, as American technology is running amuck in Southeast Asia, a discussion of American schools can hardly avoid noting . . . that these schools are the first training ground for the troops that will enforce the muted, unending terror of the status quo in the coming years of a projected American century.

Noam Chomsky, 1966

Introduction

A concrete illustration of civic illiteracy is the treatment of the U.S.-Vietnam War in American history textbooks, which prepare students to accept the basic purposes of that conflict. Although textbooks have improved factually since I co-authored an earlier study,[1] they still preserve one of education's essential purposes: shaping youth consciousness to foster support for U.S. aggression. The lessons of the war are important, for they have influenced subsequent U.S. actions in the Third World and public opinion. Since the end of the war, the dominant elite has tried to undermine the "Vietnam Syndrome," the term given to citizen fears of and opposition to U.S. wars abroad. To undermine this resistance, it has used the media and educational institutions to obtain support for policies in Central America and the Persian Gulf. History textbooks support the honorable intentions of U.S. policy in Vietnam as part of a larger ideological effort to ensure that aggression against weaker nations will not be disrupted by civically-literate youth.

Part I of this chapter reproduces a narrative history of the war in the language of 20 U.S. history textbooks published in the 1980s; this narrative history is then challenged in Part II.[2] Part III places the narrative within a theoretical framework that asserts that the dominant elite influences state policies through education and the mass media, and shapes the perceptions of youth and the public on vital issues of war and peace in an effort maintain hegemonic power. While a single historical narrative cannot capture the minor differences between individual texts, it does give an accurate representation of the major assumptions and assertions presented to students. Basic beliefs about Vietnam and the U.S. role in the world are crucial here, not minor differences among authors who still agree on the ends of the nation and its foreign policy. Aside from minor editing in terms, e.g., a single spelling for Viet Cong and Viet Minh, I have tried to faithfully reproduce the history that students would have learned had they synthesized the 20 separate texts into one narrative.

Part I: A Textbook History of the U.S.-Vietnam War

The textbook history of the war begins with French colonial rule in Vietnam, which commenced in the 1860s; it was harsh and most peasants lost their land. The French produced and marketed opium, and fostered drug addiction among the native population. There was strong resistance from the Vietnamese, but they were brutally suppressed. During World War II, Japan invaded Vietnam and drove out the French, and many Vietnamese formed guerrilla groups to fight the Japanese. The United States aided one such group: the Viet Minh, which was led by the Soviet-trained Communist Ho Chi Minh. When the Japanese surrendered in 1945, Ho proclaimed the establishment of the Democratic Republic of Vietnam, and was recognized as head of an independent state. A strong nationalist, he used the Preamble of the U.S. Declaration of Independence in his proclamation because he wanted America's support for Vietnamese independence, but that did not happen.

France returned after World War II and regained control of Vietnam. It refused to discuss independence with the Viet Minh, but it recognized Vietnam as a Free State within the French Union. This agreement broke down, however, and fighting began in 1946. Ho appealed for U.S. support, but he received no reply. Instead, the U.S. would pay more than 70% of France's war costs because it feared Ho's Communist ties and China's expansion throughout Southeast Asia. In 1954, when the Viet Minh, supported by China, won the major battle of Dien Bien Phu, Secretary of State Dulles and Vice President Nixon urged President Eisenhower ("Ike") to support the French militarily; Dulles urged a nuclear attack. But President Eisenhower realized that he had no support from Congress and other allies, so he did not escalate U.S. involvement. The French were defeated and soon left Vietnam.

The French-Vietnamese conflict ended in 1954, when the Geneva Conference divided or temporarily divided Vietnam. The North became a Communist state led by Ho Chi Minh, supported by the Soviet Union and China; the South became a "free" government under the non-Communist Ngo Dinh Diem. The United States promised to support the 1956 elections that were to unify the nation, but Eisenhower felt they would give power to Ho and the Communists. Therefore, he pledged military assistance to Diem, who declared himself president of South Vietnam, and the elections were canceled. The Viet Cong or Viet Communists as Diem called them then began their guerrilla campaign, supported by North Vietnam. Diem was a nationalist and Catholic who opposed both Communist domination and French colonialism; although Eisenhower had doubts about Diem, he supported the regime with CIA agents and money. In North Vietnam, Ho and the Communists took over and abolished all political opposition. Thousands of former landlords were killed or sent to forced-labor camps, and about one million people, mostly Catholics, fled to South Vietnam.

In 1960, the Viet Cong set up their own government, the National Liberation Front (NLF). In the early stages of the war, almost all of the rebels were South Vietnamese, who were encouraged and supplied in large part by North Vietnam; the North later took over much of the fighting. Not all Viet Cong were Communists—some were Buddhists who did not like

Diem's support of Catholics, and nationalists who wanted a united Vietnam. Since many were Communists, however, Eisenhower sent more aid to Diem, who was not a popular ruler. With his harsh policies he brutally suppressed both Communists and non-Communists, and his lack of support among the peasantry allowed the Viet Cong to gain control of most rural areas in the South by 1960.

As conditions worsened in South Vietnam, Ike increased military support to stop Communist aggression and preserve a free Vietnam. Supporting South Vietnam and other nations so they would not fall to Communism became known as the "domino theory," which was a powerful justification for further U.S. involvement. Ike also urged Diem to make reforms, but he did not. His government became increasingly unstable by the early 1960s, as the Viet Cong took over the countryside, murdering village chiefs and teachers and assassinating Diem officials and those considered traitors.

The administration of President John F. Kennedy (JFK) made Vietnam a major foreign policy commitment. Kennedy also had misgivings about Diem, but he expanded the number of soldiers to 15,000 or 17,000 by 1963 and also authorized combat air missions over North and South Vietnam. JFK was aware of Diem's lack of support, but escalating NLF victories increased his advisers' fear that South Vietnam would become Communist. He resisted advice to send more troops, but sent more advisers and supplies to offset North Vietnam's help to the Viet Cong, and also urged Diem to carry out reforms. Diem ruthlessly put down all political opponents, however, and Kennedy began to see that outsiders could not solve Vietnamese problems. He was reluctant to fully involve U.S. troops in combat because he feared getting bogged down in a land war as France had, but Diem's rule became increasingly harsh and the United States could no longer tolerate him. In late 1963, the South Vietnamese military received backing from the Kennedy Administration through the CIA for a coup; it seized power and murdered Diem and some of his family members. The United States had not sanctioned the murders, but it supported the coup, and had to choose either to let South Vietnam fall to the Communists, or expand American involvement. JFK chose the latter.

A rapid succession of military leaders replaced Diem, but none was interested in reform and most asked for American troops. Kennedy refused, at the risk of deepening U.S. involvement. Three weeks later, he was assassinated. At the time, however, he was considering expanding American involvement in Vietnam.

The Vietnam War escalated during President Johnson's term, especially after the Tonkin Gulf incident in August, 1964. Johnson (LBJ) told Congress that U.S. ships had been attacked without cause while on routine patrol. North Vietnam stated that the ships were inside its territorial waters, but LBJ denied this. After this attack, he ordered American planes to bomb the North, and Congress passed the Tonkin Gulf Resolution, giving him almost complete freedom of action in Vietnam. Only two Senators voted against it and few questioned LBJ's version of what happened. Attacks against North Vietnam's coastal islands had begun in February 1964, with American support of South Vietnamese secret operations; however, Johnson did not reveal this fact to Congress or the American public. He had the Tonkin Resolution prepared by advisers three months before the attack, and it provided his legal basis for escalating the war.

When Johnson became president, South Vietnam was almost completely dependent upon U.S. aid and controlled by the military. Each new regime was corrupt and not interested in reforms. Meanwhile, Viet Cong influence continued to grow until they controlled 80 percent of the countryside. Some 30,000 North Vietnamese troops had also infiltrated the South. LBJ's advisers laid out two unpleasant choices: further military escalation, which might bring in China and the Soviet Union, or reducing the U.S. role and leaving the fighting to South Vietnam—then the Communists would take over. The U.S. was to be trapped in this dreadful predicament for seven years.

In early 1965, Johnson ordered U.S. troops into battle because South Vietnam was being defeated. The explanation for this escalation was not clear: the simplest one given was the "domino theory." Although there were few North Vietnamese troops in the South, LBJ and his advisers recalled the failure to stand up to Hitler's aggression. U.S. "credibility" was also at stake, as other free countries needed to know that we would resist aggression. North Vietnam responded to this expansion by sending more of its regular army units and supplies to assist the Viet Cong.

The United States finally got a relatively stable government in South Vietnam in General Thieu's regime, but it was also brutal and corrupt, and the Viet Cong and the North were clearly defeating his army. The Viet Cong's strength was not in weaponry but in infiltration. The United States responded with massive technological warfare, trying to defeat a "popular movement" aided by North Vietnam, the Soviet Union, and China. Equally important, however, was the Viet Cong's success with the native population, which supported them by ambush and terror. The U.S. responded by trying to "pacify" rural areas and win the "hearts and minds" of the peasantry. But it did not get the support that Vietnamese peasants gave the highly nationalistic Viet Cong. The "pacification" program was replaced by the more extreme "relocation" campaign, by which villagers were taken from their homes into refugee centers or cities. The countryside was then devastated with bombs and chemical defoliants. These toxic chemicals caused birth defects in Vietnamese children and U.S. servicemen's offspring, and led to health problems for exposed adults.

The massive U.S. bombing of North Vietnam strengthened Communist resistance, and other military efforts were also ineffective. Beginning in 1968, North Vietnam sent 100,000 troops to the South each year to replace Communist casualties. The war shattered both the North and South. In the North, air strikes were aimed at bridges and roads, but bombs are not pinpoint weapons and villagers were often the victims. But the South felt the heaviest weight, as villages were destroyed and vast areas of the country were turned into moonscapes from "carpet bombing."

By 1967 some U.S. officials began questioning the government's policy, and Secretary of Defense Robert McNamara commissioned *The Pentagon Papers*, a study of U.S. policy in Vietnam since World War II. It revealed that the public had been misled about Vietnam for two decades as U.S. presidents secretly waged war. McNamara resigned in 1967 and was replaced by Clark Clifford, who reviewed reports and talked with leaders who had supported the war; they now thought that the

U.S. ought to get out. This caused President Johnson to reconsider his policies, as the conflict had destroyed both Vietnam
and his Great Society programs. While the war escalated,
Johnson tried to negotiate a solution, and peace efforts continued into 1968. In March of that year, with American protests against the war rising, LBJ ordered U.S. aircraft "to make
no attacks on North Vietnam." He called for peace talks, which
finally began in Paris that May. This announcement did not
alter the way the war was fought, however, and bombings i-
ncreased dramatically in South Vietnam.

In 1967, General Westmoreland had stated that victory was
near: there was "light at the end of the tunnel." But this hope
was shattered when the Viet Cong or North Vietnamese
launched the massive Tet offensive in early 1968 throughout
South Vietnam that showed astonishing power. The offensive
was very costly and they suffered terrible casualties, but it start-
led and embarrassed the American military, and Westmorel-
and was soon relieved of his command. A major battle took
place in Hue, where Viet Cong forces murdered 3,000 South
Vietnamese supporters. Although Westmoreland asserted that
Tet was an American military victory, many thought it was a
psychological triumph for the Communists. The fighting included the shooting a Viet Cong suspect on a Saigon street by
a South Vietnamese officer; televised, it did more than any
single event to undermine support for the war. Tet turned
American opinion against the war, and the media raised the
question of a "credibility gap." How could North Vietnam
launch such an attack if President Johnson was telling the truth?
Were we backing a government that did not have the support
of its own citizens? Tet revealed that the "other war"—Saigon's
effort to win the "hearts and minds" of the Vietnamese people—
was far from over.

President Nixon came to office in 1969 with a plan to bring
"peace with honor" in Vietnam, but United States involvement
was to continue for four more years, becoming bloodier and
expanding geographically. An important part of the plan was
training and equipping the South Vietnamese army to take over
most of the combat. This "Vietnamization" was accompanied
by increased bombing of North Vietnam and secret bombing
of Cambodia and Laos. It would end the war with honor, and

South Vietnam would remain independent and non-Communist. President Nixon and Secretary of State Kissinger thus restored the war to the situation of 1965, with Vietnamese fighting each other. The President actually expanded the conflict in April 1970, when he ordered a joint U.S.-South Vietnamese invasion to attack North Vietnamese "sanctuaries" inside Cambodia. He did not consult with Congress, and said the action was to shorten the war. In February 1971, Nixon ordered American support of a South Vietnamese invasion of Laos, a test of the "Vietnamization" program. It was a disaster, however: the North destroyed the South's forces.

In early 1972, North Vietnam launched a major invasion of South Vietnam as American troops pulled out. The U.S. did not have enough forces to win the war, but simply leaving Vietnam would make it seem weak and untrustworthy. "Peace with honor" was not peace at any cost, as the U.S. could not simply leave. Nixon insisted that Communist forces must leave South Vietnam, and that it must remain independent. North Vietnam did not agree: it wanted a united Vietnam under one government. One of the most difficult problems facing Nixon during this "Vietnamization" was the decay within the American military. Discipline among U.S. troops was rapidly deteriorating, with desertion, drug addiction, refusal to obey orders, and the occasional killing of unpopular officers by enlisted men.

While pursuing "Vietnamization," President Nixon tried to negotiate an end to the war. Shortly before Nixon's re-election in November, 1972, Secretary of State Kissinger announced that "peace is at hand." It did not happen, however, because of General Thieu's strong opposition, and the peace talks were suspended. The heaviest and most destructive bombing raids of the war took place in December as docks, airfields, bus and train stations were hit. Many of the targets were in heavily populated areas, and civilian casualties were high as homes and hospitals were accidently bombed. The peace talks resumed, and on January 27, 1973, an agreement was reached. All fighting was to stop and the North was to release American POWs (Prisoners of War), and the U.S. was to withdraw completely. Nixon promised that the U.S. would respond "with full force" if the North Vietnamese broke the agreement.

The Paris Agreement called for Thieu's government to remain in power, but few thought it would last long. It was actually a death warrant for South Vietnam, which could not stand long without U.S. support. Despite U.S. assurances, it was understood that it was only a matter of time before the South would be crushed by the North. The Paris Agreement did not produce peace or honor: it only removed the U.S. from the disastrous war. The agreement was broken by both sides, and within two years North Vietnam and the Viet Cong easily conquered South Vietnam. In March, 1975, North Vietnam began a final offensive against the powerless forces of the South, which disintegrated without the support of the U.S. Thieu appealed to President Ford for aid, and Ford appealed to Congress for funds but was refused. On April 30, 1975, Saigon fell to North Vietnam, and Vietnam was reunited under Communist rule.

The U.S. paid a terrible price for its involvement in the war, and the human and financial costs were staggering for both sides. Between 46,000 and 58,000 Americans died, and the war cost $110 to $190 billion. 1.2 million to 2 million Vietnamese soldiers and 2 million to 3.5 million civilians lost their lives. Millions more became refugees, and 500,000 to 1.5 million of these fled the nation. The U.S. felt a special obligation toward the Vietnamese, who had fought bravely; therefore, it took in the largest number of these "boat people." Perhaps tens of thousands lost their lives at sea. By 1979 approximately 220,000 Vietnamese refugees had come to the U.S., many of them educated and wealthy supporters of the war. The bloodbath that many feared after the Communists won did not happen, but thousands were imprisoned or resettled. The war devastated Vietnam, as millions of acres of farmland and jungle were defoliated by toxic chemicals. Today it is one of the poorest nations in the world. The U.S. tried in vain to make it a viable democratic nation, but Vietnam became a repressive regime and close ally of the Soviet Union.

Most Americans tried to forget our most unpopular war, and there was widespread cynicism toward the government and political system. Thousands of veterans were exposed to toxic chemicals, and many suffered from depression and rage. Some became addicted to alcohol and drugs and could not find or keep jobs, but most returned to normal pursuits, and the vast majority were employed. They were often met, however, with indifference or outright hostility. It took years to be accepted for what they were: patriotic soldiers who sacrificed much to support their country. After Vietnam, U.S. prestige was lower than at any time in our history, and powerful lessons can be drawn: we must find new ways to fight Communist-supported wars of "national liberation"; we should only support those who can and want to help themselves; we must never fight a conflict without a declaration of war or a clear-cut goal of victory; and the U.S. must confine itself to conflicts that Americans believe are vital to the nation's interest.

Part II: A Critique of the Textbook History: French Colonialism and Origins

The brutal nature of France's colonialism is freely admitted in the textbooks summarized above, but that tough language disappears when the U.S. takes over from the French. The U.S. does not engage in colonialism or imperialism; rather, it fears Ho Chi Minh's Communist ties and aids those who wish to remain "free." He is always referred to as a Communist, a Marxist, or a Soviet-trained leader. Ho was all of these, but there is no adequate explanation of why he and the Communist-led Viet Minh had such support. Students would not know that at the end of World War II, thousands of Vietnamese who gathered in Hanoi to celebrate the end of the war against Japan and the Allied victory were joined by U.S. army officers. A Vietnamese band played "The Star-Spangled Banner," and Ho Chi Minh, soon to be head of a united and independent Vietnam, linked his people's struggle against France to the American revolution. Ho believed that "the Vietnamese revolution was supported by the same spirit that had brought about American independence in 1776."[3]

The texts do not adequately explain why Ho Chi Minh and the Viet Minh had such overwhelming support in Vietnam, even though U.S. documents are available that would explain it. One of the many State Department reports concluded that Ho was regarded as "the symbol of nationalism and the struggle for freedom to the overwhelming majority of the population." This official view from the 1940s was confirmed by the 1972 congressional testimony of Abbot Low Moffat, the former chief of the Division of Southeast Asia Affairs, Department of State (1945-47):

> I have never met an American ... who had met Ho Chi Minh who did not reach the same belief: that Ho Chi Minh was first and foremost a Vietnamese nationalist. He was also a Communist and believed that Communism offered the best hope for the Vietnamese people. But his loyalty was to his people.[4]

Noam Chomsky confirms Moffat's view, reviewing reports from *The Pentagon Papers* that discuss efforts to prove that Ho Chi Minh was a puppet of the Russians or Chinese. One 1948 State Department report found "no evidence of direct link between Ho and Moscow"[5]; another discovered a "Kremlin-directed conspiracy . . . in virtually all countries except Vietnam."[6] Regardless of the facts, however, officials remained desperate to prove that Ho was a puppet in order to discount the indigenous nature of the Vietnamese struggle. Despite the evidence of Ho Chi Minh's leadership and respect among his people, "the internal record . . . reveals that United States government analysts recognized that Western intervention must destroy the most powerful nationalist movement in Indochina." A victory for Ho and the Viet Minh on behalf of the Vietnamese people "was regarded as inconsistent with American global objectives, and therefore it was necessary to define the Viet Minh as agents of foreign aggression."[7] Freedom and self-determination for the Vietnamese people were a threat to the dominant elite here; therefore, the Viet Minh-led, anti-colonial movement had to be crushed.

The texts present Chinese and Soviet support for the Viet Minh as if to imply that U.S. aid to France was needed to match Communist aid for those resisting the French. But when Pentagon figures for the period of U.S. escalation (1965-73) are used as a guide to the relative economic and military support given to each side in the war, U.S. aid to the French would have been forty times greater than Chinese-Soviet aid to the Viet Minh—which always relied on support within Vietnam against the French.[8] Students also are taught that U.S. leaders did not support French rule, which is pure fiction without a shred of evidence in the texts themselves. To the contrary, these texts reveal that the U.S. funded French colonialism.

The texts acknowledge that France agreed to recognize Vietnam as a Free State within the French Union in March, 1946. But as historian Marvin Gettleman and colleagues point out, France immediately broke the agreement when it formed a separate republic in the southern part of Vietnam—with no opposition from the U.S.[9] From that March agreement, Vietnam was a sovereign state and any aggression against it was a violation of international law. Students also learn that the U.S. considered a nuclear attack on Vietnam in 1954 to block the French defeat at Dien Bien Phu, but there is no discussion of this incredible fact. As with so many other admissions, the bare statement cannot do justice to the momentous possibility it revealed.

Geneva, Diem and the NLF

The view created for students about the 1954 Geneva Accords is inaccurate: the Accords did not divide Vietnam and did not create the state of South Vietnam. Vietnam was recognized as one nation, with a temporary dividing line between the Viet Minh and French forces. The "Final Declaration of the Geneva Conference" is quite explicit on this point, recognizing "that the essential purpose of the agreement relating to Vietnam is to settle military questions with a view to ending hostilities and that *the military demarcation line is provisional and should not in any way be interpreted as constituting a political or territorial boundary* (emphasis added)."[10] Despite the temporary nature of this agreement, however, the *Monthly Review* points out that "the U.S. government has never hesitated to claim the Geneva Accords as the basis of the legitimacy of the South Vietnamese state whenever it has suited its purposes to do so!"[11] In its view, this is the perspective of the former foreign policy columnist of the *New York Times*, Leslie Gelb, now an official in the Clinton Administration. Writing in the *Times* in April 1975 as the war ended, Gelb contended that "the regime of South Vietnam ... was effectively created in the summer of 1954. In the spring of 1975, it is perishing." The *Monthly Review* believes that Gelb was "wrong on two counts: the Geneva Conference did *not* create 'the regime of South Vietnam,' the United States did that; and the war now ending is *not* a civil war but a war of national liberation of the Vietnamese people against the United States."[12]

The texts' claims about the oppressiveness of the regime in North Vietnam are simply mentioned, with no context or evidence provided from the documentary record for these assertions. In November 1969, President Nixon stated that the Viet Minh killed "more than 50,000 people following their take-over in the North in the 1950s. . . . Later, he reported that 'a half a million, by conservative estimates . . . were murdered or otherwise exterminated by the North Vietnamese.'"[13] Edwin E. Moise's study of land reform in North Vietnam after 1954 demolishes the prevailing view that is rehashed in the textbooks. Moise concludes that the "number of people executed during the land reform was probably in the vicinity of 5,000 [and] the slaughter of tens of thousands of innocent victims, often described in anti-Communist propaganda, never took place." These deaths were not the result of a Communist program of revenge and murder, and an "extraordinary" fact is that the errors that occurred during that period "were not covered up, or blamed on a few scapegoats, after it was over."[14] Southeast Asia scholar Gareth Porter reveals that most of the information on the land reform abuses came from a former "substantial landholder in [northern] Vietnam" who was "employed and subsidized by the Saigon Ministry of Information, CIA, and other official U.S. sources for many years."[15] None of this history is shared by our textbook authors; without it, youth cannot challenge the texts' distortions, which have become part of the standard mythology.

The texts state that hundreds of thousands of refugees fled from North Vietnam to South Vietnam after the Geneva Conference in 1954, but there is no context provided for this fact. Many were Catholics who supported the French and later Diem. These "land people" would provide the basis for early propaganda on the evils of Vietnamese Communism, creating refugees driven to seek freedom. The role of the CIA in this movement of people is not discussed, a pattern of avoidance and ignorance about that agency that continues throughout the textbooks. Journalist Robert Scheer exposed the refugee myth as "perhaps the most important one put forth by the Vietnam Lobby, a group of anti-communist intellectual, political, and religious leaders" who supported Diem and raved "about the 'miracle of democracy'" flowering in South Vietnam." These refugees received millions in aid from "the United

States and the Catholic Relief Agency, and they became a 'privileged minority and source of support' for Diem. . . . They manufactured atrocity stories, aided in this endeavor by CIA agents."[16] Many of the Catholics who fled to South Vietnam after the Geneva Agreements had been "collaborators and even [had] been mobilized into 'an autonomous Vietnamese militia' that fought against the anti-French resistance led by the Viet Minh."[17] They thus fought for a French colonial regime that is considered oppressive even in the eyes of our textbook authors.

There are harsh comments on Diem's failings as leader of South Vietnam, and the texts admit that he would have to lose the 1956 elections called for by the Geneva Accords, and therefore refused to hold them. But such a simple note does not do justice to this fundamental violation of the Geneva Agreements. *The Pentagon Papers* state that "the French urgently sought to persuade Diem to accept consultations about the elections. . . . Britain [also] . . . joined France in urging Diem to talk with the Vietminh. But Diem refused," supported by the United States. He could not have blocked the elections had the U.S. upheld the Agreements. *The Papers* admit that before and after the Geneva Conference, the National Security Council rejected any notion of self-determination through free elections, arguing that it was "infeasible," and that "such a course of action would, in any case, lead to the loss of [Vietnam] to Communist control."[18] All of this information was known to U.S. officials; thus, they were faced with the choice of a Viet Minh victory and Vietnamese control of their own country or a policy of subversion and terrorism to impose an American-supported regime to prevent this reality.

The texts admit that Diem consolidated his power after the Geneva Conference with the aid of the CIA. From its creation in 1947, the CIA has overthrown and subverted governments perceived as threatening American (actually dominant-elite) interests in the Third World. There is nothing in these texts to help students understand why this happened in Vietnam and throughout the world. Therefore, they cannot challenge the reputed U.S. devotion to "democracy" and "freedom" with the reality of aggression and violence. Philip Agee, a former CIA agent, joins scholars like Michael Parenti in documenting this historical record, including millions in secret election funds used in Western Europe to insure that conservative forces favored by the U.S. stayed in power; and "covert actions and secret operations" to undermine internal policies, including "coups, murders [and] terrorism" in Iran, Guatemala, Cuba, Nicaragua, Angola, El Salvador and Brazil. In pursuing such policies in virtual secrecy from the public and elected officials, the CIA "violated international treaties and domestic laws." This documented history[19] of the most powerful and well-financed international terrorist organization on earth is unknown to youth because of the civic illiteracy fostered by schools, textbooks, and the mass media.

Terror and violence were the central aspects of the Diem regime, and it was this systematic terrorism that was the principal violation of the Geneva Agreements. Former Diem adviser Joseph Buttinger describes the violence used to maintain an unpopular regime in South Vietnam, including operations into regions where the NLF has great support. These resulted in the arrest of "tens of thousands of people" and the deaths of "hundreds, perhaps thousands of peasants. . . . Whole villages whose populations were not friendly to the government were destroyed by artillery. These facts were kept secret from the American people."[20] U.S. officials supported this effort, and academics worked with CIA officials to train, equip, and finance Diem's forces to carry out this terror.

U.S. officials knew that Diem was running a terrorist state. Arthur Schlesinger, Jr., a Kennedy adviser during this period, admits that "Diem's authoritarianism . . . caused spreading discontent and then armed resistance in the countryside."[21] And *The Pentagon Papers* note: "Enough evidence has now been accumulated to establish that peasant resentment against Diem was extensive and well founded. Moreover, it is clear that the dislike of the Diem government was coupled with resentment toward Americans."[22] The depth of Diem's repression is thus available in the documentary record, but students would not know this from the text history. Jeffrey Race, a U.S. Army adviser in South Vietnam whose *War Comes to Long An* is a well-respected historical study of the repression of the Diem regime and the growth of the NLF revolutionary movement, shows how the regime's violence created its own demise. Despite this, it was advised and supported throughout by the U.S.[23]

Eric Bergerud's study of the Diemist terror and the indigenous resistance supports Race's conclusions. Bergerud, who Chomsky asserts believed in the "moral validity" of the war, showed that the regime "lacked legitimacy with the rural peasantry" while the "Communist-led [NLF] enjoyed widespread support." It gained such strength because the Diem regime and the U.S. would not support "fundamental change in the social or economic makeup of South Vietnam." By the end of 1965, the NLF "had won the war in Hau Nghia province [the area of his study]." Even the CIA was forced to admit that "98 percent of the insurgents in the province were local and that they neither got nor needed substantial aid from Hanoi."[24] Faced with such realities, the U.S. turned to its only option: violence. Chomsky concurs: "For Kennedy and his circle, violence raised at most tactical problems; the client regime understood that there was no other choice, despite the negative impact on villagers when Diem's agents . . . murdered, tortured and destroyed."[25] Both Bergerud's and Race's studies reveal that the "U.S.-imposed regime had no legitimacy in the countryside, where 80 percent of the population lived . . . and that only force could compensate for this lack. Both report that by 1965, when the U.S. war against South Vietnam moved to sheer devastation, the Viet Cong had won the war in the provinces they studied, with little external support." Therefore, the only logical recourse for the Diem regime and the U.S. was "terror, then the greater incomparable violence of the invaders."[26] Diem's policies, however, are never called "murder" or "terror." The word "terror," for example, an essential part of contemporary media and political language that is always directed against nations such as Iran, Iraq, and Libya but never U.S. allies such as Guatemala and Indonesia, does not appear *once* in reference to U.S. or client practices in any of the total of forty-eight texts examined in my co-authored 1979 study and the present one.

Diem's support of the Vietnamese upper class is mentioned in the texts, yet this important issue is not examined even though it was a central factor in the nationalist struggle led by the NLF against foreign invaders. The war was a nationalist and class resistance of peasants against wealthy landowners and the military who sided with the invaders.

Kennedy and Vietnam

The texts repeat the Camelot rhetoric about the Kennedy administration, with comments on the President's high-minded concern for reform in both South Vietnam and Latin America. But the "reform" during his presidency included the use of CIA subversion and terror, gutting Third World nations' economic potential, siphoning billions in wealth to U.S. multinational corporations banks, and overthrowing popularly elected governments and replacing them with undemocratic regimes supported by the U.S., however devious and corrupt they may be. Chomsky, among others, has challenged the prevailing view of Kennedy that youth gain from these textbooks. U.S. support of national security states "dedicated to 'internal security' by assassination, torture, disappearance, and sometimes mass murder constituted one of the two major legacies" that Kennedy brought to Latin America; the other was the Alliance for Progress, "a statistical success and social catastrophe (apart from foreign investors and domestic elites)."[27] In Vietnam, there was a dramatic escalation of U.S. involvement under Kennedy, as he "moved on to armed attack" upon the civilian population in the south. "The assault that followed left three countries [Cambodia, Laos and Vietnam] utterly devastated with millions dead . . . and a record of criminal savagery that would fill many a docket, by the standards of Nuremberg."[28]

Johnson, Tonkin and Escalation

The "competing claims" viewpoint shapes the Tonkin Gulf incident. Johnson's assertions are simply repeated and students read that the President did not tell the "whole truth." The secret operations that began against North Vietnam in February 1964 are mentioned, but there is no suggestion that these violated international law. There is no outrage over the fact that a fabricated incident (Tonkin Gulf) fueled a war that led to the loss of millions of lives and the betrayal of democratic principles.

Edward S. Herman and Chomsky show conclusively that the dominant-elite media supported the mystification and lies that later would shape the history textbooks; they believe that the best coverage of Tonkin was found in the dissenting and leftist

National Guardian (later the *Guardian* and no longer published) and by the late independent journalist I.F. Stone, a critic of U.S. policies in Vietnam through his *Weekly*.[29] Stone analyzed the testimony before the Senate Foreign Relations Committee on August 6, 1964, of then-Secretary of Defense Robert McNamara, who claimed that "our Navy played absolutely no part in, was not associated with, was not was not aware of, any South Vietnamese actions [attacking North Vietnam] if there were any." His testimony to the same committee on February 20, 1968, however, revealed another version. "McNamara's [1968] version of the attack contradicts the melodramatic account he gave [in 1964]. . . . It was this graphic, but (as it now appears) untrue version which helped stampede the Senate into voting the Tonkin Gulf resolution." In 1964, McNamara told the Senate that the attack "occurred at night. It appeared to be a deliberate attack in the nature of an ambush . . . directed against the vessels [the *Maddox* and the *Turner Joy*]. *They returned the fire.*" He spoke of "unprovoked aggression," a view that "was magnified and emotionalized" by President Johnson, who talked on national television of "this new act of aggression."[30]

The truth is not what McNamara and other officials told the country. "It is quite clear that [McNamara] and Secretary [of State] Rusk . . . lied . . . to the Senate committee [in 1964], and that McNamara [was] still trying hard to lie about it [in 1968]." On both occasions, "he withheld . . . many crucial facts which cast doubt on the whole story of the August [1964] attack" that was so crucial in moving the war to another level of escalation, violence, and lying.[31] The historical record to counter the official Tonkin story has been available for decades, but the textbook authors did not use it. How can youth become civically literate about this war without the facts about one of the major events that shaped it?

The texts assert that Johnson did not want to widen the war, but also that he secretly expanded the conflict to North Vietnam. Such contradictions continue in the absence of the civic and critical analysis necessary for student understanding. It is claimed that in late 1964 and early 1965 there were 30,000 North Vietnamese troops fighting in the South alongside the Viet Cong, and that beginning in 1968, the North sent in

100,000 troops per year. The first claim is false and is contradicted by information within the texts themselves as well as by *The Pentagon Papers* and other documents. There is no mention of mercenary troops used by the U.S. in Vietnam. Up to the time of the Tet offensive in 1968, for example, Koreans, "who were particularly brutal" toward Vietnamese civilians, outnumbered the North Vietnamese in the South.[32] The second fact is also asserted without any context or evidence that might allow students to understand why this happened: it was essentially an effort to stop the brutal repression against NLF forces and supporters in the South, many of whom were being slaughtered by South Vietnamese and U.S. troops.[33]

The use and effects of toxic chemicals on the Vietnamese and American veterans and the connection to food production and starvation are briefly mentioned, but Agent Orange is not named, and the long struggle of Vietnam veterans for some form of financial restitution and health benefits is not discussed. The chemical warfare against Vietnam is a crime worthy of a Nuremberg Tribunal, but it is not deemed worthy of examination in these texts. The authors seem undisturbed by the revelation of official lies in *The Pentagon Papers*, and this source is rarely mentioned. That so little attention could be given in the 1980s to the most important government document on the conflict is an incredible omission by authors with access to this material. Despite the fact that the document revealed "that the American people had been deceived about the real situation," the authors never use the word "lie" when they refer to Johnson's (or any president's) actions.

Students learn that the United States could neither win nor understand the enemy and the struggle in Vietnam. But U.S. officials had plenty of information to assess the war correctly; however, such data had to be put through the "correct" political filter, which did not allow for Vietnam pursuing its own economic and political destiny without outside domination by the U.S. These students do learn, however, that the "heart of the problem" was that the U.S. was fighting a popular movement. This fact is not investigated in order to enhance civic literacy; perhaps it might undermine the government's assumptions and practices in students' eyes. The effort to destroy a popular resistance movement against imperialism cannot be acknowledged fully for what it was, and the texts move forward, undisturbed by the weaknesses in logic and documentation of their own narrative.

The textbooks reveal that thousands of civilians were killed in bombing raids, and Vietnam "was carpeted with [bombs] . . . vast areas . . . were turned into crater-pitted moonscapes." These are horrendous admissions, but the possibility of war crimes is not even mentioned. There is not a single allusion to the Nuremberg Trials in these texts, despite the scholarship about war crimes committed during the conflict, the International War Crimes Tribunal in Stockholm, Sweden, and the Winter Soldier investigation by the Vietnam Veterans Against the War, which featured eye-witness and personal accounts by U.S. combat troops.

The advice of Clark Clifford and other members of the political and corporate elite who changed their views on the conflict is mentioned, but there is no discussion about why this shift occurred. It was totally pragmatic and cynical, rather than a response to moral concern about destroying a people and their country. Had the U.S.-Vietnam War been quick and relatively bloodless for American troops as the invasions of Grenada, Panama and Iraq, and without major protests at home, no major government official would have opposed the war on ethical grounds. There is no discussion of the social and economic standing and influence of the leaders who advised Johnson about the war, and students are not asked whether elite self-interest and other factors were at work. The U.S. was clearly not winning and had to re-evaluate its position; thus, shifts in viewpoint had nothing to do with the war's moral premises or conduct.

Tet

The alleged murder of 3,000 South Vietnamese sympathizers by National Liberation Front (NLF) forces during the Tet Offensive in Hue in January, 1968, which was given major media attention after the My Lai massacre story broke in the U.S. in November, 1969 (nearly 21 months later), is simply passed on as the truthful version to youth. The official story is that NLF and North Vietnamese forces "deliberately . . . rounded up and murdered" these civilians.[34] D. Gareth Porter has also examined this alleged massacre and challenged its credibility. He argues that it is "one of the enduring myths of the Second Indochina War [that] remains essentially unchallenged." While "there is much that is not known about what happened in Hue," Porter states that there is enough information to show that what has been "conveyed to the American public by South Vietnamese and American propaganda agencies bore little resemblance to the truth, but was, on the contrary, the result of a political warfare campaign by the Saigon government, embellished by the U.S. government and accepted uncritically by the U.S. press." The original source of the data on Hue was a Political Warfare Battalion of the [Saigon] Army. "It is on the word of this body, whose specific mission is to discredit the National Liberation Front without regard to the truth, that the story of the 'massacre' . . . was based. Neither the number of bodies found nor the causes of death were ever confirmed by independent sources."[35]

Porter claims that American forces and not Communist executions were responsible for the greatest loss of life in Hue, concluding that the documentary evidence shows that "the official story of an indiscriminant slaughter of those unsympathetic to the NLF is a complete fabrication."[36] What happened stunned even supporters of the anti-Communist effort such as journalist Robert Shaplen, whose first-hand account supports the thesis that most of those allegedly killed by the NLF were the victims of American-Saigon assaults.

> I went to Hue and nothing I had seen during the Second World War . . . during the Korean War, and in Vietnam during the Indochina War or since 1965 was as terrible, in point of destruction and despair, as what I had witnessed. . . . Much of the city was in complete ruins. . . . *Nearly four thousand civilians were killed in Hue . . . and most of them were the victims of American air and artillery attacks.*[37]

His reports and Porter's scholarship, however, do not merit a single line in the textbook history.

The hysteria and public relations surrounding the so-called Hue massacre served a vital purpose: It obscured actual massacres that had been going on, and took people's minds off the My Lai massacre. These massacres included the CIA-sponsored "Phoenix" program, which resulted in the assassination, torture, and imprisonment of thousands of NLF guerrillas and peasants, and Operation "SPEEDY EXPRESS," a pacification program that uprooted and killed thousands of peasants in South Vietnam. Kevin P. Buckley of *Newsweek* shared his sobering conclusion on "SPEEDY": "All the evidence I gathered pointed to a clear conclusion: a staggering number of . . . civilians—perhaps as many as 5,000 according to one official—were killed by U.S. firepower to 'pacify' Kien Hoa [province]. The death toll there made the My Lai massacre look trifling by comparison."[38]

Nixon and "Vietnamization"
Nixon's "Vietnamization" program repeated the policies of the Diem period, with the Vietnamese fighting and dying and the U.S. aiding clients who had little popular support. Despite earlier comments admitting the possibility of an indigenous rebellion against Diem, the idea that the North was trying to conquer the South is maintained in the textbooks, as well as the concept of South Vietnam as a separate nation. Thus, the texts report on Nixon's continued effort to maintain an independent South Vietnam and to force Communist troops leave the South.

The textbook narrative asserts that the January 1973 Paris Peace Agreement was a "death warrant" for the Thieu regime, which could not last without U.S. support. The assertion is presented without any analysis; thus, the texts ignore the annoying fact that South Vietnam was an artificial client regime like those set up by the Nazis during World War II. In the textbooks' view, the U.S. essentially abandoned South Vietnam, and it was crushed by the North. To the final moment, the fiction of two Vietnams is sustained, with one half attempting to conquer the other. The United States undermined the 1973 Paris Accords that were to end this latest war in Vietnam, just as it had undermined the 1954 Geneva Agreements. Herman and Chomsky point out that "as the agreements were announced . . . the White House made an official statement, and Kissinger had a lengthy press conference in which he explained clearly that the United States was planning to reject every essential provision of the accords the administration had been compelled to sign." The media passed on this version "unquestioningly, thus guaranteeing that the Vietnamese enemy would appear to be violating the agreements if it adhered to them."[39] The U.S. thus disregarded "every essential provision of the scrap of paper it was compelled to sign in Paris." As in 1954 at Geneva, it subverted principles arrived at through negotiation in order to deny the legitimate aspirations of the Vietnamese people for independence and peace.[40]

The dissolution and drug abuse among American troops are mentioned briefly in the textbooks, a very inadequate explanation of a crucial development which had a profound impact on the course of the war. The widespread demoralization of U.S. ground troops, many of whom were African-American, Latino or working class, is not expanded into any discussion of why these troops were there in the first place, or why this decay occurred. Coupled with Vietnamese resistance and U.S. opposition at home, G.I. anti-war efforts and this demoralization helped to bring about the eventual U.S. withdrawal from Southeast Asia. Yet this development, which included widespread resistance and even mutinies among ground combat troops, is not examined to the extent it deserves.

My Lai

The major publicized U.S. atrocity of the Vietnam War elicits the briefest of comment, and the reported death toll ranges from 100 to 450 civilians. This massacre is morally equated with the NLF/NV murders in Hue during the Tet offensive. The nature and facts of these alleged crimes have been challenged; no scholar, however, has challenged the essential facts of what happened at My Lai. The pathetic coverage of the massacre and the contradictory casualty figures form another lesson in civic illiteracy for youth. How can they begin to make sense of the war if such a major incident is so poorly and erroneously reported?

The My Lai massacre was part of a much larger and systematic pattern of terrorism aimed at the rural peasantry who supported the NFL-led revolution against the Saigon regime and U.S. forces—but this organized terror elicits virtually no examination in the text history. Chomsky and Herman examine the central message of this massacre and the many larger and unpublicized massacres that were a regular part of U.S. military policy in Vietnam. Reviewing the dispatches of journalist Kevin Buckley, they contend that "on the matter of My Lai, misleadingly regarded in the West as somehow particularly evil (or perhaps a shocking exception), [it] was one of many that took place during Operation WHEELER WALLAWA. In this campaign, over 10,000 enemy were reported killed, including the victims of My Lai, who were listed in the official body count."[41] Buckley asserts that "the incident at My Lai [was] a particular gruesome application of a much wider policy which had the same effect in many places at many times."[42] The knowledge that massacres were routine policy is simply not raised with students, who leave the texts' discussion of My Lai with the impression that it was an isolated and regrettable incident and an exception to otherwise honorable policies.

Gettleman et al. point out that "the day the news broke [on My Lai]," the Army ordered an inquiry, which revealed that "war crimes" had indeed occurred there, including "individual and group acts of murder, rape, sodomy, maiming, and assault on noncombatants." The American Division had "suppressed" this information about the crimes, however, as part of "an elaborate cover-up of the massacre." The inquiry was itself suppressed and the Army still "refuses to release most of it to the public."[43] None of these facts finds its way into the textbook history.

The End and Lessons of the War
The casualty and refugee figures cited in the books vary greatly, as mentioned above. The divergent figures do not give one much confidence in these books' ability to help students form a truthful understanding of the conflict. The texts also state that there were 500,000 to more than 1.5 million refugees or "boat people"; many or perhaps tens of thousands died at sea. This death toll is widely exaggerated, another textbook claim that fosters civic-historical illiteracy among youth. The social class of the refugees coming to the U.S. is mentioned. In fact, many were wealthy, educated supporters of the war who were against legitimate Vietnamese efforts at self-determination and anti-colonialism; but this important point is never explored, another wasted opportunity for critical understanding.

In these texts, Vietnamese refugees are portrayed as help-less and worthy of U.S. assistance. By this logic, perhaps all refugees are equally deserving of sympathy and support, in-cluding slaveowners leaving the South during Reconstruction, Nazis escaping post-war Europe with help from the Catholic Church and CIA, and death-squad generals in El Salvador and Guatemala. Did these wealthy and educated Vietnamese share any responsibility for the murderous invasion of their own nation, or for aiding illegal actions that the United States held to be criminal at the Nuremberg Tribunal? There is no discus-sion of this question nor a deeper analysis of the "boat people" and, of course, no critical commentary about the millions of Vietnamese made refugees by the U.S.-Vietnam War. They do not deserve our concern and support, it seems, given the re-fusal of the U.S. to offer reparations and assistance as stipu-lated in the Paris Treaty.

The story of the war ends with North Vietnam "taking over" the weakened and helpless South—which had received more than $120 billion in direct economic and military aid and the support of nearly 3 million U.S. troops. The position is ad-vanced that "Congress let them down," because our represen-tatives did not want to appropriate more funds for our brave allies. This notion is not examined, and Congress, which did not oppose a single one of the 113 funding bills for the war from 1966 through 1973, is cast in an almost un-American role even though it supported the war to the bitter end. The "fall of Vietnam"— it is never called a "liberation"—came because the United States opposed an indigenous and democratic struggle for self-determination against foreign aggression. But students learn that a fundamental lesson was "clear to nearly everybody," namely that the U.S. could not simply withdraw from its responsibilities in the world. Only irrational critics and extremists could possibly assert that the basis of U.S. involvement in the world is domination of smaller nations to benefit the economic-political interests of the dominant-elite here. Although the texts state that Vietnam's land and people had been destroyed and its agricultural economy was ravaged, students are assured that this was done in an effort to make Vietnam a viable democratic nation; sadly, it ended up as a "repressive" state allied with the Soviet Union. There is no analysis of U.S. responsibility for what eventually transpired.

Concern is voiced in the textbooks for the disaffected youth who became bitter and disillusioned about our government and political system because of the war; they and the nation would not soon recover. But, one could ask, why shouldn't they be bitter and disillusioned, and why should the nation soon recover from what it has done? As many veterans remind us, the wounds from the war cannot be healed without a truthful reckoning of our responsibility as a government and a people. The textbooks lament the distrust and cynicism directed against the government, but given the lies and contradictions admitted even in these texts, and the indisputable evidence of official lying found in *The Pentagon Papers* and other sources, distrust and cynicism are healthy responses to the government's cynical betrayal of democratic ideals, its citizens, and the truth.

The veterans who chose "to obey the call of their country" or, more accurately, to obey the dominant-elite that claims to speak for the country, are victims of a process of civic illiteracy that begins in our schools. They did not answer the genuine call of a nation to defend freedom, but a call by an elite that defines its narrow self-interest as the nation's, and influences youth to sacrifice their lives in undemocratic and immoral causes. While the bitter legacy of the war endured by U.S. veterans is briefly mentioned in the text history as one the lessons of the conflict, it is surprising that there is no examination of the controversial POW/MIA issue. Rutgers University professor H. Bruce Franklin, an Air Force veteran and an anti-Vietnam War activist, reveals the bankruptcy of the dominant view in his book: *M.I.A. or Mythmaking in America.* At that time (1992), most people believed that "Americans prisoners of war [were] still being held as captives in Indochina."[44] This faith is not simply based "on political rhetoric, rumors, and the POW rescue movies," but also on material that puts forth "a coherent and superficially plausible pseudohistory compounded by self deception, amatuer research, anecdotes, half truths, phony evidence, slick political and media manipulation, downright lies, and near-religious fervor." The anguish over POWs and MIAs "permeates the society, running especially strong in the working class"; it remains "the most important concern of many Vietnam veterans, displacing their own problems with unemployment, homelessness [there are thousands of homeless Vietnam vets], Agent Orange, and inadequate medical care."[45] All of these legitimate problems have been eclipsed by an unproven and blindly supported claim—testimony to the prevailing view of the conflict which serves to keep youth and citizens civically illiterate.

In spite of the national obsession with U.S. MIAs, there has been little recognition of the human cost of the war for Vietnamese families and veterans. Journalist Philip Shenon reported that the Vietnamese have some 300,000 missing from the war. They have also attempted in gentle ways to remind those here who are eager to pursue the MIA issue that "the sacrifice of Vietnamese families was greater than that of families in the U.S." If we compare the number of Vietnamese killed and wounded (1945-1975) in terms of the two countries' relative size, the equivalent toll for the U.S. would be some 31 to 37 million dead and wounded. Such an awesome human loss should cause citizens here to ponder at last the tragic legacy of this conflict. Although "the chances of finding a soldier's remains are virtually nonexistent, nearly 1,000 northern Vietnamese families apply to the Government each month for the chance to travel south to look for clues to the fate of missing relatives."[46] This reality should be kept in mind when we read about Vietnam's unwillingness to help U.S. officials find the remains of American servicemen, and the Clinton administration's decision to formally recognize that nation after more than two decades of U.S. economic and political harassment.

The textbook lessons on the war do not deal adequately with the struggles faced by returning American veterans. Walter Capps, former director of the Center for the Study of Democratic Institutions, calls our attention to the great many suicides among Vietnam veterans—which are greater in number than the combat death toll, the hundreds of thousands who still suffer "delayed stress syndrome," the 2.5 million who were exposed to Agent Orange, the thousands who have been in jail and prison, and the 7,465 women who also served there.[47] The latter, along with Vietnamese women, receive not a line of mention in the textbooks. Carol Lynn Mithers points out that women fought and died both sides, especially the Vietnamese: "Eight American women died in Vietnam; by 1968, according to the North Vietnamese government, 250,000 Vietnamese women fighters had been killed and 40,000 disabled."[48] Since the shooting war continued for another seven years, it is evident that the casualties are much higher. The American women who served in Vietnam were "overwhelmingly white and middle class." They were all volunteers, many of whom "specifically requested assignment to Vietnam. Like the men who served, however, most knew nothing about . . Vietnam [or] the politics of the war raging there."[49] Thus, civically-illiterate men and women ended up fighting and dying in a conflict and country they knew little about—a tragic ending to the long indoctrination they had received.[50]

The lessons in these textbooks are many, but not one suggests that those who planned, executed, and lied about this aggression are war criminals as surely as those this nation and its allies tried at Nuremberg. The one lesson students ought to have learned is that the United States must stop invading smaller nations, but this is never presented as a possibility for civic learning. The essential message in the texts and major media sources such as the *New York Times*, is to wage war differently and quickly next time (as the Gulf War demonstrated) and never to ask whether the U.S.-Vietnam War was unethical, unconstitutional, and undemocratic, as well as an affront to humanity and the ideals that educators share with students.

The textbook history avoids all of the dissenting lessons suggested by Chomsky. In "Visions of Righteousness," he raises issues that youth will not find in the textbooks. For example, Chomsky states that "in one of his sermons on human rights, President Carter once explained that we owe Vietnam no debt and have no responsibility to render it any assistance because 'the destruction was mutual.'" One of the "most astonishing statements in diplomatic history," it created no stir "among educated Americans" and did not diminish "Carter's standing as patron saint of human rights."[51] If youth can be made to believe that this was a "mutually destructive" war, then the ideological assault against the Vietnamese will continue in the textbooks and mass media. Chomsky contends that the "American system of indoctrination is not satisfied with 'mutual destruction' that effaces all responsibility for some of the major war crimes of the modern era. Rather, the perpetrator of the crimes must be seen as the injured party." Since the essential government and textbook history version of the war is that the United States was "simply defending [itself] from aggression, it makes sense to consider ourselves the victims of the Vietnamese."[52]

Final Thoughts
The history of the war in these texts reveals many terrible facts and strategic deceptions. They are similar to Robert McNamara's lament about Vietnam, in which he states that his "exceptional . . . vigorous, intelligent, well-meaning, patriotic" colleagues in the Kennedy and Johnson administrations—recall "the best and the brightest"—were "wrong, terribly wrong" about the war, although they acted "according to what we thought were the principles and traditions of this nation."[53] However, the textbooks essentially reproduce the dominant-elite viewpoint of the conflict. The fundamental integrity of the nation and of our leaders is not subject to critical examination; it is naturally assumed that the United States was in Vietnam for honorable reasons. The possibility that the intentions of the dominant elite that led the country into war were *not* honorable, and were essentially played out in aggression against Chile, El Salvador, Grenada, Guatemala and Nicaragua, is simply out of bounds and not open for civic and historical examination. The doubt and uncertainty that the texts claim would "plague" the nation for years are seen as problems for educators and political leaders, not a marvelous opportunity to debate moral and political issues in a democracy, and that doubt and uncertainty are necessary for debate to occur is not considered. The struggle for such a democracy, therefore, cannot be aided by these history texts.

Part III: The History Textbook Treatment of the U.S.-Vietnam War: A Dissenting Theoretical Explanation

The textbook treatment of the U.S.-Vietnam War is an example of civic illiteracy, through which education's most important civic function has become the preparation of students to support U.S. aggression against the Third World. The textbook narrative that appears earlier in this chapter must also be placed within a theoretical context to help us understand the dominant-elite view of the war. A dissenting perspective is provided by insights on ideological hegemony that are often associated with Antonio Gramsci, who has been called "the greatest Western Marxist theorist of our century." His important theoretical and political insights have in turn been enriched by those of Paulo Freire and Chomsky.[55]

Gramsci defines hegemony as the "'spontaneous' consent given by the great masses . . . to the general direction imposed on social life by the dominant [economic] group."[56] In the United States, as elsewhere, this means the dominant elite that shapes national and international policies, especially on life-and-death issues such as war. It is able to establish its views of society, war, and patriotism as the acceptable and most important ones for citizens, by influencing beliefs and ideas disseminated by schools and the media. The "national security" argument is perhaps the most powerful single example of Gramsci's theory. The needs of multinational corporations are presented as the interests of the nation, and as necessary to the defense of the country and the "free world." The underlying "truth" embedded in this ideology is that, despite resorting to questionable means, the United States acted in Vietnam, as it does everywhere in the world, from honorable moral and political motives. National leaders may stumble and err in the pursuit of noble ends, but they are always trying to do good and speak on behalf of all Americans. In Vietnam, as in the Persian Gulf, the country is committed to freedom and democracy. These are fundamental assumptions conveyed to students, but which Chomsky and others have challenged.

Chomsky's criticism of how the mass media manufactures agreement for this conception of the "national interest" should extend to our textbook authors, whose "institutional task . . . is to create the system of beliefs which will insure the effective engineering of consent."[57] Peter McLaren agrees with this assertion and aims his criticism directly at educational institutions: "The prevailing image of America that the schools . . . have promulgated is a benevolent one in which the interests of the dominant classes supposedly represent the interests of all groups. . . . the values and beliefs of the dominant class appear so correct that to reject them would be unnatural, a violation of common sense."[58]

Gramsci's theory of hegemony is complemented by the insights of Paulo Freire. In his major theoretical work, the *Pedagogy of the Oppressed*, Freire asserts that subordinate groups are dominated by social situations and educational institutions that make their inferior status appear legitimate. His work reminds us that education is always political, and the dominant elite always uses schools to further its own agenda. But education can also become a subversive element in the struggle over ideas, if the elite's power and influence are challenged and people begin to define the world in critically conscious terms.[59] It can aid the process of civic literacy by helping youth to look at the world accurately, free of the nationalism and patriotism that now shape history textbooks and lessons. Freire, Gramsci, and Chomsky hold that all people have the intellectual potential for civic literacy; they can think critically about issues such as war and change the conditions that produce it—and the world. The educational system is largely a hindrance to such understanding, however, because it serves to make the interests of the dominant elite appear natural and good in the eyes of youth. This "natural" process is reflected in the textbook history on Vietnam.

An analysis of Freire and Gramsci's work reveals two basic ways in which dominant-elite views are passed on in U.S. education: an ideological form, in which the dominant elite shapes the fundamental beliefs about the social order and schools, and an ideational form, by which the content of historical issues blocks students' civic literacy. This latter process determines what is taught, and discussed. Curricular materials such as textbooks play a vital role because they can nurture or stifle critical thought. As Michael Apple argues, the actual content or ideational form reflected in textbooks is extremely powerful: "*How* is this 'legitimate' knowledge made available in schools? By and large it is made available through something to which we have paid far too little attention—the textbook. . . . the curriculum in most American schools is not defined by courses of study or suggested programs, but by one particular artifact, the standardized, grade-level-specific text."[60] Even though many high school students learn nothing about the U.S.-

Vietnam War in history classes, their textbooks remain the primary source for information on this epic tragedy. They are also training manuals for civic illiteracy on conflicts in Grenada, El Salvador, Nicaragua, Panama, and the Persian Gulf.

Gramsci's and Freire's theoretical insights are enriched by Herman and Chomsky's propaganda critique. Since history texts are an educational medium within the mass media, the Herman-Chomsky model is a powerful tool for examining textual content as a part of the larger purposes of schools. While the textbooks describe some of the problems and ruthless nature of the war, such facts are presented within the constraints of premises that maintain the integrity and honor of our country, its institutions, and leaders. Herman and Chomsky challenge this "defense-of-honor" position in their study of the media. The textbooks can be placed alongside the media because their essential task is to convince students that the Vietnam aggression was a defense of democracy and freedom that did not work; it was a mistake, a tragedy. The possibility that the war was "outright criminal aggression—a war crime—is *inexpressible*. It is not part of the spectrum of discussion [and] the idea is unthinkable."[61] Neither the media nor the texts and school lessons, however, simply "parrot" the official government line. The texts, for example, touch on many unsavory facts about U.S. aggression—though never termed as such—and criticisms are made of the means employed and the horrible results. But this treatment of the war does not confront Chomsky's conclusion: "We have no problem in perceiving the Soviet invasion of Afghanistan as brutal aggression. . . . But the U.S. invasion of South Vietnam in the early 1960s . . . cannot be perceived as what it was."[62]

Notes

1   William L. Griffen and John Marciano, *Teaching the Vietnam War: A Critical Examination of School Texts and An Interpretive Comparative History Utilizing The Pentagon Papers and Other Documents* (Montclair, New Jersey: Allanheld and Osmun, 1979); reissued as *Lessons of the Vietnam War* (1984). This chapter builds upon that work.

2   The textbooks used in this chapter were obtained from the Teaching Materials Center, State University of New York at Cortland, and the Ithaca High School, Ithaca, New York: Carol Berkin and Leonard Wood, *Land of Promise* (Glenview, Illinois: Scott, Foresman, 1983); Daniel Boorstin and Brooks Mather Kelly, *A History of the United States* (Lexington, Massachusetts: Ginn, 1986); Paul Brandwein and Nancy Brauer, *The United States: Living in Our World* (San Francisco: Harcourt Brace Jovanovich, 1980); Richard C. Brown and Herbert Bass, *One Flag, One Land*, Volume II (Morristown, New Jersey: Silver Burdett Co., 1987); Joseph R. Conlin, *Our Land, Our Time* (San Diego: Coronado Publishers, 1985); Richard N. Current, T. Harry Williams, Frank Freidel, and Alan Brinkley, *American History: A Survey* (New York: McGraw-Hill, 1987); James W. Davidson and John Batchelor, *The American Nation* (Englewood Cliffs, New Jersey: Prentice Hall, 1989); Henry N. Drewry, Thomas H. O'Connor and Frank Freidel, *America Is*, 3rd Edition (Columbus, Ohio: Merrill, 1984); Henry Graff, *America: The Glorious Republic* (Boston: Houghton Mifflin, 1988); Robert P. Green, Jr., Laura L. Becker, and Robert L. Coviello, *The American Tradition: A History of the United States* (Columbus: Merrill, 1984); Diane Hart and David Baker, *Spirit of Liberty: An American History* (Menlo Park, California: Addison-Wesley, 1987); Winthrop D. Jordan, Miriam Greenblatt, and John S. Bowes, *The Americans: A History of a People and a Nation* (Evanston, Illinois: McDougal, Littell & Co., 1985); Glenn M. Linden, Dean C. Brink, and Richard Huntington, *Legacy of Freedom: A History of the United States* (River Forest, Illinois: Laidlaw Brothers, 1986); Pauline Maier, *The American People: A History* (Lexington: D.C. Heath, 1986); Ernest R. May, *A Proud Nation* (Evanston: McDougal, 1985); James J. Rawls and Philip Weeks, *Land of Liberty* (New York: Holt, Rinehart, and Winston, 1985); Donald A. Ritchie, *Heritage of Freedom* (New York: Macmillan, 1985); Melvin Schwartz and John R. O'Connor, *The New Exploring American History* (New York: Globe Book Company, 1981); Robert Sobel, Roger LaRaus, Linda DeLeon, and Harry P. Morris, *The Challenge of Freedom* (River Forest: Laidlaw, 1986); Howard B. Wilder, Robert Ludlum, and Harriet McCune Brown, *This is America's Story* (Boston: Houghton Mifflin, 1983). In this chapter, or textbook history synthesis, I have tried to reproduce the authors' view of the war as a synthesis of all the works, as if a class of American history students had woven together the twenty

texts into one narrative of the conflict. Support for the text study came from the Faculty Research Program, State University of New York at Cortland.

3   Walter H. Capps, *The Unfinished War: Vietnam and the American Conscience* (Boston: Beacon Press, 1982), 31-2.

4   Testimony of Abbot Low Moffat before the Senate Foreign Relations Committee, May 11, 1972, quoted in Griffen and Marciano, 60.

5   *The Pentagon Papers, Senator Gravel Edition* (Boston: Beacon Press, 1972, Vol. I, 243, hereafter noted as *GE*. Quoted in Noam Chomsky, *For Reasons of State* (New York: Vintage Press, 1973), 52.

6   *GE*, I,5,34, quoted in Ibid.

7   Chomsky, xv.

8   *Congressional Record*, June 3, 1974, 17391.

9   Marvin E. Gettleman, Jane Franklin, Marilyn Young, and H. Bruce Franklin, *Vietnam and America: A Documented History* (New York: Grove Press, 1985), 49.

10   "Final Declaration of the Geneva Conference" quoted in "Historic Victory in Indochina," *Monthly Review*, Vol. 27, No. 1, May 1975, 5.

11   Ibid., 6.

12   Leslie Gelb, "The U.S. and Vietnam: The Accretion of Failing Policy, *New York Times*, April 6, 1975, quoted in Ibid., 6-7.

13   Nixon quoted in Noam Chomsky and Edward S. Herman, *The Washington Connection and Third World Fascism: The Political Economy of Human Rights, Volume I* (Boston: South End Press, 1979), 341.

14   Edwin E. Moise, "Land Reform and Land Reform Errors in North Vietnam," *Pacific Affairs*, Spring, 1976, quoted in Ibid., 344.

15   D. Gareth Porter, "The Myth of the Bloodbath: North Vietnam's Land Reform Reconsidered," *Bulletin of Concerned Asian Scholars*, September, 1973, quoted in Ibid., 343-4.

16   Robert Scheer, *Ramparts Magazine Primer on Vietnam* (San Francisco: Ramparts Press, 1966), 21.

17   Chomsky, "The Pentagon Papers as Propaganda and History," in *The Pentagon Papers: Critical Essays*, eds. Noam Chomsky and Howard Zinn, *GE*, V, 188.

18   *GE* I, 239.

19   Philip Agee, "The CIA," Taped lecture, October 6, 1988. See William Blum, *Killing Hope: U.S. Military and CIA Interventions Since World War II* (Monroe, Maine: Common Courage Press, 1995).

20   Joseph Buttinger, *Vietnam: A Dragon Embattled*, 2 Vols. (New York: Praeger, 1967), 976.

21   Arthur Schlesinger, Jr., quoted in *GE* I, 252.

22   *GE* I, 252.

23   Jeffrey Race, *War Comes to Long An* (Berkeley: University of California Press, 1972), 196-7.

24   Eric Bergerud, *The Dynamics of Defeat: The Vietnam War in Hau Nghia Province* (Boulder: Westview Press, 1991), 82.

25   Chomsky, *Rethinking Camelot: JFK, the Vietnam War, and US Political Culture* (Boston: South End Press, 1993), 59.

26   Ibid., 57.

27   Ibid., 25.

28   Ibid., 25-6.

29   Edward S. Herman and Noam Chomsky, *Manufacturing Consent: The Political Economy of the Mass Media* (New York: Pantheon, 1988), 209.

30   "All We Know Is That We Fired The First Shots," *I.F. Stone's Newsweekly*, March 4, 1968.

31   Ibid.

32   Chomsky, *Rethinking Camelot*, 43.

33   Douglas Kinnard, *War Managers* (Hanover, N.H.: University Press of New England, 1967), 37; and George McTurnan Kahin, *Intervention: How America Became Involved in Vietnam* (New York: Alfred A. Knopf, 1986), 307-8, cited in Chomsky and Herman, *After the Cataclysm: Postwar Indochina & The Reconstruction of Imperial Ideology: The Political Economy of Human Rights: Volume II*, 321-2.

34   Chomsky and Herman, Ibid., 345.

35   D. Gareth Porter, "The 1968 'Hue Massacre'," *Congressional Record–Senate*, February 19, 1975, 3515.

36   Ibid., 3519.

37   Robert Shaplen, *Time Out of Hand* (New York: Harper and Row, 1969), 412.

38   Kevin P. Buckley, "Pacification's Deadly Price," *Newsweek*, June 19, 1972, 42-3, quoted in Griffen and Marciano, 133.

39   Herman and Chomsky, *Manufacturing Consent*, 230.

40   Ibid., 232.

41   Chomsky and Herman, *The Washington Connection and Third World Fascism*, 317.

42   Kevin Buckley, "Pacification's Deadly Price," *Newsweek*, June 19, 1972, quoted in Ibid.

43   Gettleman, et al., 404-5. See Seymour Hersh, *My Lai 4: a report on the massacre and its aftermath* (New York: Random House, 1970).

44   Bruce Franklin, *M.I.A. or Mythmaking in America* (Brooklyn: Lawrence Hill Books, 1992), xii.

45   Ibid., 5-6.

46   Philip Shenon, "The Vietnamese Speak Softly of 300,000 Missing in the War," *New York Times*, November 30, 1992.

47   Walter H. Capps, *The Unfinished War: Vietnam and the American Conscience* (Boston: Beacon Press, 1982), 1.

48   Shelley Saywell, *Women in War* (Toronto: Penguin Books, 1985), 131, cited in Carol Lynn Mithers, "Missing in Action: Women Warriors in Vietnam," in Carlos Rowe and Rick Berg, eds., *Vietnam and American Culture* (New York: Columbia University Press, 1991), 81.

49   Mithers, 75.

50   A courageous minority cut through the civic illiteracy and resisted in Vietnam and military units throughout the world. See Richard Moser, *The New Winter Soldiers: GI and Veteran Dissent During the Vietnam Era* (New Brunswick, New Jersey: Rutgers University Press, 1996).

51   Chomsky, "Visions of Righteousness," in Rowe and Berg, 21.

52   Ibid.

53   Robert McNamara, *In Retrospect: The Tragedy and Lessons of Vietnam*, with Brian VanDeMark (New York: Times Books, 1995), xv-xvi. For commentary on McNamara's views, see R.W. Apple, "McNamara Recalls, and Regrets, Vietnam," *New York Times*, April 9, 1995; Max Frankel, "McNamara's Retreat," *New York Times Book Review*, April 16, 1995; and Carol Brightman and Michael Uhl, "Bombing for the Hell of It," *The Nation*, June 12, 1995.

54   Eugene Genovese, "On Antonio Gramsci," in James Weinstein and David Eakins, eds., *For a New America: Essays in History and Politics from Studies on the Left, 1959-1967* (New York: Random House, 1970), 285.

55   See Paulo Freire, *Pedagogy of the Oppressed*, Richard Schaull, ed. (New York: Herder and Herder, 1972). Freire's seminal work has moved thousands of teachers and citizens to reflect on the educational and social premises and practices in this country.

56 Antonio Gramsci, *Selections From The Prison Notebooks*, eds. Quintin Hoare and Geoffrey Nowell-Smith (New York: International Publishers, 1971), 12.

57 Noam Chomsky, in *Language and Power*, C.T. Otero, ed. (Montreal: Black Rose Books, 1988), 674.

58 Peter McLaren, *Life in Schools: An Introduction to Critical Pedagogy in the Foundations of Education*, 2nd Edition (New York: Longman, 1994), 175. See chapter 4 for more on McLaren.

59 See Richard Schaull, "Foreward" in Freire, 13-15.

60 Michael Apple, *Teachers and Texts: A Political Economy of Class and Gender Relations in Education* (New York: Routledge, 1988), 85.

61 Herman and Chomsky, *Manufacturing Consent*, 252.

62 Chomsky, *Necessary Illusions: Thought Control in Democratic Societies* (Boston: South End Press, 1989), 150.

Chapter 6

The Persian Gulf War

Introduction

This chapter discusses civic illiteracy in the context of the Gulf War. Part I reviews the war from the yellow-ribbon or dominant-elite perspective; Part II offers a dissenting critique based on evidence rarely encountered in the mass media and schools. The yellow-ribbon perspective of those in the Bush administration who planned and executed the war, and the intellectuals who defended it, dominated the media-educational discussion of this conflict. Before reviewing this dominant perspective, however, some comparisons with the U.S.-Vietnam War are in order.

As in Vietnam, the United States was in the Persian Gulf trying to do good, and standing for law and order and justice. The belief that this country respects these principles is fostered by the media and school history lessons, but nothing could be further from the truth. For example, since World War II the United States has wreaked devastation on Angola, Brazil, Chile, Cuba, El Salvador, Grenada, Guatemala, Nicaragua, Panama, South Africa, Vietnam, and other nations. These actions resulted in the deaths of millions of people, and were condemned by the United Nations, the Organization of American States (OAS), the World Court, and many U.S. citizens. As in Vietnam, racism was crucial to the Persian Gulf conflict. In the 1960s, we heard about Asians' lack of respect for life; in 1991, it was Arab terrorists who assault civilized and humane values. As with Vietnam, the media and the schools primed the citizens and students to dehumanize the "enemy," one of these institutions' essential functions. The media acted the role of cheerleaders for the attacks on Iraqi troops and people, functioning as an arm of the State. This situation was not fundamentally different from that of the Vietnam War, despite the media mythology of their self-appointed role as critic of U.S. policy in that war.

As with the U.S.-Vietnam War, the planners of the Gulf War came from the same dominant elite that David Halberstam identified as "the Best and the Brightest"[1] in the Kennedy and Johnson Administrations: white, wealthy males with powerful ties to the military-industrial complex that Eisenhower warned the American people about in his farewell address. As in Vietnam, the fundamental premise of the Gulf War was economic and political: the dominant elite wanted to maintain control of the region's natural resources, especially the "black gold" of oil that has been critical to U.S. and Western interests for decades. Both Vietnam and the Persian Gulf were testing grounds for terrifying and sophisticated weapons of mass destruction. As in Vietnam, there was uncritical acceptance of the claim that only "military targets" were being bombed. As in Vietnam, there was no real opposition to the imperial presidency and national security state in Congress. During the Vietnam War, for example, it was not until May 10, 1973, *fully eight years after U.S. combat troops went to Vietnam*, that the Congress voted for a bill to reduce or end military activity. Their role then and during the Gulf War was reduced to cheerleading or lamenting what was happening, rather than mounting a principled challenge to unconstitutional and lawless acts by the Chief Executive. Aside from six members of the House who voted against the Congressional resolution supporting Bush and the troops in the Gulf, and the introduction of a Resolution for Impeachment by Representative Henry Gonzalez, Democrat of Texas, Congress did not challenge the fundamental premises of the Gulf conflict.

Finally, as with Vietnam, the ultimate "enemy" was the American people, who must be conditioned to accept aggression by another name. In this New World (or Business-as-Usual) Order, propaganda took on an Orwellian character: the Gulf War diverted people's attention from oppression and anguish at home to military and economic exploits abroad.

Part I: The Dominant-Elite/
Yellow-Ribbon View of the Gulf War

I have taken the dominant-elite, yellow-ribbon view of the war from the editorial page of the *New York Times*, which the magazine of media criticism *Lies of Our Times* called "the most cited news medium in the U.S., our paper of record." The *Times* influences civic literacy as surely as school history lessons. Its view of America and world events complements the national reports and theorists cited in chapters 1 and 2; despite some tactical criticisms of policy at times, it presents the U.S. as engaged in honorable efforts to support democracy and freedom throughout the world. The selection of the *Times* is deliberate, for its important ideological role in the mass media clearly reveals the dominant or yellow-ribbon perspective.

I will present the *Times*'s view at three different editorial points in the evolution of the war: shortly before the U.S. bombing began (January 10, 1991), right after it began (January 17), and at the war's conclusion (March 1). On January 10, just prior to the Congressional debate on the war, the paper stressed the themes of democracy, dialogue, and commitment to high ideals.

> Iraq's intransigence invites an angry vote. What members of Congress owe America, however, is neither anger nor truculence but their best judgement on what best serves the vital interests of the United States.[2]

Six days before the war began, the Times asserted that "those interests would not be served by the offensive use of military force to expel Iraq from Kuwait." It cautioned that it would be wrong "to confuse patriotism with blind loyalty to the President. A strong America is a democratic America, functioning in accordance with the constitutional design. The larger patriotism is to be wise, not merely tough."[3]

Neither the Congressional debate nor the *Times*, however, discussed the thesis that these "vital interests" are those of a dominant elite with the power and legitimacy to define and pursue them as it sees fit. Since there is no public debate in the mass media or the schools about what the vital interests of the country are, or who decides what they are, it is impossible for youth to develop the critical civic literacy that might challenge the dominant perspective. At the time of the editorial, President Bush had moved more than 500,000 troops to the Gulf region without any debate or resolution in Congress. The *Times's* message is clear: the U.S. must stand up to Iraqi leader Saddam Hussein's aggression, but in a manner that respects our legal and historical principles. An accurate civics lesson, however, would have revealed that constitutional guidelines on war have been systematically undermined and ignored since World War II by all presidents, who have pursued countless military actions that violated the Constitution, with no fear of impeachment and little outcry.

Despite its ambivalence on some specifics of the government's Gulf policy, the *Times* supported the official position, then articulated as "Operation Desert Shield": the protection of Saudi Arabia and other nations in the area from further aggression by Saddam Hussein. It did not "shrink from the ultimate prospect of war," however, "for there are circumstances that justify, even compel, the sacrifices of war," but stated that "those circumstances are not now present," and the nation's "vital interests in the Middle East . . . are in no imminent danger." The nature of the interests is never examined; they are simply defined by the dominant elite that controls and speaks for the nation. Contending that "Saddam Hussein's crimes offend most Americans, most Arabs and most of the world," the *Times* did not believe that "the right response now is . . . a U.S.-led attack . . . [and] to sign off instead on a blank check, leaving it to the President to fill in a future date, would be a dereliction of constitutional duty."[4] Despite this caution, however, its position was not substantively different from that of the Bush administration: Hussein was evil and must be opposed; the President should be supported because he seeks honorable ends; and the U.S. position is just. The expected role of educators is to ensure that youth support these fundamental premises.

The *Times* dropped its caution on January 17, the day after the bombing began. "Saddam Hussein could not have missed, or misunderstood, the message that the rest of the world has sent him . . . since his troops devoured Kuwait last August. He surely cannot have missed the message delivered last night by the waves of bombers and missiles. It was a message on behalf of honorable goals." The "honorable" view captures the dominant-elite's position on the war and the founding principles and history of our country. When it comes to the national security state and the use of violence to sustain it, the *Times* is as "red, white and blue" as William Bennett. It claimed that U.S. bombing raids

> are not to destroy Iraq or kill thousands of civilians. . . . They are to free Kuwait, as President Bush said gravely last night; to insure stability in the region; to avert Saddam Hussein's chokehold on the world's energy supply, and to manage the crisis in a way that establishes a resolute, decent precedent for maintaining collective security in the post-cold-war world.[5]

The concerns the *Times* raised just prior to the Congressional debate on the war melted away after the U.S.-led bombing attacks.

At the end of the war, the *Times* spoke with its authoritative victory voice, pointing out that "American and allied forces suffered dozens of casualties, not thousands, in winning their lightning victory over Iraq's sadistic blusterer. It's a glowing moment for the soldiers and pilots of many nations, and their plain-spoken commander, General Norman Schwarzkopf." These forces, it stated, "have earned the admiring gratitude of millions in this and other countries. The skill and coordination first in the long air war and then of the assaulting armies was as stunning as the speedy outcome." It admitted that it and others "who agreed with the President's goals but thought he was pressing too fast, have to acknowledge that his choices at treacherous junctures proved as successful as they were bold."[6] Here again is a key principle in the dominant-elite notion of civic literacy and responsibility: it means agreeing with the ends of the national security state, while occasionally challenging its problematic means.

The *Times* asserted that the entire Gulf campaign "was possible because . . . Bush turned simultaneously to the United Nations Security Council for declarations condemning Iraq, imposing an enforceable embargo, calling for restoration of Kuwait's Government and holding Saddam Hussein accountable." Citizens and youth, minimally aware that the United States was acting with U.N. authority, had almost no knowledge of the bribery and coercion that were used to get the

Security Council to support the conflict.[7] The questionable or problematic aspects of the conflict did not interfere with the Times's overall admiration for what eventually happened. It pointed out that after the November 6, 1990 elections, "Bush ordered a doubling of the 150,000 troops already deployed. The timing was politically suspect and the explanation was murky." He "provoked understandable Congressional criticism—especially when he appeared to circumvent its war powers by going first to the United Nations for a resolution permitting the use of force against Iraq."[8] Congressional criticism was extremely weak and disorganized, however, and did not interfere with Bush's plans for war. The great "debate" in Congress was an after-the-fact approval for what was already in place; appearing to be a democratic and civic dialogue, it was actually an empty one with no power.

Saddam Hussein "misread the debate as a sign of division and infirmity. More wisely, . . . Bush recognized it as a source of strength. After a debate notable for reasoned eloquence, Congress gave the President, narrowly in the Senate, authority to wage war." But Bush was not given a declaration—a fact that the mass media and political figures ignored in their rush to support the conflict and the so-called democratic process. In a key point that highlights the true nature of official "dissent" in the United States on the crucial issue of war, the *Times* pointed out that once the debate ended, "the opposition quickly closed ranks behind the cause." When it comes to war, Congress, the media, and influential educators offer no principled opposition to the state's basic policies; they merely have tactical differences that end once the dominant-elite policy is decided upon. In conclusion, the *Times* asserted that Bush was an "unchallenged winner in an enterprise of high risks and high ideals. With this outcome, he holds a formidably strong hand in seeking support for his peace aims." It claimed that "this was a war that had to be won. That it was won so swiftly and with so few allied casualties is cause for pride, and gratitude." In this dominant-elite view, it is assumed that the U.S. pursues high ideals of democracy and justice; this premise is rarely challenged in the mass media or our schools, which both ensure that little critical examination of these "high ideals" will be undertaken.

During the war, the Portland, Oregon chapter of the Physicians for Social Responsibility published two war prayers: Bush's Presidential Proclamation of January 16, 1991, which captured the official and dominant-elite U.S. position in the war; and Mark Twain's "War Prayer," written in 1905 in response to the imperialist and racist war against the Filipinos. Bush's proclamation reflects the yellow-ribbon view that mesmerized our youth and nation:

> At this moment, America, the finest, most loving nation on Earth, is at war, at war against the oldest enemy of the human spirit, evil that threatens world peace. . . . the triumph of the moral order is the vision that compels us. . . .
>
> We pray for God's protection in all we undertake, for God's love to fill all hearts, and for God's peace to be the moral North Star that guides us.
>
> So I have proclaimed Sunday, February 3rd, a National Day of Prayer. In this time of crisis, may Americans of every creed turn to our greatest power and are united together in prayer. . . .
>
> Let us pray for our nation. We ask God to bless us, to help us, and to guide us through whatever dark nights may still lie ahead. And, above all, let us pray for peace, peace which passeth all understanding. On this National Day of Prayer, and always, may God bless the United States of America.[10]

Readers should recall that escaping slaves on the Underground Railroad looked for the North Star at night to mark their way to freedom. Comparing their struggle for freedom to the Gulf War slaughter dishonors that struggle and those who risked their lives for it.

Readers should compare Bush's ideological defense of American aggression and self-righteous nationalism with Mark Twain's "War Prayer," which forces us to think about what actually happened during the Gulf War. I did not find a single mention of Twain's prayer in the mass media, and I doubt if many students heard it in their schools.

> It was a time of great and exalting excitement. The country was up in arms, the war was on, in every breast burned the holy fire of patriotism; . . . in churches the pastors preached devotion to flag and country, and invoked the God of Battles, beseeching his aid in our good cause. . . .

Then an aged stranger entered the church and put "the unspoken and real meaning of the prayer into words."

> O Lord, our Father, our young patriots, idols of our hearts, go forth in battle—be Thou near them! O Lord, our God, help us to tear their soldiers to bloody shreds with our shells; help us to cover their smiling fields with the pale forms of their patriot dead; . . . help us to lay waste to their humble homes with a hurricane of fire; help us to wring the hearts of their unoffending widows with unavailing grief; help us to turn them out roofless with their little children to wander unfriended the wastes of their desolated lands in rags and hunger and thirst, . . . Lord, blast their hopes, blight their lives, protract their bitter pilgrimage, make heavy their steps, water their way with tears, stain the white snow with the blood of their wounded feet! We ask it, in the spirit of love, of Him Who is the Source of Love. . . . Amen.[11]

Twain's prayer cuts through the ideological hegemony about God and patriotism to the heart of the matter. The Gulf War was seen as such a conflict, a Christian, White and Western Holy War against the Arab "Infidels," and many Americans reveled in the slaughter.

When the editorials of the *New York Times* are laid side by side, they are seen to be variations on the theme articulated by the dominant-elite and educational apologists such as William Bennett and Diane Ravitch. The essence of this position was articulated by the *Times* in its Veteran's Day editorial in 1991, when it proclaimed that "if any war could be called 'just,' the Gulf War qualified."[12] The United States is portrayed as a unique place worthy of the title of the "most loving nation on earth," and also of God's protection as the savior of freedom and democracy. It is a beneficent nation that brings blessings to all. Until this view is challenged at its roots, civic illiteracy will dominate our nation and schools.

Part II: The Persian Gulf War: A Dissenting View

Introduction
What follows is an alternative and challenge to the dominant yellow-ribbon perspective that was found in every community and school in the nation. Historical amnesia was the first lesson of the war, as few knew (or know) anything about British imperialism, the creation of Iraq and Kuwait as nations, U.S. support for Iraq during its war with Iran in the 1980s, and

U.S. actions shortly before the invasion of Kuwait in August, 1990. Without this context, it remains impossible to critique the Bush administration and support for the war.

Western Imperialism and the Formation of Iraq and Kuwait

A historical context is provided by Joe Stork and Ann M. Lesch, two Middle East scholars who argue that "the scale and timing of U.S. intervention have submerged the important issue of Iraqi aggression and Kuwaiti sovereignty within the large issue of Arab self-determination against Washington's efforts to impose its hegemony over the Gulf region and the Arab world," a domination masked by U.S. rhetoric about international agreements, freedom and democracy.[13] This domination was not open to critical dialogue, as the yellow-ribbon mentality prevented citizens, students and teachers from questioning what happened in the Gulf. Few in the United States knew (or know now) that in 1922, Sir Percy Cox, a British official in the Gulf, "unilaterally set the boundaries between Kuwait, Saudi Arabia and Iraq." This action "deliberately limited Iraq's access to the Gulf."[14] Although Iraq became formally independent in 1932, British "influence remained dominant until the nationalist revolution of 1958." Stork and Lesch contend that the reason Iraq's argument had so much "currency in the Arab world . . . [rested on] the powerful sense that the political and economic order prevailing in the region . . . has been constructed and maintained primarily for the benefit of the Western powers. Behind this perception is oil."[15] This analysis was reflected in the gut level, street response of many Americans that the war was indeed "about oil." This, insight, however, was not explored in a civically-literate manner by the mass media and educators.

Ramsay Clark, former Attorney General and an activist who opposes U.S. foreign policies, points out that dominant-elite interests in Iraq and the Gulf emerged after World War I, as the increasing importance of Middle Eastern oil "coincided with the rise of nationalism in the region and the decline of the British and French colonial powers—and not coincidently, with the rise of the American century." The U.S. took over from the British and used Arab regimes and Iran against each other so that the oil corporations could profit from division among the countries. In 1953, however, this elite domination was threatened in Iran when Mohammed Mossadegh nationalized British oil facilities. The U.S. responded to this nationalist "threat" with an embargo followed by a CIA coup that overthrew Mossadegh and put the Shah of Iran on the throne as a client and ally of the United States.[16] The arbitrary creation of Kuwait as a nation is crucial to British and U.S. imperialism in the Middle East and the ensuing conflicts that exploded with the Gulf War; it has been used by the Western elites as a lever against Iraq, "which was abundantly rich in oil." Thus, the policies that led to the Gulf War are the result of efforts to keep the "oil-rich . . . southern Gulf states" under outside control. Making sure that the oil-burning industrial countries . . . exercised that control became the central preoccupation of first British, then American, foreign policy."[17]

Iraq has been the focus of CIA subversion since at least 1958, when "a popular, nationalist revolution" overthrew the monarchy that had been put in place by the British in 1921. Iraq then helped found the Organization of Petroleum Exporting Countries (OPEC), which challenged the status quo of Western oil monopolies that had been prevalent for decades. The CIA responded to this "threat" with a "health alteration committee," which plotted the assassination of Abdel Karim Kassem, leader of the 1958 revolt. In 1963, he and thousands of his supporters were killed in a CIA-backed coup.[18] In 1972, Iraq was the target of CIA operations because it had nationalized the U.S.-British-owned Iraqi Petroleum Company. After this nationalization, the United States declared that Iraq was a supporter of international terrorism. During the Iran-Iraq war, however, it was removed from this list.[19]

Most Americans first heard about the Iraq-Kuwait conflict after the Iraqi invasion in August 1990; at that time it was framed as a simple case of aggression. The actual history is much more complex, however, and some of it emerged in the 1980s. One of the serious conflicts that emerged from the Iran-Iraq War "was a long-standing Iraqi-Kuwaiti boundary dispute involving . . . oil fields." Hussein argued that the Kuwaitis were taking "more than their fair share [of oil] from the disputed territory. . . ."[20] During the Iraqi invasion, the Kuwaitis reportedly left behind top-secret documents that proved these Iraqi claims and substantiated the charge that Kuwait had supported

U.S. and Western efforts to destabilize Iraq. A Kuwaiti security official met with CIA Director William Webster in 1989, a meeting at which they reportedly agreed "to take advantage of the deteriorating situation in Iraq."[21] The CIA contends that the memo is a forgery, and Iraq was not discussed "at that meeting."[22] This incident was ignored by the mass media, reflecting a common pattern in the United States: evidence documenting illegal acts surfaces, but is denied by authorities—who are then are revealed as liars when citizens examine that evidence. But the damaging facts are then forgotten, and they have no impact on the civic dialogue about the event in question.

Despite the image of Kuwait presented in the mass media, the reality was that the ruling Sabah family ran the country and "denied basic human rights to citizens and immigrant workers alike." When a rare election was held, only a minority of Kuwaiti men could vote. Violations of human rights were frequent, and foreign workers, who made up most of the labor force, were denied citizenship.[23] Kuwaiti women had "no civil [or political] rights, and the treatment of immigrant women [was] abominable."[24] Kuwait's royal family has supported U.S. and British oil companies for decades, "using their country's vast oil reserves to bludgeon poorer and more populous OPEC members into line when they tried to negotiate fairer prices from the oil companies. They have also recycled billions . . . from oil sales into U.S. banks. In return, the al-Sabahs' throne is guaranteed by the U.S. military and the CIA."[25] After the Iran-Iraq War ended, Kuwait was used by the United States in "a campaign of . . . 'economic warfare' against Iraq." During this time, Iraq attempted "to resolve its differences" with Kuwait, but it was continuously rebuffed. "Kuwait maintained what all observers agreed was an attitude of arrogance and intransigence" that was recognized throughout the Arab world.[26] This relevant history remains unknown by nearly all U.S. citizens and students, and civic literacy about this oppressive regime is non-existent.

U.S. Support of Saddam Hussein and the Iran-Iraq War

Persian Gulf developments in the 1980s, especially U.S. support for the Iraqi invasion of Iran, were unknown to nearly all citizens and students. The relevant historical context was missing from discussions in the schools. Citizens were rarely told that the U.S. "ignored or abetted" many of Saddam Hussein's terrible acts—including his internal war against the Kurdish minority in Iraq, the invasion of Iran, and the use of chemical warfare. The historical amnesia and ideological conditioning about Hussein and preparations for the Gulf War were crucial to the later and "essential task," which was to undermine and end the "Vietnam syndrome" that affected the American people—"the reluctance of many Americans to support military intervention" abroad.[27] Undermining a resistance to interventionist policies is a fundamental aspect of the promotion of civic illiteracy, and the mass media and education have played crucial roles in this ideological effort.

During the 1980s, the United States gave economic support to Hussein while "conspiring with others to undermine him." The Kuwaitis were involved in all of these activities, and they "actively supported" Hussein against Iran by loaning him billions to purchase weapons that his Iraqi regime could not otherwise have obtained, and "enthusiastically participated in the economic campaign inspired by Western intelligence agencies against Iraqi interests." This history was essentially unknown in the U.S., and people marched behind Bush when he called for war against Saddam. During the Iran-Iraq War, which left more than one million dead and wounded, there was no anguish at home about U.S. exploitation of "national and ethnic divisions" in the area. The U.S. government encouraged Iraq's invasion of Iran after the Shah was overthrown, to counter "the alarming rise of Khomeini-style fundamentalism." It also supported both sides during the war, officially banning arms sales but secretly providing weapons to each.[28]

By 1984, the U.S. had become Iraq's principal trading partner, and the Reagan administration authorized increased intelligence support for its conflict with Iran. Also in 1984, Vice-President Bush and other officials urged "large-scale financing" of U.S. exports to Iraq. By 1986, a CIA team had been sent to advise the Iraqi military; and "finally, with its 1987 decision to protect Kuwaiti oil tankers in the Gulf, the United States became directly involved in the war on Iraq's side."[29] The Iraq-Iran War ended in August 1988; "almost immediately, Iraq's standing in the Western world began to change" as U.S. plans for a Persian Gulf War targeted Iraq as the enemy. The U.S. "announced . . . that Iraq had used poison gas against the Kurds[30]; [soon after] . . . the Senate voted unanimously to impose economic sanctions that would cancel technology and food sales to Iraq. Though the bill never became law, it was both a threat and a humiliation that could only be seen in Iraq as hypocritical." This began "nearly two years of anti-Iraqi propaganda" that included an early 1990 condemnation of Iraq's production of illegal weapons. The propaganda attack by the Bush Administration and the media continued, even as the United States was shipping billions of dollars of military and technological equipment to Iraq.[31]

Journalist Stuart Auerbach revealed the ongoing relationship between the Bush administration and Hussein that continued to the day before Iraq invaded Kuwait. Presidents Reagan and Bush allowed Iraq to buy "$1.5 billion of advanced products . . . from 1985 to 1990," including helicopters that were used to "spray poison gas on Kurdish rebels in 1988." As one official stated after the Persian Gulf War began, the Administration "had no problem with Iraq until the day after Saddam's troops walked into Kuwait."[32] This support was buried under the propaganda barrage against Hussein and his regime that began in 1990. There occurred a well-organized effort to support him when it was in the dominant-elite's interest to do so; however, when he moved in an independent direction, he suddenly became a menace to the "free world" and all civilized values. This blatant reversal did not cause many citizens to question U.S. leaders and policy—a testimony to the civic illiteracy that is nurtured by the media and schools. By 1990, therefore, the context had been established and the propaganda was in place to portray Saddam Hussein as a maniacal leader bent on aggression in the Gulf region, even before his forces invaded Kuwait in August of that year.

The Persian Gulf War

The prevailing view of the war is that Iraq caused it by invading Kuwait; the United States simply responded by defending Kuwait against Hussein's aggression. But Noam Chomsky argues that the history leading up to the war itself is quite clear, though it is not found in the prevailing view. The U.S. "indicated . . . that it had no serious objection" to Hussein settling border problems with Kuwait "by force and intimidating other producers to raise the oil price. Saddam interpreted this as a 'green light' to take all of Kuwait, thus demonstrating that he was not only a torturer and killer, which is fine by U.S. standards, but an independent nationalist, an authentic crime." He was then punished for this "unacceptable behavior." At no time was Bush interested in peace, as the course was set for war and he would not be deterred even by genuine efforts to settle the conflict diplomatically.

Hussein's tyranny and the U.S. double standard are documented, but were not examined in the mass media or educational institutions. Chomsky argues that "fascist killers and tyrants are quite acceptable as long as they [keep] the world safe for profit—but suddenly become beasts who must be exterminated when they reveal a lack of appreciation for the doctrine formulated with characteristic lucidity by Winston Churchill: that 'rich men dwelling at peace within their habitations' must be guaranteed their right to rule the world."[33] Since citizens and youth knew virtually nothing of the actual U.S. efforts cited by Chomsky, the propaganda about Hussein and the war was undisturbed by any real challenge. A civic literacy that would allow youth to understand and question this double standard did not arise because the critical insights of Chomsky and other dissenters are not found in school history lessons and mass media commentary. Therefore, youth remained easy prey for the official version of the war.

The Role of the United Nations During the Gulf War
Bush lauded the role played by the United Nations during the war. Former U.N. official Erskine B. Childers disagrees, arguing that the war did not have the freely given blessing of the world body. Operation Desert Storm was not a U.N. action: "Some member governments have been economically high-pressured into contributing to, and others in facilitating, this war in the hope that its 'U.N.' mask may cover them." The U.N. Charter states explicitly that all possible "measures not involving the use of armed force" have to be exhausted before any military action is taken, and such action must be decided on by the Security Council. This was not done; "thus, any resort

to the war being a joint and legal U.N. venture was simply ideological window dressing by the Bush administration in order to cast its actions in a favorable light. This was not even seriously attempted." Bush unilaterally doubled the number of U.S. forces in November 1990 without any discussion with the Security Council. He had no "U.N. warrant whatsoever," yet he claimed to be "acting under the U.N."[34] The historical amnesia and double standard about the Gulf War also extend to the U.N.'s previous stances on regional questions, especially the U.S. position on issues involving Israel and the Palestinians.

Bush's effort to obtain U.N. sanctions against Iraq for violating international agreements begins to reek of hypocrisy when we learn of the U.S. record on sanctions and other measures before the U.N. regarding Israel. While each step of Hussein's that challenged the U.N was broadcast widely, "no protest was heard" when Israel refused to allow the U.N. Atomic Energy Agency to inspect its nuclear plants, which are "well known to be making nuclear weapons since the early 1960s—while Iraq was regularly allowing the agency to inspect its nuclear plants (including 1990)." Bullying the U.N. Security Council into supporting sanctions and war against Iraq did not change the essential issue: the United Nations has been used as an instrument of U.S. foreign policy, and will be ignored when it challenges U.S. aggression, and lauded when it supports that end.[35]

Ramsay Clark backs up Childers's view, asserting that "the fig leaf of U.N. approval was a fraud" as Security Council resolutions were obtained through "what would constitute criminal bribes, coercion, and extortion in any system of government desiring integrity in voting."[36] These U.N. actions are documented but they are unknown to most students and teachers who rely on the mass media and school history lessons for their information on world affairs. Examination of the actual record is necessary in order to put the reborn faith in that international body and international law into some perspective.

The U.S. Constitution and Impeachment Resolution

Article I, Section 8 of the Constitution gives Congress the right and power to declare war; President Bush violated this clause in order to wage war against Iraq. Asserting that the Constitution was "shredded" during the Gulf conflict, Clark reminds us that the right to declare war deeply concerned the Founding Fathers; one of them, James Madison, wrote that "The Constitution supposes, what the history of all governments demonstrates, that the executive is the branch of government most interested in war, and most prone to it. It has, accordingly, with studied care, vested the question of war in the legislature."[37]

A Resolution of Impeachment against Bush was introduced in the House by Representative Henry Gonzalez; there was a virtual media blackout regarding it and no effort was undertaken to examine its serious allegations so that students might meet their civic and democratic responsibilities. Gonzalez stated that he "did not pledge an allegiance to the President, but to the Constitution, which is the highest law of the land. The Constitution provides for the removal of the President when he has committed high crimes and misdemeanors, including violations of the principles of the Constitution. The President has violated these principles." He claimed that Bush did not receive "a declaration of war . . . and in contravention of the written word, the spirit, and the intent of the U.S. Constitution has declared that he will go to war regardless of the views of Congress and the American people." Gonzalez declared that Bush "planned, prepared and conspired to commit crimes against the peace by leading the U.S. into an aggressive war against Iraq in violation of . . . the U.N. Charter, the Nuremberg Charter, . . . and the Constitution of the U.S."[38] The lack of critical dialogue on this resolution did not result from any factual basis, but rather from an ideological conditioning that refuses to acknowledge crimes of aggression by the United States and the dominant elite that rules it.

The Gulf War and the National Security State
The Gulf War must be seen in the context of the national security state, which allows little room for a democratic and civic dialogue on vital matters. This reality is missing in the mass media and school history lessons, which teach students about the "genius of American democracy" with its balance of powers. These explanations, however, do not address the hundreds

of executive-ordered U.S. military actions that have occurred
with no formal vote or debate in the country or Congress.
Reviewing the Gulf War process of planning and executing
military moves and then informing Congress after the fact,
journalist George Wilson states that the United Nations gave
Bush "the international equivalent of the Tonkin Gulf resolution that Lyndon Johnson employed to legitimize" the Vietnam War. "Bush, like Johnson before him . . . managed to keep
Congress and the public out of the crucial decision process
until after he committed almost as a big a force to the Persian
Gulf as Johnson sent to Vietnam." In fact, the last-minute debate just prior to the war was a feeble attempt to raise the
issues of war and constitutionality that should have been raised
long before any troops were sent to the Saudi desert.[39] Those
who proclaim their allegiance to civic literacy and American
constitutional democracy should have vigorously protested the
process leading to this conflict, but such principled opposition was absent.

Historian of education Clarence J. Karier contends that the
Gulf War "clearly indicated that the American National Security State, which had been in the making ever since the Japanese attacked Pearl Harbor, had finally come of age." This war
clearly demonstrated U.S. military might, but "more impressive was its ability to control the media, manipulate the public
and negate any possible opposition." The smashing military
victory allowed Bush to "proudly [announce] that America had
finally overcome its Vietnam syndrome." Citizens are evidently
"abnormal" when they resist imperialist wars such as Vietnam,
but "normal" when they go along with them. The Gulf War
took us back to the Tonkin Gulf era and Vietnam when the
Pentagon manipulated public opinion through staged events.
This time, however, the military command—with much help
from a cheering and fawning media—kept strict control through
the use of simulation combat-like videos, not repeating the
same mistake of Vietnam by showing the killings of women
and children, and not even counting the enemy dead.[40] Karier's
concern goes to the heart of the issue raised in chapter 3: the
aggressive and violent American national security state reflects
not the common good of citizens, but the illegitimate and particular interests of a dominant elite that claims to speak for

that good. The premises and policies associated with this state are not challenged by schools and the media, because the ideological blinders about it are so powerful that most accept its premises and policies uncritically.

The Gulf War was an example of U.S. imperialism, a phenomenon that remains unexamined in the mass media and schools. The underlying aim of the imperialist struggle in the Middle East, according to Chomsky, has been "incomparable energy reserves of the region." A fundamental aim of U.S. policy in the region, therefore, "has been to ensure that no independent indigenous force (or foreign power . . .) might gain substantial influence over the oil reserves of the region. These are to be dominated by the U.S., its regional clients, and its oil corporations."[41] This is the economic prize underneath the political rhetoric that seeks to justify why the U.S. goes to war. The fundamental economic reason for the Gulf War is no different than that articulated by former Marine Corps General Smedley D. Butler about his role in pacifying the Caribbean:

> I helped make Mexico safe for American oil interests in 1914. I helped make Haiti and Cuba a decent place for the National City Bank boys to collect revenue in. . . . I brought light to the Dominican Republic for American sugar interests in 1916. I helped make Honduras 'right' for American fruit companies in 1903. Looking back on it, I might have given Al Capone a few hints.[42]

Chomsky views the Iraqi invasion of Kuwait as strikingly similar to the U.S. invasion of Panama—a similarity that had to be suppressed for fear that citizens and youth would see the important links between the two wars. Thus, no one wanted to talk about how Hussein's deeds matched the U.S. invasion of Panama about one year earlier—ostensibly to arrest former CIA ally General Manuel Noriega for his illicit drug dealing in the hemisphere. "It is also easy enough to draw further parallels between the puppet government installed by the Iraqi invaders . . . and the regime of a tiny minority of white businessmen and bankers in Panama, coordinated by a parallel structure of U.S. military and civilian 'advisors' at every level." The fundamental difference between the two invasions is that the Panama invasion was carried out by the United States and was therefore understandable and necessary, whereas Iraq's invasion of

Kuwait is not in the interest of the U.S., and therefore "was nefarious and in violation of the august principles of international law and morality."[43] The Gulf War followed the classic double standard of international conduct, but the dominant-elite apostles of civic literacy like William Bennett were noticeably silent when it came to condemning this evident hypocrisy.

The United States had much more trouble defending its position internationally—under much more criticism—than domestically, where civic illiteracy prevented citizens and youth from challenging the lies about U.S.-Iraqi relations. The first of the various ideological challenges was the easiest: "portray Iraqi dictator Saddam Hussein as a vicious tyrant and international gangster," which is "plainly true." The second was a bit more difficult: "to gaze in awe at the invader of Panama and manager of what the World Court determined to be 'the unlawful use of force' against Nicaragua as he denounced the unlawful use of force against Kuwait and proclaimed his undying devotion to the U.N. Charter." The ideological conditioning was reflected by the press, which fell in line as it "solemnly observed that 'Bush demonstrated that the U.S. is the only superpower . . . [able] to enforce international law against the will of a powerful aggressor,' and reiterated our unwavering commitment to the rule of law and the sanctity of borders." Forgotten in all this bravura about the President's wonderful policy decisions are "the invasions of Panama and Grenada, the war against Nicaragua, the attack against South Vietnam and the rest of Indochina, the invasion of the Dominican Republic and the huge campaign of international terrorism against Cuba."[44] This is the real historical context in which any discussion of the "rule of law" and human rights should have occurred, but it was not brought out in the mass media and was virtually absent from our schools, save for the courageous efforts of some dedicated and principled educators.

The Gulf War: Consequences and Reflections
The human and physical destruction from this brief and devastating war should move any civically-literate citizen to anger and grief; that it did not is tragic but eminently reasonable when we realize that years of educational and media hegemony by the dominant elite has left most Americans numb to such

horrors. The human toll is horrific, especially for young children. One estimate (November, 1995) concluded that "as many as 576,000 Iraqi children may have died since the end of the [war] because of economic sanctions imposed by the Security Council." One of the authors of the study, conducted for the U.N. Food and Agricultural Organization (F.A.O.), asserted that "Iraq has now sunk to the levels of poor developing countries, with underweight among children comparable to those in Ghana or Mali." Several U.N. organizations including the F.A.O. have "expressed concern" to the international body, and for two years the F.A.O. warned that Iraq "risked widespread starvation."[45]

The number of Iraqi military deaths was staggering, especially when compared with U.S. combat losses. General Schwarzkopf stated that "we must have killed 100,000. . . . There's a very large number of dead in these units. A very, very large number of dead."[46] European estimates were higher, with one estimate as high as 200,000 Iraqi military fatalities.[47] The United States reported that 148 of its forces were killed in combat; 37 of these died from "friendly fire."[48] Reflecting on this death toll, former Army intelligence analyst William M. Arkin asked whether America would "ever face up to the true impact" of what happened. The war that "earned a reputation for being clean, smart and humane, was perhaps the most efficient killing machine in history."[49]

The Iraqi invasion of Kuwait also caused extensive civilian loss of life and other destruction. One source estimates that 10,000 people were detained and 1,000 killed by the invading Iraqi forces, with "widespread arrests, torture and summary executions." There were perhaps 1,000 rapes committed against Kuwaiti women, resulting in some 300 pregnancies; there may have been more but many women fled the nation for abortions elsewhere. Palestinians and other foreign workers who were seen as collaborators with the Iraqis also suffered at the hands of returning Kuwaitis; in February, 1994, Amnesty International said 120 people were still being held and that torture had been reported. The physical destruction in Kuwait was extensive, as the Iraqis "looted, plundered, burned and destroyed many buildings, mainly in Kuwait City," leaving approximately $19 billion in total damage throughout the country; the total cost of reconstruction in Iraq has been estimated at between $100 and $200 billion.[50]

Michael T. Klare, who writes extensively on issues of war and technology, pointed out that the Gulf War was "the most firepower-intensive conflict since World War II." The destruction, that resulted, however, was mainly hidden from the American public. The moral issues involved "by the introduction of high-tech conventional weapons and their use in defense of a 'new world order'" were avoided because U.S. citizens refused to see these weapons for "what they truly are—highly effective killing instruments that are designed to produce nuclearlike levels of destruction without arousing popular revulsion." One of the key objectives of the conflict was "to break the will of the Iraqi resistance quickly, and thus avoid a long-drawn out war like Vietnam that would generate widespread opposition at home. In this sense, the relentless pounding of Iraqi positions was as much a response to the still-potent 'Vietnam syndrome' as it was to military conditions in the gulf."[51] Revulsion over what the United States did in Iraq rarely surfaced during and after the war, however, as the media and educators joined the high-tech, yellow-ribbon admiration society. In addition to the moral and political bankruptcy of the Gulf War, even the so-called technical genius of American weapons has been called in question. A massive and secret 4-year study done by the Government Accounting Office (GAO) concluded that the claims made by the Pentagon and its major military contractors about the precision of impressive new weapons were in fact "overstated, misleading, inconsistent with the best available data, or unverifiable."[52]

One dissenting scholar, Stephen Slade, believes that we have to "go back to the great colonial wars when European technology decimated Third World countries to find a parallel" to the slaughter that happened in the Gulf. Although one cannot know who will suffer next from the New World Order, "perhaps none will dare to cross the path of the world's only superpower. Perhaps Bush's NWO will be like Pax Romana—decades of peace through superior firepower. . . . Perhaps this wave of euphoria will begin to ebb." Perhaps citizens will eventually "realize that the price of the NWO is war and endless preparation for war—and the responsibility for death on a grand scale."[53] Except for a minority of educators and citizens, and dissenting media sources such as Pacifica Radio, *The Nation*, *Progressive*, and *Z Magazine*, these reflections about the New World Order were not made part of the public discourse, and their truth claims were not tested by civically-literate citizens.

The Distinguished Professor of Psychiatry and Psychology at the City University of New York, Robert J. Lifton, has written extensively on issues of war and peace. Discussing the nature of the conflict shortly after it ended, Lifton described an "America . . . now in the full flush of triumph," a mood that "poses grave problems for the state of our national soul. Our claim to glory can hardly erase, psychologically or morally, some highly unpalatable features of our behavior." The video-game mentality pushed by a compliant media and educational system legitimated the slaughter of the war. Lifton concluded that the nation had become "quickly dominated by an ugly pattern of war psychology that justified the killing of large numbers of defenseless people. . . . What then emerged was an aggressive patriotism." Citizens saw this as "a blessed country but also as the agent of an all-powerful technological deity. Militarized high-tech becomes equated with absolute virtue, and as possessors of that virtue we have the duty to be the most powerful of world policemen." This "militarized nationalism reached a troubling crescendo during [Bush's] address to both houses of Congress . . . when (as the *New York Times* reported), he 'basked in the atmosphere of triumph, which produced cheers at his every mention of the military.'"[54]

Journalist George Bradford argues that the Gulf slaughter and contemporary U.S. politics raise profoundly troubling issues that were not examined by the media and schools. He asserts that George Orwell's insights in *1984* about the "credulous and ignorant fanatic" party member help us see that this cheering Gulf War fanatic "is no longer Orwell's 'party member' but the loyal citizen of 'democracy.' . . . The contemporary Thought Police have done an impressive job so far. . . . Probably no war in history has been more carefully packaged and controlled." The awesome destruction of the Gulf War proved that "there is little humanity" remaining in the nation. But one must be honest about the soldiers doing the killing. "They are not 'our troops' but the Empire's. They do its bidding, either enthusiastically or silently. As long as they simply followed orders, one cannot support them." For Bradford, "America is today's Nazi Germany, Bush its Hitler, the Marines its stormtroopers. There is no honor in following orders . . . particularly if the cause is ignoble."[55] Few youth were given the civic opportunity to think about Bradford's thesis, even to reject it. How could we presume that there is any civic literacy, therefore, when there is no examination of such critiques of the war?

The ideological conditioning to get citizens ready to support the slaughter of Iraqis had a long history—from the wars against Native Americans to Vietnam. There is a racist and imperialist "arrogance [that] manipulates a population that has grown up in the blue light of the mass media, a population in whom therefore the ability to think critically and reach an understanding based on deep ethical foundations [and relevant historical facts] has been deformed and distorted." Bradford's assertion was not examined by the mass media and schools, thus depriving students of strong and controversial views that might have helped them sharpen their critical understanding of the war. His harsh truths should be part of any dialogue on the conditions of conformity and passivity that led to the war, but they were not. There was a calculated effort to turn citizens' eyes away from "an America in ruins, its economy and infrastructure collapsing . . . its foreign adventures sordid and confused." These conditions appear to people today in "the way Weimar Germany [in the 1920s] looked to many Germans. Like the Germans, the loyalties and ideological illusions of Americans have been eroded by all the aspects of imperial decline, but they have not found any real community, values or authentic loyalties with which to replace the nationalist mystique."[56]

The Mass Media and War Propaganda
The mass media deserve special attention, for they propagandized the public and youth in a manner that undermined any attempt at civic literacy. One study surveyed the relationship between television viewing and factual knowledge of the war and found "strong public support" for it, but the support rested on a foundation of civic illiteracy about the region's history

and U.S. policies there. "Despite months of television coverage [on the Gulf region and conflict], most people . . . were alarmingly ill-informed"; the Bush administration was "the beneficiary of this profound misunderstanding." Most respondents believed "that the U.S. should intervene with military force to restore the sovereignty of *any* illegally occupied country." This means that respondents "are unaware of other occupations in the Middle East—or anywhere else. This is important, because such awareness would undercut the moral cornerstone of the war policy." But most were not aware of this important contradiction in American policy. The survey asserted that "the public are not generally ignorant—rather, they are *selectively misinformed*." Most respondents believed that the United States "should forcefully intervene against leaders that slaughter significant numbers of civilians. If that moral position was applied consistently, the U.S. would have invaded many countries that the State Department has actually supported"[57]—thus demonstrating the deeply contradictory double standard that pervades all civic learning in this country.

The survey indicated that "*the more TV people watched, the less they knew*." Thus, the authors concluded that "if the news media had done a better job in informing people, there would have been less support for the war." The results showed "*a strong correlation between knowledge and opposition to the war*. The more people knew . . . the less likely they were to support the war policy." This reaction is what one should expect from a civically-literate citizenry: critical and informed judgments about national and international issues. But the important study indicates that such critical civic literacy for youth is politically problematic: youth might understand and then oppose official policies, something the dominant elite and its influential educational allies cannot allow. The study claims that the "media have . . . failed in their 'duty to be objective,' since they appear to be communicating facts that support America's policy and playing down those that do not."[58] This was an important study, but I disagree with the authors' premise: the media did not fail, because in reality their duty is to promote civic illiteracy rather than objectivity, and to pass on the dominant-elite ideology. But the authors' critique of the essential message for youth and citizens is accurate. The media demonized Saddam Hussein, cheered on the winning team that crushed his troops and people, and essentially invoked the imperialist and racist principle of Manifest Destiny—the American cause was divinely anointed.

Another dissenting view of the media was offered by scholar and media critic Norman Solomon, who highlighted their role in preparing and then propagandizing the public—especially when it came to ignoring civilian casualties of U.S. bombing, which was "routinely followed by immediate denial of responsibility," a key element of the psychological and political structures that supported the war. "The very magnitude of its brutality . . . required heightened care to turn the meaning of events upside down. Those who massacre are the aggrieved; those being slaughtered . . . are depicted as subhumans." The rage that was carefully crafted "against the butcher of Baghdad [and one-time faithful ally of Reagan and Bush] is probably the most ingenious manipulation of the propaganda alchemists. Every reflex of hate, fear and rage is gathered in the person of the Great Satan himself, 'Saddam.'" In this process, the "rage and feelings of powerlessness, the miseries and humiliations of living in a society dominated by powerful and most anonymous forces, are channeled into a partly choreographed, partly spontaneous fury against the external enemy."[59] Rather than help youth to understand and change the conditions that produce such rage and powerlessness, schools and media complement each other, creating and sustaining a lack of civic understanding and involvement that deflects challenges away from those in power and the institutions they direct to those enemies they select.

The hegemonic media and educational onslaught that garnered public support for the Gulf War has also been analyzed by Richard A. Brosio, who discusses the ease with which the Bush administration planned and executed American involvement after Iraq's invasion of Kuwait in August, 1990. He reminds us that "there occurred no widespread, articulate opposition against a policy that had not been widely discussed" in the country. The mass media "were overwhelmingly hawkish as the crisis developed," in the mold of "classic yellow journalism. The American people, by and large, were persuaded that the administration's former ally . . . was now one of the gravest threats to the Western way of life since Hitler." Brosio goes on to state that "the success . . . capitalism and imperialism enjoyed during [that] period . . . is a brutal demonstration of the [dominant elite's] power, not only on the battlefield, but also as an indication of hegemonic efficacy." He cautions those critical theorists who stress contestation between capitalist power and the democratic imperative "not to take leave of obvious empirical facts."[60] One of these facts is that the combined years of conditioning by media and schooling left most youth and other citizens unable to resist the calls for war and glory—they were reduced to civically-illiterate victims.

War Crimes in the Gulf War
Despite extensive documentation proving that the Bush administration committed war crimes during the Gulf conflict, such crimes are a non-issue, ignored by the mass media and educators. Mark Sacharoff, scholar and author of a work reviewing U.S. war crimes in Vietnam, believes that the "massive air strikes [in Iraq] were far from lawful and humane." They violated a number of international agreements and conventions on war, including the Geneva and Hague Conferences and the Nuremberg Principles, which include a ban on "'wanton destruction of cities.'" This truth is irrelevant in the fantasyland of U.S. moral supremacy and civic illiteracy, where such charges rarely disturb the citizenry and are held in contempt by influential leaders.

Sacharoff raises the double-standard argument discussed earlier: "whenever someone raises the war crimes issue and cites these well-established laws, many respond by claiming that nations cannot abide by them in modern warfare. . . . Yet, at the same time we hear indignant protests about the atrocities in Kuwait, the mistreatment of POWS." The dominant elite, influential educators, and media commentators follow this pattern. Though it is a perversion of the ethical principles we teach youth, the patriotic state institutions have stupefied citizens to the point where they will accept this double standard. Sacharoff asserts that "impartial international lawyers can hardly pretend that the unremitting bombardment of a city with no remaining military targets upholds the principle of proportionality, a principle necessary for a just war." The clearest evidence of the carnage produced by the war and the culpability of United States in war crimes came with the media coverage of the "seven-mile convoy of Iraqi trucks and other vehicles, utterly ruined, their drivers' charred bodies slumped over. . . . Some U.S. soldiers referred to it as a 'turkey shoot.'"[61] This televised slaughter did not bring calls for international tribunals, nor cries of revulsion from educational, political, or religious leaders—most of whom applauded it or remained silent. Aside from a minority of courageous and committed educators, classrooms were silent as well—an indication of the depth of civic and moral illiteracy in our schools.

Ramsay Clark helped to organize the Commission of Inquiry for an International War Crimes Tribunal to deal with the allegations of illegal acts by the United States. This Commission of Inquiry was "an international effort to gather evidence . . . and determine whether war crimes had been committed by the United States." The detailed preliminary charges were "based on evidence already available as measured by international laws defining crimes against peace and war crimes." To gather such evidence, the Commission held hearings and meetings throughout the United States and in more than 20 countries, taking evidence from eyewitnesses, scholars, and experts.[62] The Tribunal members who presided at the final hearing "were 22 judges . . . from 18 nations. . . . They included a former deputy prime minister, elected national legislators, sitting judges, . . . the president of a labor union, political party heads, an African-American Vietnam veteran, . . . and several lawyers' association presidents. Several had endured lengthy prison terms for acts of conscience and political beliefs. Many are authors." The final judgment of the Tribunal "found the United States and its principal officers guilty on all 19 charges of war crimes. Although ignored by the U.S. media the event received major coverage by the international press."[63]

According to Clark, the major principles proclaimed at the Nuremberg Tribunal apply to the Gulf War and to actions of U.S. leaders. These principles are clear:

> Any person who commits an act which constitutes a crime under international law is responsible . . . and liable to punishments. . . .

> The fact that internal law does not impose a penalty . . . does not relieve the person who commits the act from responsibility. . . .

The fact that a person who committed an act . . . acted as Head of State or responsible Government official does not relieve him from responsibility under international law. . . .

The fact that a person acted pursuant to order of his Government or of a superior does not relieve him from responsibility under international law, provided a moral choice was provided to him.[64]

Conclusion

It is a bitter and tragic commentary on the state of civic life in America that the relevant history leading up to the Gulf conflict and allegations of war crimes received no hearing in the mass media or schools; one might have expected such actions, judging from the rhetoric of civic literacy that dominant-elite educators routinely urge as necessary for an informed citizenry. The Persian Gulf War was simply the most recent example of how national security state propaganda overwhelms any alternatives. The extent to which a critical and civically-literate hearing did take place in the schools rested upon the shoulders of a dedicated minority of educators, to whose efforts we now turn.

Notes

1   David Halberstam, *The Best* and *The Brightest* (New York: Random House, 1972).

2   "The Larger Patriotism," *New York Times*, January 10, 1991.

3   Ibid.

4   Ibid.

5   "What the Bombs Said," Ibid., January 17, 1991.

6   "This Aggression Will Not Stand," Ibid., March 1, 1991.

7   See Erskine B.Childers, *War News*, March 2, 1991, and *Middle East Report*, March-April 1991, No. 169, Vol. 21, No. 2.

8   *Times*, March 1, 1991.

9   Ibid.

10 *The Folded Crane: Newsletter of the Portland, Oregon Chapter of the Physicians for Social Responsibility*, March 1991.

11 Ibid.

12 "For Veterans, A Prouder Time," *New York Times*, November 11, 1991.

13 Joe Stork and Ann M. Lesch, "Why War?," *Middle East Report*, November-December 1990, No. 167, Vol. 20, No. 6, 11.

14 Ibid., 12.

15 Ibid., 13.

16 James Ridgeway, "Imperious George," interview with Ramsay Clark, *Village Voice*, December 8, 1990.

17 Ibid.

18 Ramsay Clark, *The Fire This Time: U.S. War Crimes in the Gulf* (New York: Thunder's Mouth Press, 1994), 4.

19 Ibid., 7.

20 Michael Emery, "How Mr. Bush Got His War: Deceptions, Double-Standards and Disinformation," Open Pamphlet Series, quoted in "The War That Didn't Have to Happen," *Village Voice*, March 5, 1991.

21 Kuwaiti Intelligence Memo cited in Clark, 16.

22 George Lardner, Jr., "Iraqi Charges Alleged Kuwaiti Memo Proves a CIA Plot Against Baghdad," *Washington Post*, November 1, 1990.

23   Clark, 110.

24   Ibid., 116.

25   Ibid., 13.

26   Ibid., 14.

27   Tom Mayer, "Imperialism and the Gulf War," *Monthly Review*, Vol. 42, No. 11, April 1991, 5-6.

28   Emery.

29   Clark, 7.

30   Ibid., 19.

31   Ibid., 20.

32   Stuart Auerbach, "U.S. Sold High-Tech Devices to Saddam Day Before Invasion," *Washington Post*, March 12, 1991.

33   Noam Chomsky, "Third World: Don't Lift Your Head," *Guardian*, April 3, 1991.

34   Erskine Childers, *War News*, March 2, 1991.

35   Ibid.

36   Clark, 169.

37   James Madison, *Letters and Other Writings of James Madison, Fourth President of the United States*, Volume II (New York: R. Worthington, 1884), 131, quoted in Ibid, 157.

38   Henry Gonzalez, "Terms of Impeachment," *The Texas Observer*, January 25, 1991. It stated that (1) "Bush . . . violated the equal protection clause of the Constitution" by having "the poor and minorities fight a war for oil to preserve the lifestyles of the wealthy." (2) He violated the Constitution, federal law and the U.N. Charter by "bribing, intimidating and threatening others, including members of the U.N. Security Council." These documented facts brought no cries of outrage from those dominant-elite apologists who supported the war and were well aware that support for the conflict was "purchased." Gonzalez also claimed that Bush "prepared, planned and conspired to engage in a massive war against Iraq employing methods of mass destruction that will result in the killing of tens of thousands of civilians, many of whom will be children." This planning violates a number of international agreements, including the Nuremberg Charter and the U.N. Declaration on Human Rights.
The history prior to the war was also part of the Impeachment Resolution. Bush followed "a course of action that systematically eliminated every option for peaceful resolution of the Persian Gulf crisis." He approached Congress for a declaration of war when "500,000

American soldiers' lives were in jeopardy—rendering any substantive debate by Congress meaningless."

39 George Wilson, "Dealing With Saddam in the Shadow of Vietnam," *Washington Post*, December 2, 1990.

40 Clarence J. Karier, "The Educational Legacy of War," Lecture, Nazareth College of Rochester (N.Y.), July 15, 1992.

41 Chomsky, "Nefarious Aggression," *Z Magazine*, October 1990, 18.

42 *New York Times* interview, August 21, 1931, quoted in James Loewen, *Lies My Teacher Told Me* (New York: The New Press, 1995), 214.

43 Chomsky, 19.

44 Ibid., 19-20.

45 Barbara Crossette, "Iraq Sanctions Kill Children, U.N. Reports," *New York Times*, December 1, 1995.

46 James Gerstenzang, "Tens of Thousands of Iraqi Soldiers' Bodies Left Behind," *Los Angeles Times*, March 1, 1991.

47 James Adams, "Iraqi Toll Could Be 200,000," *London Times*, March 3, 1991, cited in Clark, 38.

48 Ibid., 38.

49 William M. Arkin, "The Gulf 'Hyperwar'—An Interim Tally," *New York Times*, June 2, 1991.

50 Gregory Quinn, "The Iraq Conflict (1990-)," in Michael Cranna, ed., *The True Cost of Conflict: Seven Recent Wars and Their Effects on Society* (New York: The New Press, 1995), 34-5.

51 Michael Klare, "High Death Weapons of the Gulf War," *The Nation*, June 3, 1991, 737-8.

52 GAO Report quoted in the *New York Times*, July 9, 1996.

53 Stephen Slade, "Can We Stop the Next 'New World' Slaughter?," *Guardian*, March 20, 1991.

54 Robert J. Lifton, "Last refuge of a high-tech nation," *Guardian*, March 12, 1991. See also his *Home From the War: Vietnam Veterans: Neither Victims Nor Executioners* (New York: Basic Books, 1985), and *The Genocidal Mentality: Nazi Holocaust and Nuclear Threat* (New York: Basic, 1990).

55 George Bradford, "These Are Not Our Troops; This Is Not Our Country," *Fifth Estate*, Spring 1991.

56 Ibid.

57 Justin Lewis, Sut Jhally, and Michael Morgan, "The Gulf War: A Study of the Media, Public Opinion and Public Knowledge," Center for the Study of Communication, University of Massachusetts, Amherst, March 1991.

58 Ibid.

59 Norman Solomon, "Media Denies, Anesthetizes, Inverts War," *Guardian*, February 13, 1991.

60 Richard A. Brosio, *A Radical Democratic Critique of Capitalist Education* (New York: Peter Lang, 1994), 313.

61 Mark Sacharoff, "War Crimes in the Persian Gulf," *Fellowship*, April/ May 1991, No. 625.

62 Clark, xxxix.

63 Ibid., 195.

64 *Principles of the Nuremberg Tribunal*, 1950, quoted in Ibid., 173.

Chapter 7

Civic Literacy and the Gulf War: Critical Pedagogy and an Alternative Vision

There is no better way to love one's country, no better way to fulfill its greatness, than to entertain critical ideas and engage in the pursuit of social justice at home and abroad.

Michael Parenti

Introduction

This final chapter covers four areas: (1) an introductory discussion of general principles of civic literacy as applied to the Gulf War; (2) three examples of what teachers did to challenge the dominant-elite version of that war; (3) some dissidents' views on democracy, society, civic literacy, and change; (4) final thoughts on what must be done to foster civic literacy in our country and schools.

Those educators who foster civic literacy against great odds deserve our gratitude, respect, and support, because real civic literacy has *never* been accepted by the dominant-elite and its educational allies. We must not confuse the minority of teachers who struggle for civic literacy *within* institutions, however, with those *running* the institutions, who have not fostered a civic literacy that can truly challenge national and international policies. We must not confuse the real heroes and heroines with powerful leaders and influential educators who oppose change, and only accept it when forced upon them by students and citizens. The next time we hear rhetoric about fostering critical thinking and civic literacy from political officials and influential educators, it would be well to recall that such people responded to the student civic struggles in the 1960s by ignoring, opposing, and maligning them. The critical pedagogy and civic literacy I envision are captured by *Rethinking Schools*, a marvelous educational journal published in Milwaukee. In its critique of the Gulf War (March 2, 1991), written in the midst of nearly unanimous and "resounding endorsement" of Bush's policies against Iraq, the editors indicated that

> amid the . . . yellow ribbons, the resurgent national pride and relief that so few Americans died, it will be hard to challenge U.S. policies that led to the war.
>   But we feel compelled to raise such a challenge. We are saddened that such a large majority of Americans acquiesced in or enthusiastically supported this war.

Readers were asked to consider what the war "taught our children; lessons which contradict what they most need to learn." Educators are supposed "to help our children develop a passion for justice and a capacity to reason critically," but the media overwhelmed the public with "military briefings and bombing raids, while providing little analysis of the historical patterns of colonial domination and U.S. policies that have shaped Middle East politics." The commentaries and debates on the war

> were so bereft of intellectual and moral rigor that we deprived [children] of the chance to think deeply about the issues. And it is a sad reality that the schooling most of our children receive does little to help them develop the intellectual independence they need to wrestle with the challenges of controversy.[1]

What students learned from the media and educators during the Persian Gulf War, therefore, was not civic literacy by any reasonable definition of the term.

Rethinking Schools argued that "children need to have courage in their convictions. But they were given the example of anti-war politicians whose opposition crumbled in the face of the pro-war fever which gripped the country." The lesson that children should learn is that "peaceful conflict is nobler than violence. Yet we favored war over negotiation." They also "need values which will not allow technology to cheapen human life. But we have given them weeks of carnage masquerading as a Nintendo game." Although it is vital that our children "learn to be critical of racial inequality and celebrate diversity," behind the war was "thinly concealed racial prejudice. Our young people saw how quickly we condone the slaughter of people of color. As we adorned our schools with yellow ribbons, little thought was given to the young Iraqi men lying dead in their trenches, or the Iraqi children crushed inside the ruins of bomb shelters."[2]

The editors stated that "the moral blinders which made it easier for the U.S. public to accept the slaughter in the Middle East are rooted in the most sorrowful episodes in our nation's history. The African slave trade, the genocide against American Indians, the war of 'Manifest Destiny' to annex one-third of Mexico, the incarceration of Japanese-Americans during World War II were all justified by racist assumptions." Although contemporary U.S. foreign policy may be "more subtle, [it] is fundamentally no different." The editors called for civic literacy and a principled dissent from the government's aggressive policies, providing a basis for the critical perspective that some teachers raised during the war:

> As long as our students remain oblivious to the culture and experience of other peoples, and unaware of the vulnerability of other countries to the actions of our government, they will remain captives of a national chauvinism that blunts their moral sensibilities.[3]

The clash of these moral sensibilities with patriotic war fever shows a conflict between what many teachers, sadly, do in the name of teaching history, civics, and critical thinking, and what should be done to counter the lies and distortions that have defined this and other U.S. wars.

During the opening week of the war, I soon realized that my college students' civic illiteracy precluded a critique that could be defended with anything resembling historical evidence. Virtually none of them had the slightest understanding of the conflict (or, for that matter, the Vietnam War); they had been made civically illiterate by a hegemonic educational system and mass media. This bitter truth must be faced with the deepest compassion and understanding, but such feelings must not be allowed to distract one from the essential issue: like many citizens and teachers, these youths did not have the critical tools of inquiry to examine vital international issues—and to teach their future students about them.

Only 1 undergraduate student out of 70 had an informed and clear perspective on the issue and could defend it with reference to historical facts. His brother was in the Marines in the Saudi Arabian desert, but he was critical of the war, based on reading he had done since the Iraqi invasion of Kuwait. The other undergraduate students could not take *any* position and defend it in a critical dialogue; these future teachers were ignorant of the most basic facts of the Middle East and U.S. foreign policy. This lack of any critical perspective on any of the issues involved in the war was profoundly disturbing; yet, it was understandable, when one considers the ideological conditioning they had received from schools and the mass media. Barring a dramatic change in reading habits once they leave the college community (which is highly unlikely), it is clear that these future teachers will not be able to help students become civically literate about war and patriotism because they are civically illiterate themselves. Most of my graduate students were practicing teachers, and were slightly better informed; many, but not all, read a daily newspaper (but none read the *New York Times* regularly) and watched daily newscasts. But they too were not civically literate on the basic facts of the conflict. None of the graduate and undergraduate students had examined the war through such dissenting sources as *The Nation*, *Progressive*, or *Z Magazine*; and not a single one had ever heard of Noam Chomsky.

What Some Teachers Did to Foster Civic Literacy During the Gulf War: Three Examples

I wish to share three examples of classroom practice during the Gulf War that illustrate how some teachers assisted their students to question the dominant-elite, yellow-ribbon perspective. Even within the existing structural limitations of present schooling, committed and informed teachers can and do foster the civic literacy that is necessary in a democracy.

Bill Bigelow teaches history and social studies in a predominantly African-American and working-class high school in Portland, Oregon. Bigelow asserts that when events such as the Gulf War explode, "teachers need to be instant experts . . . students have a right to expect that we will help them understand what's going on." When school began in September, 1990, Bigelow candidly admits that he was "ill-prepared to be much of a resource" on the emerging conflict. But he did what any reasonable teacher should do: with the help of others, he educated himself about it, and engaged his students in a rigorous dialogue to help them sharpen their civic literacy skills.[4] It is not magic, but knowledge, commitment, time, and critical reflection that make for powerful lessons in the classroom, and Bigelow represents the best of these important educational and pedagogical qualities.

He followed some basis classroom principles to get at the controversial issues on the war: "The only ground rule is that we should remember we are a community of learners and everyone has a right to his or her opinion. Students raise their hands to speak, with whomever has just spoken calling on the next speaker. I interject occasional questions, but if I want to make a point I raise my hand and wait to be called on like everyone else." This reasonable process reflects mainstream pedagogy; what distinguish Bigelow's efforts, however, are the critical knowledge and solidarity that he brings to the dialogue with his students. He was able to assist them in dealing with these tough issues because he was informed about them. In such a dialogue, students will use the time "to express confusion, outrage, sadness or to convince others of the correctness of their positions. They learn a lot from listening to each other, but unless they get new information and analysis, these discussions become repetitive and tiresome."[5] Bigelow's and Freire's pedagogies are absolutely crucial, for a student-centered, process-oriented discussion will not spontaneously move to more critical and historically accurate discussions without the intervention of an informed and reflective teacher.

Bigelow is forthright about his own failings.

Early on I relied too heavily on news articles and videos of nightly newscasts. It was a mistake as our discussions tended to mirror the shallow, ahistorical mainstream media reports. These rarely transcended descriptions of this bombing mission or that press conference and left us with none of the larger "why" questions answered, or usually even asked.

In a Freirean dialogue between teacher and student that begins where the students are but moves them through the criticism and contradiction inherent to all views, Bigelow encouraged his students to "constantly ask why . . . look for the people behind the rhetoric and statistics, and . . . not to begin from the assumption that our government is always right or that American lives are worth more than Arab lives."[6]

He asked students to share what came to mind when they thought of "Arabs." He got the common responses, including "terrorists, rich sheiks, [and] camel riders." To raise critical questions and thinking, he showed a video of "Popeye the Sailor Meets Ali Baba and the Forty Thieves," a cartoon that "portrays the Arab masses as helpless, uninteresting victims, terrorized by heartless thugs. The prognosis is grim, save for the presence of justice-loving, militarily-potent Americans . . . represented by Popeye." He then showed slides from a trip that he had taken to Jordan, the West Bank, and Gaza, in order to introduce students to the Palestinian-Israeli struggle. It also "erased the cartoon Arabs from students' minds and replaced them with real people: doctors, teachers, pharmacists, students, community organizations." This is a vital point, because the image of enemies is always an abstraction. For example, they are "terrorists," not Iraqis or Salvadorans, and are rarely portrayed as individual people with names, residences, occupations, and families. The classes also read a short story by a young Palestinian student "which exposed students to the history and anguish of Palestinians in West Bank refugee camps. The goal was to give voice and persona to a people too often depicted as the inferior, inscrutable 'Other.'" To get beyond the abstract explanation of what happened, he suggested that teachers could use similar eyewitness accounts of the various elements of the Gulf crisis, including one on "the degradation and brutality visited on Kuwaitis by the occupying Iraqi army. [It] also chronicles the determination and creativity of the Kuwaiti resistance."[7]

One way to analyze why the United States became involved in the war "is to test official explanations against past U.S. conducts. Such a route might also lead students to a broader understanding of U.S. foreign policy." Students (and teachers) become truth-seeking reporters who try to ask tough but fair questions that challenge the dominant explanations for the war which were passed on in the media and schools to secure uncritical approval of American foreign policy. Fostering such a truth-seeking team of students is quite difficult and presupposes substantive critical knowledge on the teachers' part, a rarity given the yellow-ribbon ideological hegemony to which they were subjected. Bigelow's insights on the Gulf War and his classroom pedagogy are extraordinary, especially compared with the commonplace historical understanding and civic literacy. His critical commitment to this process is not what the Bradley Commission, William Bennett, and Diane Ravitch have in mind when they advocate civic and historical literacy. For example, students analyzed the Bush Administration statements about why the United States was involved in the Middle East. These various assertions included pronouncements about "creating a New World Order," and the statement that Hussein's invasion of Kuwait was "intolerable because it violate[d] the U.S. *principle* of support for national sovereignty [professed but not practiced]—a principle underscored by numerous U.N. resolutions." Bigelow had a simple and elegant way to test this so-called commitment: he worked with students to see "how the United States responded to other invasions and occupations." He reviewed what the U.S. did in Nicaragua, Israel, Namibia, and Iraq, and discussed the U.N. reaction to each case.[8]

Bigelow raised a key question with students as they struggled to understand the roots of U.S. involvement in the Middle East: "Who stands to gain?" Together, the class discussed the "beneficiaries from U.S. involvement in the Gulf." Bigelow helped students to think about the human beings behind the news reports, since so much of the military information was in "a deadening techno-commentary. . . . General Powell, for example, could have been talking about a rat or a cockroach." Students critiqued the language used during the war with Edward S. Herman's "Doublespeak" column in Z Magazine—"a wonderful resource to provoke students to critically read propaganda masquerading as news. Why, for example, is Iraq's invasion of Kuwait labeled as 'aggression' but the U.S. invasion of Panama dubbed 'Operation Just Cause'?" One can't help students to make the link between Iraq and Panama, however, unless one is informed about both issues and is able to challenge the dominant-elite explanation that America was simply trying to do good in both countries. Bigelow and other teachers who present alternative views are able to do so because they are well-informed about the dissenting perspectives on such events. They help students critique the mass media and government precisely because they are familiar with the writings of Herman, Noam Chomsky, and other dissidents. This effort to critique the dominant-elite perspective is crucial. Bigelow asserts that "English and social studies classes could pore over speeches, news conferences, and press releases reading for doublespeak. They could function as truth detectives ferreting out duplicitous or obtuse statements and revising them with clarity and honesty as the criteria."[9] In theory, any teacher could take this approach to truth-seeking; that few did during the Gulf War is a testimony to the depth to which they have internalized dominant-elite propaganda.

Bigelow related community responses to the war as well. In Portland, students walked out of schools to protest the conflict, and marched with thousands of others in "nightly protests after the bombing of Iraq began." Some of his students also attended "'pro-troop' rallies—many of which explicitly supported U.S. intervention." Regardless of their views, he encouraged all his students to be "history makers" and not mere "spectators" on world events.[10] This is an important point, as the journey toward critical dialogue with students must begin at their starting place; their positions will be dictated by their own history and ethical concerns, and not by the critical perspective of those who wish them to move beyond this starting point. Respecting and engaging them as they think through their own stated ideals and fears, whether pro- or anti-war, is a crucial aspect of fostering civic literacy in the classroom and community.

Bigelow claims that "the more we use our classrooms to analyze war, oppression, and exploitation, the more important it is to allow—even encourage—our students to act. To keep students' passions and belief bottled up is to turn our classrooms into factories of cynicism and despair." Although teachers are not "political organizers," students should learn to see themselves as "*agents* of change, not objects of change." Hope should be the subtext of every lesson we teach—especially now."[11] This is an eloquent summary of the efforts of one teacher who has worked in schools and communities, through his teaching and in articles in *Rethinking Schools*, to nurture the ideals of civic literacy so that his students will be able to make informed and humane decisions about the national and international events that shape their lives.

A civically-literate challenge to the Gulf War was also accomplished by Maria Sweeney, a fourth-grade teacher in a middle- to upper-income suburban school district in northern New Jersey that had a 25 percent Asian-American and 75 percent European-American student population. Sweeney was a "new, untenured and vulnerable" teacher in an "extremely rigorous district."[12] This tenuous situation made her efforts even more astounding, an example of the kind of civic and educational courage that should be emulated by all, but is in fact only demonstrated by a few. She believes that what she did during the war "was clearly risky, but I wouldn't have considered otherwise"—a remarkable statement given her teaching situation. When she shared what she was doing with colleagues "who were also against the war," she was advised "to 'be careful' or 'cool it' and that they would never do the same." What prevents those colleagues (some of whom were tenured) and others like them from raising critical questions with their students and communities? What truly separates Sweeney from so many others in the profession; what divides those who speak truth against power from those who state the same truth privately but recoil from voicing their convictions to others?

Sweeney's civic literacy lessons began before the U.S. bombing commenced, using current events and social studies to review the geography and history of the Persian Gulf, with special attention to the history of colonialism. Her students were only nine and ten years old; therefore, she "had to do this very generally and simply so that they would have some knowledge of the region and understand the economic [interests] the U.S. and other major powers had/have there." Sweeney did not think she had expertise on the region and conflict and simply tried her best—another important practice which complements basic knowledge and fosters a climate conducive to dialogue with students. The notion that ordinary teachers can inform themselves and question the policies set up and explained by the dominant elite and its experts is part of civic literacy. Like Bigelow, Sweeney truly did her best and learned as she taught, which is one of the hallmarks of outstanding teachers.

Sweeney discussed Kuwaiti politics with her students. They learned that it is "ruled by elite men, . . . most people can't vote, few are citizens, there are no opposition groups," [and there are] "extreme disparities in wealth." These reflections were extremely important, given that they and few Americans knew anything about Kuwait and viewed it through the lens provided by the Bush administration. She facilitated a dialogue on Kuwait with students by relying on information from *MERIP* (*Middle East Report*, a fine source of historical and political information), and complemented this with "many photos of Arab kids" which were displayed in her room. As with Bigelow, she humanized the abstract "enemy": she "wanted . . . students to have images of the children in Iraq and to be able to sympathize with them. I think photos are very important when working with children and I use them often."

Historical and political issues were addressed as well, using such alternative sources as *The Nation*, WBAI (a Pacifica Network radio station that opposed the war, unlike NPR), the above-mentioned *MERIP*, and dissenting letters and op-ed pieces from the *New York Times* and her local newspaper. The class discussed views on "why the [U.S.] invasion would be a disaster, what the real reasons were for our involvement (not to preserve democracy which didn't exist in Kuwait) and some alternatives to war (sanctions, etc)." As did Bigelow, Sweeney widened the range of views for her students beyond those given by the mass media and colleagues, creating a "free marketplace of ideas" that does not exist in the media and most schools. Sweeney stated that she "used all the above sources and this simple technique of explaining leftist views and opinion sources once the war began." Then her students began "writing what they understood (summary of information) and then what they thought (their opinions), combined with small and large group discussions." Sweeney was honest and candid about her views: "When the kids asked me what *I* thought, I told them without any reservations or beating around the bush. I never tried to hide my bias." This position contrasts sharply with the pretense of neutrality and objectivity of teachers, educational reports, and theorists who claim to support critical thinking and civic literacy, but who always end up supporting the government when it commits acts of war against other countries.

Sweeney drew some insights from a *Nation* article on "how the U.S. practically bribed much of the Security Council to get it to vote in favor of the invasion." She created "a very informal simulation with my class having a number of kids sit on the Council [while she] played the role of a U.S. official. I went around to various members and offered goodies for a vote in our favor. The kids got the point." Most Americans, including teachers, did not.[13]

The day after the bombing began, Sweeney came to class and shared her feelings. "I told the children that when I heard that we'd begun the bombing, I went out for a long walk and cried. . . . I wasn't afraid to tell the kids this because I wanted them to begin seeing the war as a tragedy. I immediately began asking them to imagine what was happening to the people who lived in Iraq." Here was an important effort to critique the abstract notions of "enemy" that her students and most Americans had. She asked her students to "write pretend diary entries as though they were children living in Iraq at that time," in an effort to "to humanize the Iraqi people." If all teachers followed this simple but powerful principle and lesson, students would be more civically literate, sensitive and able to challenge the criminal policies and violent deeds done in their name. Students were given a critical perspective on the media's role; they learned that there was "only controlled media access to the war and talked about how that would keep the U.S. public from knowing what was really going on in Iraq." She shared her belief that "the nightly news' coverage of the Vietnam War had galvanized many here to turn against and protest that war," and also brought in material she had obtained from alternative media sources. The class talked about the "very pro-war" coverage of the conflict in the daily press and television using examples, including many press clippings that she and her students collected.

Sweeney's civic efforts were not confined to the classroom. She attended an antiwar rally in Washington, and again shared

her involvement with her students. She moved beyond classroom civic literacy to a more activist involvement that included
peaceful assembly/protest, another rare and courageous act
that was not emulated by most teachers. She brought in photos
of the demonstration, as well as the various chants and songs
and what some of the speakers had said. She thought the
speeches "were very moving" and told students about them;
they "were touched and encouraged by the event."

In a country swept up with uncritical patriotic fever, Sweeney
explained to her students why she would not wear a yellow
ribbon and critiqued the "yellow ribbon mania around our
town." She believed that "the way to support 'our troops' was
to bring them home as soon as possible." In the midst of this
mania which overwhelmed citizens' critical sensibilities,
Sweeney exhibited a bold civic courage informed by knowledge; one wishes that masses of teachers had followed her example, rather than succumbing to a civic illiteracy that simply
reinforced students' brainwashing to "support the troops" (i.e.,
the government). Sweeney also attended a four-part teach-in at
the local Unitarian Church on the conflict, and brought those
insights back to her classes. All in all, her in-class reflections
and dialogue with students and her community activism against
the war were amazing educational and civic efforts. To my
knowledge, not a single student in my own classes during the
same period (some 150 in all) engaged in any similar efforts.
In the United States, there was civic illiteracy for most and a
heroic civic virtue by a few, including Sweeney and Bigelow.
Such efforts provide the spark and spirit of hope.

The last example comes from the Alternative Community
School (ACS) in Ithaca, New York, a public middle and secondary school open by lottery to all in the community who wish to
attend. In January, 1991, students at the ACS asked for a course
dealing with the conflict. It was a team-taught course given by
teachers Chris Sperry (history/social studies), Diane
Carruthers (social studies), and principal Dave Lehman, which
resulted in a summary report prepared on the role of the media during the Gulf War.[14] The content of the course was structured around student questions about the war and the Middle
East.

In a letter to the author, Chris Sperry discussed the background and context of the development for the course, which

was "one of the more impressive reflections of ACS's commitment to civic literacy and pedagogy which values student experience." At the time of the war, he was teaching a year-long
course on "War and Peace" that traditionally covered South
Africa, Vietnam, Central America and Nuclear War/Peace.
Diane Carruthers was teaching a year-long course on World
Geography. "There was such interest in the situation in the
Gulf by January 1991 that we decided to scrap our planned
curriculum and create a whole new nine-week course focused
on students' questions about the war." When some 50 students
signed up for the course, ranging from learning disabled students to National Merit Scholars, Dave Lehman volunteered
to co-teach with Carruthers and Sperry so that they could break
the larger group into three smaller sections for discussion and
projects. Sperry believes that such a "responsiveness to real/
immediate/alive social issues and events is not found in most
school situations," and he is right. He continues: "The flex-
ibility and commitment to student interest and exploring current issues in depth to the point of scrapping curricular plans,
are key components of civic literacy education within a
school."[15]

The teachers had a number of basic objectives, including
addressing "students' questions about the war"; creating "an
understanding of the [war's] historical and cultural contexts";
helping to "develop critical thinking skills" by examining "various points of view" and the media presentation of the conflict; developing students' "research, organization, writing, and
independent study skills through the completion of a research
project"; and writing about "their opinions on the war."[16]

The course was organized to maximize student involvement
in the development of central themes and questions, and in
the pedagogy that would unfold between the three teachers
and students. The course was divided into three pedagogical
units: history and culture of the Middle East and the war; invited guest speakers from the community who had some expertise or interest in the topic; and student presentations on
media research. Students' questions were divided into various
categories: "history and culture of the Middle East, history of
the war, Saddam Hussein and U.S. decision making, . . . weapons systems, the military and the draft, . . . economics . . . the
Israeli-Palestinian conflict, comparisons to past wars, the me-

dia, public opinion, opposing perspectives, peace and anti-war movement, and future projections and questions."[17]

Questions raised on the theme of "comparisons" were related to the media study, and which reflected a large concern by the students about the truth of media presentations on this and other important international events. Some of the questions were: "Can we really compare Saddam Hussein to Hitler? Can we really compare the War in the Gulf to Vietnam? What comparisons can be made between the Gulf War anti-war movement and that during the Vietnam era? What comparisons can be made in media coverage during the Gulf conflict, during Vietnam and past wars?" Students and teachers developed a dialogue based on a specific "media watch" that was based on students' analysis of newspaper, television, and radio coverage in a number of countries, with individual students examining a different media source for each day of a three-week period in order to obtain the most detailed information possible. Based on their observations, they made an international comparison on the issues and time devoted to each.[18]

The students' media questions were tough and pointed: "What is the nature of 'media censorship' (U.S. and Iraq)? . . . How are they biased? Are the media telling the truth? Who controls them? How have they become an arm of the government? Why do the media lie about the size of the anti-war movement? . . . What comparisons can be made with media coverage in past wars? Are there discrepancies between our media and Iraq's coverage of casualties?" The media group presented its research, and the entire class discussed the coverage from the *New York Times*, the *Ithaca Journal*, *Newsweek*, *Kayhan* (an Iranian weekly), "ABC Nightly News," "NBC Nightly News," "As It Happens" (a Canadian radio program), and "Radio Havana." Students counted the exact duration of coverage or words used in their particular media source for each of the categories developed. This analysis was done because they questioned the way the war was being covered and "felt they were being manipulated by the media to think a certain way." The data they compiled allowed them "to give concrete examples of how they were being manipulated," and revealed some dramatic differences in coverage allotted, e.g., between the *New York Times*, "Radio Havana," and the Iranian weekly *Kayhan*.[19]

Guest speakers from the community who presented a wide range of opinion on the war during the course: an anti-Vietnam War activist who had been jailed for his activities but who now supported the Gulf War; a pacifist who presented non-violent alternatives to war; an Arab American who shared insights on the conflict; an Army Captain from the Cornell University ROTC who discussed the weapons used in the war; an African-American activist who discussed his community's perspectives; a Cornell professor who discussed foreign policy implications; and a media researcher who examined that aspect of the conflict. Readings for the course were also compiled on the basis of the students' questions and concerns, and included collections of political cartoons from major newspapers, *Scholastic Updates* on the war, *Newsweek* articles and op-ed reflections; and articles and op-ed pieces from the *New York Times.*

It is evident that the ACS students and teachers engaged in an exceptional dialogue, especially when one considers what happened in most schools during the Gulf War conflict—although the print media examined did not include the radical and dissenting critiques found in Bill Bigelow's and Maria Sweeney's lessons. Sperry pointed out that "given the left/liberal family background of most ASC students, e.g., Jesse Jackson won the school's 1988 presidential election by a landslide, most, if not all the students in the course were well-versed in anti-war rhetoric and, to a lesser extent, knowledge." He agrees that a "full airing of radical perspectives is critical to civic literacy . . . in our school's context development of real critical thinking on the part of our students was dependent upon having credible presentations by people, and other sources, which challenged most students' knee-jerk beliefs. This meant having a thoughtful military presenter [the Cornell University ROTC Captain] to challenge many of their assumptions that all military personnel are Rambo-type warmongers."[21]

Sperry also pointed out that "many ASC students are very aware (and critical) of the overtly left-wing (I hope radical) political orientation of their teachers and the school." He states that "the legitimacy of our teaching emanates from the students' belief that our greatest priority is helping them to develop their own . . . critical thinking abilities." In this process, the students "assess our sincerity by the range of perspectives and voices we invite them to consider. It is creative and powerful to present oneself as a teacher with values, beliefs, commitments, and political passion—and to win their trust that our greatest commitment is to the development of their reasoning and valuing abilities."[22] I deeply admire the efforts that the ASC teachers and students put into this course; their courage, insights and integrity should be emulated by all citizens, educators, and youth.

The media research and course ultimately proved to be a worthwhile and informative project for the students. Sperry stated that they

> found the data collection difficult at first and boring later on, but they all felt it was an important learning experience. They found themselves looking at news differently; analyzing what the news was covering, and focusing on what was left out of the news coverage. Their final exhibition of learning was to present a short analysis to the whole class on how their program or periodical covered the war in comparison to the other media sources.[23]

The Gulf War course reflects the educational efforts that are commonplace at ACS, which is a member of the national Coalition of Essential Schools, a group that has embarked on a series of educational reforms throughout the country under the leadership of Theodore Sizer at Brown University. Teacher and student efforts during the war (and on a myriad of other issues) are a hallmark of this exceptional and fine school, which stands out amidst the deadening conformity and civic illiteracy that is too often found in American education.

Dissident Views on Democracy, Society, Civic Literacy, and Change

There are essential principles about society, democracy, and civic literacy that we should apply if we truly wish to challenge the national security state and the civic illiteracy that sustains it. A basic one has been articulated by Noam Chomsky:

> A society is democratic to the extent that its citizens play a meaningful role in managing public affairs. If their thought is controlled, or their options are narrowly restricted, then evidently they are not playing a meaningful role: only the controllers, and those they serve, are doing so. The rest is a sham, formal motions without meaning.[24]

It is within the context of active and substantive democratic participation by citizens in the policies that profoundly shape their destinies that all assertions about America, war, and peace must be examined.

In their work on society and education, Samuel Bowles and Herbert Gintis critiqued the guiding principles of American capitalism as the basis for their view of educational reform. They assert that "many modern progressive educators have seen a more equal and liberating school system as the major instrument for the construction of a just and humane society"; civic literacy must be a part of this proposed construction. The authors disagree with some progressive educators, however, and "are more than a little skeptical of these claims. The social problems to which these reforms are addressed have their roots . . . in the normal functioning of the economic system," which they assert is profoundly undemocratic and not conducive to egalitarian participation by citizens.[25] Their critique of the hierarchical and undemocratic American economic system is entirely relevant to a discussion of civic literacy and critical reflection on the premises of our political economy and the national security state. While the civic dialogue envisioned by Bowles and Gintis and fostered by Bill Bigelow, Maria Sweeney, Chris Sperry and others at ACS is necessary and important, it is not sufficient unless the root cause of civic illiteracy is also attacked: the dominant-elite control of the national security state, for which civic illiteracy provides the ideological support.

Bowles and Gintis also assert that educational alternatives which do not confront the lack of economic democracy "have served to deflect discontent, depoliticize social distress, and thereby have helped to stabilize the prevailing structure of privilege."[26] Reform efforts for civic literacy therefore also fail because they do not address the fundamental nature of this society; a genuine civic literacy among students and citizens would constrain the dominant elite from acting selfishly and maintaining its own interests. They believe that "only revolutionary [educational] reforms . . . have [the] potential" to assist in any basic transformation of the economic and political system. Therefore, such deep reforms are necessary if this genuine civic literacy is to be part of a broader democratic movement within the nation. They argue further that "implicit in the need for such reforms is the understanding that educational change must contribute to a fundamental democratization of economic life" at all levels of the country. This level of educational change is predicated on having critically educated and civically literate citizens and students, for an accurate understanding of society and its ills is essential to any activism that seeks to radically change them. The authors also believe that any "success in the protracted education struggle [which would involve a struggle for genuine civic literacy] will require an acute awareness of both the dynamics of contemporary social change and an alternative to the contemporary social order."[27] In the absence of the necessary assistance of civically aware teachers, parents, and other citizens, there will be no spontaneous student understanding of the American national security state, nor any challenge to its policies.

Carol Edelsky complements Chomsky's and Bowles's and Gintis's insights about democracy in her discussion of the premises that should form the basis of any democratic system of governance and civic literacy. Edelsky, an Arizona State University educator, argues that "a democracy is a system [that involves] participation among equals, negotiation among equals, not participation where a few are more equal than the rest." This system must rest on "*significant* participation, not just having a vote on options already determined behind the scenes, but being a part of what is now done behind the scenes." This principle is crucial to any substantive civic literacy, for without the active and critical involvement of informed students and citizens, there can be no meaningful public involvement in the momentous decisions of war and peace. Such significant participation does not occur in the United States, however, because "in a system where wealth buys the right to overrule majority wishes, where wealth buys the power to make decisions that affect the life and livelihood of everybody else, you can't have a democracy. In a system where corporations are so privileged that they can write the laws as well as decide which laws they'll obey, you can't have a democracy."[28] Without a movement that challenges corporate rule, there is little hope for a substantive civic literacy that can sustain the people's right to active involvement in a democratic process.

Edelsky claims that "politics is about who gets what, where, and how. . . . Democracy is *one* way to decide who gets what. It's one *political* approach to *economy*, to the allocation of societal resources." A civically-literate education to protect and sustain such a democracy "would aim at helping put an end to the systems of domination that create the condition we have now—a condition of decidedly unequal influence over who gets what. The last thing we need, therefore, in creating education for bringing about democracy is to do something that further entrenches some system of domination." Among such retrogressive actions is the proposal that schools and corporations should form partnerships that would enhance the civic literacy of our youth, which Edelsky believes would only entrench the system of domination that already exists and undermine any meaningful and civically literate challenge to the multinational corporate state.[29]

Strengthening that already powerful state is not

> the way to educate for democracy, for putting an end to systems of domination—including corporate domination—that prevent us from having a democracy. Instead, the first step is to see those systems of domination, to become aware, to see how *systemic* (not idiosyncratic) privilege linked to a system driven by profit prevents us from participating equally and meaningfully—that is, from having a democracy."[30]

Edlesky's reflections remind us that the system of domination, which is tied to the national security state, demands a critical civic education that allows students to question its premises and practices. Without this kind of civic literacy, the conservative and liberal history, schooling, and civic literacy will continue to shape any discussion of democracy and society. A critical and accurate understanding of how the political economy actually works, as well as its impact upon the issues of war and patriotism, is the necessary but not sufficient condition for challenging the dominant-elite's current ideological hegemony in the nation and schools.

The basis for such a democratic civic literacy was put forth in eloquent and passionate terms by Howard Zinn. Drawing from the insights of English writer and social critic George Orwell, Zinn believes that "if you can control history, what people know about history . . . you can order their thinking.

You can order their values. You can in effect organize their brains by controlling their knowledge."[31] This control is what has happened with American aggression in the world: the dominant-elite view has created a civically-illiterate youth who have little knowledge of these actions. Therefore, they can be easily manipulated because their historical amnesia is such that they offer little critical challenge to what is told to them.

The guiding premises about society and history that should shape our civic literacy efforts include the proposition that "we should have history that does reflect points of view, in other words, history that is not objective. We should have history that enhances human values, humane values, values of brotherhood, sisterhood, peace, justice, and equality." Zinn believes that the closest approximation of these values is "enunciated in the Declaration of Independence. Equality, the right of all people to have life, liberty, and the pursuit of happiness. Those are the values that historians should actively promulgate in writing history. In doing that they needn't distort or omit important things."[32] It appears that educators and historians could endorse these general principles, but their concrete application in the real world of international policies remains controversial. This controversy should be shared with youth in their history and civic studies, but during the Gulf War, as with other contested issues, the material and insights presented by Bigelow and other educators were lacking. This omission in education and public debate gives credence to Zinn's concerns.

Zinn also asserts that "whatever progress has been made in this country on various issues [and the principles he and others have articulated above], . . . whatever human rights have been gained, have not been gained through the calm deliberations of Congress or the wisdom of presidents or the ingenuous decisions of the Supreme Court. [These have] come because of the actions of ordinary people, of citizens, of social movements. Not from the Constitution."[33] This is a crucial fact of social-historical change: civic literacy advances have come through the efforts of dissident teachers, students and citizens, and not through the dominant elite and its educational apologists.

Zinn's critical historical principles are not rooted in pessimism, however; they point to another fundamental precondition of social and educational change: the committed involvement of people in forging their history against the pressures of oppressive elites and institutions. The principle articulated here is the recognition that even radical change builds upon the work of generations past, and that "the roots of one era branch and flower in subsequent eras. Human beings, writings, invisible transmitters of all kinds, carry messages across the generations." For Zinn, this principle leads him to "think back over the decades, and look around. And then it seems to me that the future is not certain, but it is possible."[34]

In recent autobiographical reflections on his own activism and struggle, Zinn has elaborated on this long-range vision by drawing upon the history of the past few decades, especially the period since the 1960s.

> I think of my students at Boston University and of young people all over the country who, anguished about the war in Vietnam, resisted in some way, facing police clubs and arrests. And brave high school students like Mary Beth Tinker and her classmates in Des Moines, Iowa, who insisted on wearing black armbands to protest the war and when suspended from school took their case to the Supreme Court and won.

Many think that such aware and involved youth have disappeared, but Zinn disputes this view. He claims that "even in the seventies and eighties, when there was widespread head-shaking over the 'apathy' of the student generation, an impressive number of students continued to act." During those years, "young women were becoming more involved in demanding sexual equality, freedom of choice for abortion, control of their own bodies. Gays and lesbians were speaking out, gradually wearing away the public's longtime prejudices."[35] Beyond those activists, however, "there was a much larger population of students who had no contact with any movement, yet had deep feelings about injustice."[36] Zinn implores us to take a much longer historical and philosophical view on the pressing contemporary concerns, acknowledging their urgency and depth but not succumbing to a prevailing view that nothing can be done.

Zinn's view of change and hope is based on actual historical movements, not on some "pie-in-the-sky" notion devoid of any evidence. He is sustained, as he travels around the country, "by how favorably people reacted to what, undoubtedly, is a radical view of society—antiwar, anti-military, critical of the legal system, advocating a drastic redistribution of the wealth, supportive of protest even to the point of civil disobedience."[37] He is encouraged by the "change in *consciousness*" that he has witnessed in the nation, even as he recognizes that "racial hatred and sex discrimination are still with us, war and violence still poison our culture, we have a large underclass of poor, desperate people, and there is a hard core of the population content with the way things are, afraid of change." If we are only able to see the existing and deep ills that divide the nation and the world, however, "we have lost historical perspective." It is the principle of "*long-term* change that . . . we must see if we are not to lose hope. Pessimism becomes a self-fulfilling prophesy; it reproduces itself by crippling our willingness to act."[38] It is "not just foolishly romantic" to sustain hope in terrible times; hope "is based on the fact that human history is a history not only of cruelty, but also of compassion, sacrifice, courage, kindness." These latter qualities are brought out when we act in humane ways based on principled convictions that cause us to oppose injustice and war in order "to live *now* as we think human beings should live"; to do so, "in defiance of all that is bad around us, is itself a marvelous victory."[39]

Zinn's links his historical principles regarding social change to educational and pedagogical principles. In an interview with *Rethinking Schools*, he states that he still believes, "based on a lot of contact with high school teachers over the past few years, that while there's a danger of becoming overly assertive and insensitive to how others might view you, the most common behavior is timidity. Teachers withdraw and use the real fact of outside control as an excuse for teaching in the orthodox way." This timidity is all too true of my graduate students, who are nearly all teachers. By their own admission, even those who are tenured have rarely if ever challenged dominant-elite views on issues, thus substantiating Zinn's view. He believes that

> teachers need to take risks. The problem is how to minimize those risks. One important way is to make sure that you present material in class making it clear that it is subjective, that it is controversial, that you are not laying down the law for students. Another important thing

is to be extremely tolerant of students who disagree with your
views. . . . I don't mean tolerant in the sense of not challenging such
ideas, but tolerant in the sense of treating them as human beings.[40]

The tough decision is how to challenge teacher timidity without engaging in the teacher-bashing that is all too prevalent in
the country. One must say with compassion, but truthfully, that
most teachers never critically examine the controversial issues
that Bigelow, Sweeney, and Sperry did. Nearly all the rhetoric
about civic literacy and critical thinking is just that: talk with
no substance.

Michael Apple has discussed such educational and pedagogical principles in a recent work, *Official Knowledge: Democratic
Education In A Conservative Age.* Supporting those who point
out "that curriculum and teaching always end in an act of personal knowing," and that "no matter how grounded our critical investigations are (and *must be*) in an equally critical understanding of the larger relations of dominance and
subordination of this society," he reminds us that "it ultimately
comes down to a recognizing that we, as persons, participate
in these relations." We must try to "say 'no'" to those who are
antidemocratic and "act to affirm what is less dominative and
more caring."[41] Thus, the struggle for civic literacy will come
down to what teachers, parents, youth, and citizens actually do
with their critical knowledge and civic literacy. As with Zinn,
Apple's insights have been built upon decades of activism and
scholarship; he proposes a tough critique of the dominant-elite
view of America and education, and puts forward a non-ro-
mantic and sensible program that can muster the support of
educators, parents, and youth who will become actively involved
in practical struggles to develop the kind of civic literacy necessary for a vibrant democracy. This task takes critical understanding and hard work: there is no substitute for either.

In addition to his excellent insights about teaching the Gulf
War, Bill Bigelow has written about critical pedagogy, civic
literacy, and educational/social change. He believes that "teaching should be partisan," and "as a teacher I want to be an agent
of transformation, with my classroom as a center of equality
and democracy—an ongoing, if small, critique of the repressive social relations of the larger society." Such "ideological"
teaching is what Bennett and Ravitch warn Americans about.

When done to support the dominant-elite's view of America and their conservative views, it brings no concern for political proselytizing of youth; but when put forth by progressives like Bigelow, it brings cries that they are undermining civic literacy and politicizing the classroom. Bigelow recognizes that his "vision of teaching flies in the face of what has been and continues to be the primary function of public schooling in the United States: to reproduce a class society, where the benefits and sufferings are profoundly unequal."[42] With this pedagogical stance, one must be ever aware of the dangers for teachers who present the full narrative of American injustice. One danger is that students might become "terribly cynical as they come to understand that the enormity of injustice in this society and in the world is just too great. They have to know that it is possible—even joyous, if I dare say so—to work toward a more humane society."[43] Here, as in Zinn's work, is the combination of the historical bad news about injustice and the good news that many have fought to change it and our students can be part of that liberating movement.

Bigelow thinks that "all teaching *is* partisan. Whether or not we want to be, all teachers are political agents because we help to shape students' understandings of the larger society."[44] Thus, nothing is value free in the classroom or country, and the sooner we recognize and act on this truth the better off teachers and students will be as they approach civic and historical issues. But as Bigelow states, these classroom struggles for civic literacy must always be set within the larger social context:

> No matter how successful we are as critical teachers in the classroom, our students' ability to use and extend the analytic skills they have acquired depends on the character of the society that confronts them. Until the economic system requires workers who are critical, cooperative, and deeply democratic, teachers' classroom efforts amount to a kind of low-intensity pedagogical war.[45]

In this pedagogical war, critical teachers can easily divorce themselves from larger movements for radical social change, though they "depend on these movements to provide . . . students with living proof that fundamental change is both possible and desirable." It is a tragic fact that this truth has been denied by the teaching profession throughout American his-

tory. Bigelow concludes: "It seems to me that you cannot emphasize too strongly how teachers' attitudes to teach humane
and democratic values in the classroom should not be isolated
from the social context in which schooling occurs." These are
wise words, indeed, from an outstanding and committed
educator.[46]

Some Final Thoughts on Civic Literacy in the Country and Schools

The civic illiteracy and social ills discussed in this book will
not be ended without a long and protracted struggle in the
schools, streets, and other public spaces in this country. The
fundamental principle for active struggle is perhaps best stated
by Noam Chomsky, who believes that we are faced "with a kind
of Pascal's wager: assume the worst, and it will surely arrive;
commit oneself to the struggle for freedom and justice, and its
cause may be advanced."[47] Given the choice that Chomsky describes, it is clear what educators and citizens need to do if
they are make the rhetoric of ideals about civic literacy into a
reality. Ultimately, dissidents who wish to change the country's
policies will do so by their actions: speaking, teaching, writing, organizing, marching, and civil disobedience. We will either create the world we imagine in our grandest poetic mo-
ments, or continue the long and sure slide into barbarism and
violence. What teachers do in their classrooms and communities, therefore, will contribute either to this barbarism or to
the liberation that a genuine civic literacy demands.

As one of the most important activist-theorists in the world
who has given much thought to the issues that shape this book,
Chomsky has made some specific suggestions for those who
wish to promote civic literacy and radical social change. When
asked by the editors of the *Harvard Educational Review* to respond to the possibilities of a radically different and progressive social order, he commented:

> As everyone has always known, the best way to defend civil liberties is
> to collectively build a movement for social change that has broad-
> based appeal, that encourages free and open discussion, and offers a
> wide range of possibilities for social agency. The potential for such a
> movement surely exists. Many positive changes have taken place in

the last thirty years as a result of popular movements organized around
such issues as civil rights, peace, feminism, and the environment. . . .
"Broad-based" also implies that along with the general public, scien-
tists, engineers, technicians and skilled workers, educators, writers
and artists also need to be deeply involved in the development of the
intellectual resources necessary for providing plausible, concrete,
short- and long-term solutions to the problems of our advanced industrial society.[48]

The role of educators in this diverse effort by skilled people
is crucial, as they shape the minds of those future engineers
and other workers to think rationally and compassionately on
vital issues—or, alternatively, to help advance the civic illiteracy
that has made so many otherwise skilled citizens profoundly
ignorant of the most basic national and international issues.
In this struggle for change, Chomsky says "people can organize, initiate demonstrations, write letters, and vote. They can
form unions and other grass-roots organizations . . . even an
opposition political party so that we'll at least have a two-party
system. . . . The systems of private tyranny—totalitarian in character . . . can be dismantled and democratized. What concen-
trated privilege can't live with is sustained pressure that keeps
building, organizations that keep doing things, people that keep
learning lessons from the last time and doing it better the next
time."[49] All this activity does not happen unless citizens are
civically literate, and possess the critical skills to demystify
the propaganda of the dominant melite and its educational
apologists.

June Jordan argues passionately and powerfully that we must
go back to the struggles of the 1960s—which have been distorted by the dominant-elite media—in order to recapture moral
fervor and militancy. We need more of such qualities in these
difficult times: more critique, more creative disruptions of
business as usual, more challenge to authorities—especially the
national government and its stand on war and patriotism. She
states that "none of us . . . has proven ourselves as wise, as
effective, as persevering as the myriad and mostly anonymous
Americans who fought to desegregate the privileges of freedom and who stopped a war."[50] Thus, part of any contemporary struggle for civic literacy would be to learn what actually
happened during the 1960s and early 1970s, not the Rush
Limbaugh version of that era. What occurred in the human

rights struggles of Blacks and the anti-Vietnam War and feminist movements can be a foundation, so that present insights
can be developed that will form the strategy for attaining a
critical civic literacy. Jordan continues:

> The neglected legacy of the Sixties is just this: unabashed moral cer-
> titude, and the purity—the incredibly outgoing energy—of righteous
> rage. I do not believe that we can restore and expand the freedoms
> that our lives require unless and until we embrace the justice of our
> rage. And, if we do not change the language of current political dis-
> course, if we do not introduce a Right and Wrong, a Good or Evil
> measurement of doers and deeds, then how shall we, finally, argue
> our case?[51]

Jordan's discussion of the Poetry for People Program in Berkeley, California reflects the Freirean belief—founded on actual historical evidence—that all citizens are capable of a civic
literacy and active involvement in forging a genuine democratic
dialogue about the issues that shape their lives. Its guiding
principle should be the same for the struggle for civic literacy:
"every man or woman can be enabled to use language with the
precision and the memorable impact that poetry requires. In
this way, the writing and publishing and public presentation
of poetry becomes a process of empowerment for students as
well as a catalyst for coalition politics of a practical and spontaneous nature."[52] The principle of civic literacy for the people
is a revolutionary idea in a system that has blocked this truth
since the Founding. With the proper education and support,
all youth can be critical and civically literate members of a
democratic and just society.

Moved by the activists and scholars cited in this book, over
the past three decades I have struggled with my own thoughts
on civic literacy, education, and war. I believe that any challenge to the civic illiteracy in education that supports the national security state must be mounted both inside (within
schools and colleges) and outside (in public spaces, including
the streets). The inside approach means keeping alive the best
in the critical liberal tradition—a theoretical spirit of inquiry
in ourselves and students, and a concern for literacy, reflection, and historical inquiry, both of which are absolutely necessary to confront the momentous issues we face. These are
necessary but not sufficient in order to educate for civic lit-

eracy, peace, and justice. The outside approach reflects the extent to which we are engaged beyond the classroom as critical educator-citizens, informed about these issues and involved with others in local, regional, national and international struggles. We must expand our notion of political involvement and commitment, lending our tools of intellectual analysis to those struggles for peace and justice. We must reverse the essential role of educators in this country as servants of power, apologists for the dominant elite, and functionaries who go about their work while others are oppressed and killed.

Without the most far-reaching and revolutionary change in historical knowledge and consciousness among current and future teachers, there is little chance that they will be involved as thoughtful citizens and educators in judging what is done in their names by the violent and aggressive national security state. Dissident teachers at all levels of schooling must raise critical issues and questions with students, with a profound understanding of the educational and socio-economic realities that now prevail in the United States. We cannot afford a naive assessment of the relative strengths of the dominant-elite and radical perspectives. Educators must embrace the view reflected by Chomsky, Freire and Zinn: given the facts and a dialogue about them, students and citizens will see the truth about what the national security state does and act against it. We must soberly assess why this has not happened, however, and reject those overly optimistic "contestation" analyses in education and society that simply do not fit the facts.

The courage, intellect, militancy, spirit and force with which we must struggle for civic literacy and democracy have been articulated by the late activist and lawyer, William Kunstler. Legal defender of many dissident activists who challenged the national security state's violent policies, in his last public speech Kunstler laid out a civically literate and civilly disobedient view that should be considered by anyone seeking social transformation and real democracy:

> There is a time to act. There is a time to break the law—wasn't that how we were formed in the first place? Don't we celebrate that, every July? . . . to paraphrase . . . Roosevelt, the only thing they have to fear is us. And that's the truth of the matter. There is only one thing that moves government, on any level—it's utter, stark fear. And if you will

recall when Richard Nixon sent the troops into Cambodia in April of 1970 . . ., the United States went on a tear that culminated, as you know, in four young people being shot down at Kent State, in two at Jackson State, and in the closing down of 300 colleges and universities. And it forced the President of the United States to [withdraw] the troops from Cambodia. . . . Electoral politics doesn't bother them that much. They always think that there are enough lunatics out there to vote them back in. . . . So all of us have to do what we have to do. Some of us do things that others will not. In Chicago I remember Dave Dellinger saying, Some of you may break the law, some of you may write letters to the editor; in between there may be varieties of actions. Do what you can do, what your conscience, your will, your state of mind, can lead you to do. But do it.[53]

Here is some sound advice from a true citizen of the country and the world, one who fought for democracy, civic literacy, and peace. Educators and students would do well to emulate his insights, activism, and spirit.

Notes

1 "One Big Nintendo Game," Rethinking Schools, March/April 1991, 2.

2 Ibid.

3 Ibid.

4 Bill Bigelow, "Fighting for the Truth: The Gulf War and Our Students," *Rethinking Schools*, March/April 1991, 1.

5 Ibid.

6 Ibid.

7 Ibid., 7.

8 Ibid.

9 Ibid., 17.

10 Ibid., 18.

11 Ibid.

12 Following quotes are from Maria Sweeney's reflections on her teaching during the Gulf War, detailed in a letter to the author (July, 1995).

13 For more evidence of this bribery, see Ramsey Clark, *The Fire This Time: U.S. War Crimes in the Gulf*, 153-56,169,204-5. The article to which she referred was Alexander Cockburn, "Beat the Devil," *The Nation*, March 18, 1991.

14 Chris Sperry and students, "What the Media Covered about the War in the Persian Gulf," Alternative Community School, Ithaca, New York, March 29, 1991.

15 Chris Sperry, letter to author, February 10, 1996.

16 "What the Media Covered."

17 Ibid.

18 Ibid.

19 Ibid.

20 Ibid.

21 Sperry letter.

22 Ibid.

23 Ibid.

24 Noam Chomsky, *Deterring Democracy* (New York: Hill and Wang, 1991), 6.

25 Samuel Bowles and Herbert Gintis, *Schooling in Capitalist America: Educational Reform and the Contradictions of Economic Life* (New York: Basic Books, 1976), 245.

26 Ibid., 246.

27 Ibid., 263.

28 Carole Edelsky, "Education For Democracy," *Language Arts*, Vol. 71, April 1994, 252-3.

29 Ibid., 253.

30 Ibid., 254.

31 Howard Zinn, *Failure to Quit: Reflections of an Optimistic Historian* (Monroe, Maine: Common Courage Press, 1993), 10.

32 Ibid., 11.

33 Ibid., 69.

34 Ibid., 164.

35 Zinn, *You Can't Be Neutral on a Moving Train: A Personal History of Our Times* (Boston: Beacon Press, 1995), 198.

36 Ibid., 199.

37 Ibid., 206.

38 Ibid., 207.

39 Ibid., 208.

40 "Why Students Should Study History: An Interview with Howard Zinn," in *Rethinking Schools: An Agenda for Change*, eds. David Levine, Robert Lowe, Bob Peterson, and Rita Tenorio (New York: The New Press, 1995), 98. This is a book of articles and interviews put out by the teachers/writers who edit the educational journal *Rethinking Schools*.

41 Michael Apple, *Official Knowledge: Democratic Education In A Conservative Age* (New York: Routledge, 1993), 14.

42 Bill Bigelow, "Inside the Classroom: Social Vision and Critical Pedagogy," *Teachers College Record*, Vol. 91, No. 3, Spring 1990, 437.

43 Ibid., 445.

44 Ibid.

45 Ibid., 447.

46 Ibid.

47 Chomsky, *Deterring Democracy*, 64.

48 "A Dialogue with Noam Chomsky," *Harvard Educational Review*, Vol. 65, No. 2, Summer 1995, 143.

49 Ibid., 143-4.

50 June Jordan, *Technical Difficulties: Selected Political Essays* (London: Virago Press Limited, 1992), 144.

51 Ibid., 146.

52 Ibid., 176.

53 William Kunstler, "comments," July 27, 1995, reprinted in *The Nation*, October 2, 1995, 341. Dave Dellinger was one of the Chicago 7/8 anti-war activists. They were arrested and brought to trial for their protests at the 1968 Democratic Convention.

Index

Z

John Marciano is an Associate Professor at SUNY Cortland, where he teaches courses in the social and historical foundations of education.

COUNTERPOINTS publishes the most compelling and imaginative books being written in education today. Grounded on the theoretical advances in criticalism, feminism and postmodernism in the last two decades of the twentieth century, Counterpoints engages the meaning of these innovations in various forms of educational expression. Committed to the proposition that theoretical literature should be accessible to a variety of audiences, the series insists that its authors avoid esoteric and jargonistic languages that transform educational scholarship into an elite discourse for the initiated. Scholarly work matters only to the degree it affects consciousness and practice at multiple sites. Counterpoints' editorial policy is based on these principles and the ability of scholars to break new ground, to open new conversations, to go where educators have never gone before.